THE DEVIL AND
SECULAR HUMANISM

The Devil and Secular Humanism

THE CHILDREN OF THE ENLIGHTENMENT

Howard B. Radest

 PRAEGER

New York
Westport, Connecticut
London

Library of Congress Cataloging-in-Publication Data

Radest, Howard B., 1928–
  The devil and secular humanism : the children of the enlightenment
/ Howard B. Radest.
    p.   cm.
  Includes bibliographical references and index.
  ISBN 0-275-93442-X (alk. paper)
  1. Humanism.   2. Enlightenment.   I. Title.
B21.R27   1990
144—dc20   90-38843

British Library Cataloguing-in-Publication Data is available.

Library of Congress Catalog Card Number: 90-38843
ISBN: 0-275-93442-X

First published in 1990

Praeger Publishers, One Madison Avenue, New York, NY 10010
An imprint of Greenwood Publishing Group, Inc.

Printed in the United States of America

The paper used in this book complies with the
Permanent Paper Standard issued by the National
Information Standards Organization (Z39.48-1984).

10 9 8 7 6 5 4 3 2 1

FOR KAREN
AND
THE STUDENTS OF THE HUMANIST INSTITUTE

Contents

Preface

Ordinarily, I would introduce myself. Since, however, my experience is woven into the chapters that follow, this would be redundant. But I do want to begin with thanks to my many colleagues and friends who, over the years, have enriched my life and work. There are hundreds of them. Since they play a role in the story that follows, and since naming some would risk ignoring others as significant, let me express a deeply felt gratitude to all of them. I trust that my criticisms of Humanism will not be overly offensive. They are offered in a spirit of reconstruction and from an abiding faith in Humanist values.

Repeatedly, I have found myself drawn back to the Enlightenment. I had not expected it to play so major a role in my analysis. Years ago when I did some research on Condorcet under the guidance of Horace Kallen and Saul Padover at the New School, I was fortunate to become familiar with Enlightenment ideas and thinkers. I drew upon that experience as I developed my current thinking. As I tried to understand the virulence of the attack on Humanism, I came to understand that Enlightenment values were really the enemy of Humanism's attackers. Most particularly, the Enlightenment trinities—liberty, equality, and fraternity and life, liberty, and the pursuit of happiness—set the modern world on a career that has yet to run its course. It is understandable that these values should be felt as dangerous to those who are privileged, or to those for whom liberty and equality are sources of insecurity. The confrontation of our age—and it will carry into the twenty-first century—is between those who enjoy the modernism the Enlightenment set in motion and those who fear the possibilities that it entails.

Humanism is the incarnation of Enlightenment values and the legitimate descendent of an age of reason and freedom. Themes I set out to explore are that contemporary Humanists have not fully grasped the cultural, historic, and personal import of their own history; that others, understanding this all too well, attack Humanism; and finally, that two hundred years of experience have revealed the inadequacies of the Enlightenment and the need to reconstruct it. Together they describe the mission of modern Humanism.

I have drawn on the history and philosophy of Humanism and on the experience of a lifetime with Humanist colleagues here and abroad in Ethical Culture, Unitarian-Universalism, Humanistic Judaism, Religious and Secular Humanism, free thought, and rationalism. Above all, I have benefited from the work of my students and my fellow instructors in The Humanist Institute. Together, we have begun the fascinating task of uniting for the sake of the education of Humanist leadership. In our seminars and in our faculty colloquia over the past seven years we have set out to rethink Humanism. A number of the ideas that find their way into this essay were initially offered at the Institute. Obviously, the responsibility for them is mine but, insofar as they are valid and usable, they are the outcome of a collective wisdom and insight.

Finally, I want to say a word or two to those who are not (or who are not yet) Humanists. Certainly, I appreciate the strength of traditional loyalties and my criticism of the traditions is not intended to disparage the integrity of those who still find meaning and value in them. At the same time, I cannot help but urge giving tangibility to democratic and scientific values in a world so tempted to irrationality. However this is accomplished—whether by the reconstruction of the traditions themselves or by taking the newer pathways named Humanism—we cannot survive as slaves and victims and we cannot meet our needs out of ignorance.

As I write, Eastern Europe is in turmoil, the Soviet Union faces an unknown future, China is turning backward toward tyranny, addiction and poverty afflict the United States, and bigotry threatens the Middle East. In addition to this is the reality that technological power could end the human adventure on this planet in moments. An equally impressive list of the possibilities for achieving peace and a just world could be drawn. In other words, we face serious choices in the public and private worlds we inhabit. The values of Humanism are dedicated to the making of choices that offer us hope. The intention of this essay is to examine, analyze, criticize, and finally to reaffirm this offer and to invite others to join in its development.

THE DEVIL AND
SECULAR HUMANISM

1

First Person Singular: From Philosophy to Biography

I've been a Humanist for more than forty years. Like you, I have heard the accusations and defenses of Humanism. Its followers have been party—not always willingly—to arguments between fundamentalists and secular Humanists, between creationists and evolutionists, and between progressives and conservatives. When under attack, unfortunately, Humanists are often found speaking in voices as raucous and strident as their opponents. Ideas are reduced to simple-minded slogans. This will not do. It serves neither those of us who are committed to modern Humanism nor those of us who just want to know what Humanism is all about. Let me try then to find my own voice on the subject and attempt to avoid mere partisanship.

Humanism has been around for thousands of years. When, caught up in the excitement of a culture on the rise, its celebration of human powers has seemed so self-evidently right, argument for and against Humanism simply did not arise. So it must have been—excluding women, slaves, and proletarians—for fifth-century Athens, the Renaissance, or revolutionary America. At other times, things were so dismal and hopeless that the argument for the goodness and creativity of human powers could only seem inane.

At times, Humanism has come to us embedded in religion and in politics, at other times in the arts, and at still others in the sciences. Often it has been known by other names—as in Socrates' skepticism, Democritus' materialism, Jefferson's Deism, Ingersoll's secular religion, or Comte's "religion of humanity." Today, for the first time in history, Humanism has also emerged as a movement in its own right, with its own organizations, vocabularies, and even sectarian quarrels. At the same time, Humanism is still found where it always existed, as part of the fabric of history and culture. Obviously, my story will be complicated, but worth telling.

Those of us who call ourselves Humanists have hardly helped to clarify the situation. We are unable to arrive at common meanings. So we are secular and religious, Marxist and non-Marxist, socialist and libertarian. We use adjectives like naturalistic, scientific, evolutionary, and ethical. Still, I have no doubt that we inhabit a common neighborhood, although its boundaries are unclear and the conditions of residence are difficult to define. Adding to the confusion, Humanism is also found as a sub-theme elsewhere, such as in Catholic Humanism[1] or in the anti-Stalinist socialism of worker management in Yugoslavia.[2] Some Humanists reject their fellows. Those who claim a belief—however vague—in a deity are seen as false Humanists by their secular comrades. Then too, there are Humanists who jealously guard their own definitions of democracy, equality, freedom, or moral responsibility and use them to attack the Humanist credentials of others.

I confess that I share the ambiguities that beset my subject. No doubt I have even helped to create them by yielding to the temptations of partisanship. I have flirted with many of the adjectives that are said to define a genuine Humanism; at other times I impatiently want to do away with them all. More than occasionally I am bored by fruitless debates and frustrated by my inability to convince others of what is the manifest wisdom on the subject—my own wisdom obviously. When I am in such a mood it is very easy to ride roughshod over the differences that exist. I make my own claim all the more assertively because I am not clear about what I am claiming. I am tempted to say, "Humanism is. . . . " and then to list appropriate—or at least habitual—predicates. But that will not do. The outcome of the exercise is predictable. I only convince those who are already convinced. Instead, I think we need to discover what is hiding behind the passionate certainties on all sides. Usable ideals are needed, never more urgently than today. Among the best possibilities for finding them is through Humanism. That would seem to invite disciplined inquiry, but how this is to be done has its own problems, particularly in an arena where there are no neutrals.

Once upon a time, I thought that the way to deal with ideas was from a distance. As a philosopher, I learned that *ad hominem* argument was poor argument and that intensity of belief demonstrated nothing but intensity itself. To hold something to be correct, however genuinely, does not solve the problem of its correctness, or the problem of personal integrity. I can be honestly wrong and honestly right. If anything, the experience of the 1960s confirmed my skepticism of passionate devotion as proof of certainty. Nearly everywhere, I met those—young and not so young—for whom an inner state of certainty was sufficient warrant for the truth. More recently, I meet with misguided tolerance. All claims are reduced to opinion and all opinions are treated as equal. It seems that truth itself has ceased to be available and has been replaced by conflicting psychological states. The sign of this deterioration is the language of the subjective truth, of "my" truth as distinct from "your" truth. Not surprising, is the effort in less tolerant circles to recapture "the" truth out of a profound dismay at how shaky things become when mere opinion is all we are said to have. But this effort is only another psychological state, one which I have called the "fundamentalist temptation."[3] Symptomatically, current debate about Humanism is angry and endless, confrontational and foolish. For those who are not party to these battles, the result is indifference, even disgust, or perhaps amusement. As I approach my subject I admit the dangers of confusing my desire for something to be so with a judgment that it is so. It has never been easy to maintain the notion that inquiry demands that we seek out the evidence and assess its weight. It is most difficult when interests on all sides are blinded to anything but partisan advantage.

At the same time we all know that ideas do not spring full-blown from the head of Athena. My experience does make a difference. Where and when and who I am—and who I have been with—must shape what I believe and disbelieve, what I value and what I consider unimportant, and what I accept or deny as evidence. Nor is this only the case where biography is itself a party to the idea—as in human relationships and loyalties. Even in more austere disciplines that think to deal with the universe "as it really is," we cannot claim to have accounted for subjectivity, as we once thought to do, by "correcting for bias" or by mustering sufficient data to strike an average or locate a mathematical limit. It is no doubt an injustice to the history of astronomy, and yet not that far off the mark, to say that Ptolemy looked to the heavens and saw a circle while Brahe looked to the heavens and saw an ellipse. Plato heard the "music of the spheres," while a modern cosmologist hears a "big bang." Even where the "facts" may be said to adjudicate these claims, future "facts" will reveal our entanglement with imagery and metaphor, as we believe was the case with our predecessors.[4]

I am oppressed by the illusions of objectivity and by the inevitabilities of subjectivity. This is a caution against claiming too stridently what must be approached gently. The problems of human knowledge are further complicated by issues of faith, politics, moral judgment, and ideology—the same issues that whirl around Humanism. My theme invites confusion— even if its content could be clearly defined by some authoritative body or tradition—which it cannot. An attempt to understand Humanism and to find its place in the dialogue of faiths asks for trouble. Even to call Humanism a "faith" can start an argument. Some Humanists would accept the description, others would reject it—repelled by connotations of religion or irrationality. It is also easy to confuse the personal commitments of a lifetime with what must be true about the world, and with what must be best for everyone else. At the same time, it is a temptation, particularly for

Humanists and others with a liberal temper, to evade the dangers of arrogance with exaggerated self-criticism. Both the mood of arrogance and the mood of self-depreciation are very much alive in Humanist circles—claims of self-evidence mingle with endless self-doubt.

Serious reflection on Humanism will soon reveal the problem of trying to know what it is about. Earlier in my career, I met the problem by seeking to hide my voice behind an anonymous "third person," thinking to overpower subjectivity by massing information and reasoned analysis. My appeal was to evidence or to common sense. A complementary strategy called for winning the argument by citing the opposition much as St. Thomas set up his own views by inviting the enemy to be a party to the inquiry.[5] Just as with Thomas, I was able to conclude, strangely enough, where I began, as I knew I would. Usually, after the initial pleasure of winning an argument, this left me dissatisfied, not least because on reflection it raised questions about the genuineness of my inquiry. Nor was this simply a question of honesty. If Humanism has any common reference point, it is to disciplined intelligence, and to the distinction between hypothesis and creed. Yet it seemed to me that while trying to give the appearance of the former, I was really proclaiming the latter. And that would not do!

More recently and in response to this recurrent dissatisfaction, I have found myself accepting incompleteness as a fact of life. Closure appears in my decisions and actions, but not in my inquiries. I learned to admit to myself that I was only stopping—interrupting, as it were—but that I really did not have a "conclusion" to offer. Aesthetically, if not intellectually, this is troubling for I can no longer find the contentment that grows from shaping the drama of ideas with a beginning, middle, and end. More constructively, however, this failure to conclude has become an invitation to a dialogue in which all parties are expected to move. It has the advantage of integrity.[6] This has its dissatisfactions too, because the risks of decision and action cannot be evaded when issues of moral judgment or of politics are at stake. This dual situation of action and inquiry lends an element of adventure and fear to my experience. A voice within cautions that dialogue can easily become an excuse for abdicating the responsibilities of choice. I confess, however, that I can do no better than to seek—never successfully—to expose as much as I can, as much as I know. Each time I think I have reached a conclusion, the horizon recedes; each time I think I have "put it all together," I discover another question.

The more I reflect on any idea, let alone an idea affected by passions, the more I realize that a turn to biography is essential to understanding. In biography, I find a bridge between self and other, passion and existence, the inner and the outer. A biography entails connections with others and is never only a meditation. I become aware of the actions of others and of my interactions with them. This is obviously true of family, friends, and colleagues. I also understand that I have been shaped by those whom I do not and never will know and by events both large and small. In short, biography is a meeting point of the objective and the subjective, of the reflective and the active. I think that for human beings it is the only such meeting point.

Let me then approach my subject by recalling my experience. Nearly forty years ago, I began work as the Leader of an Ethical Culture Society. Founded in 1876, Ethical Culture has evolved as a type of humanism, and Ethical Culture Leadership as a type of Humanist professional, even a type of Humanist clergy. To be sure, in the early 1950s, Humanism was not often used as a description of Ethical Culture. Given the mood of post-war America, we called ourselves a "liberal religion" and noted our affinities to Unitarianism, Reform Judaism, and the Society of Friends. When I began, I was attracted to the ideal of building a purely ethical religion with a group of people, a "congregation" or, to use more recent but less accurate language, a "community." Ethical Culture promised the possibility of eliminating the paraphernalia of traditional faith which to me only mystified rather than clarified. I had had the usual childhood training—somewhere between Jewish orthodoxy and conservatism—and had gone through the usual adolescent rejections. Now I was ready to move onto a middle ground that avoided affronting my intelligence while seizing upon the genius of religious institutions—the building of relationships between strangers. Ethical Culture Societies were "gathered" groups unlike churches, synagogues, or mosques, which were peopled by those who had inherited their membership. Above all, Ethical Culture appealed to the social idealism in me and in those with whom I came to work.

I found myself in good company, scholars like Joseph Blau, Horace Friess and David Muzzey, as well as reformers like Henry Neumann and Algernon D. Black, to name Ethical Culture Leaders who bridged the generations from the founder to my own.[7] I saw myself in the tradition of Emerson, who had called for an ethical religion. To me, working in suburbia in the 1950s, that seemed a necessary corrective to the religiosity that characterized the shopping mall church and synagogue of that decade. I shared—or tried to—the vision of Felix Adler, the founder of Ethical Culture, and saw myself too as heir to the passion of the Israelite prophets and the nineteenth century reformers.

It was refreshing to be able to do the work of faith without the need to argue about another world with its Gods and superstitions. The narrowness of traditional faith and the dishonesties it demanded affronted me. I did not have to explain and interpret ancient texts in order to square scientific inquiry and religious claim as in the debate over "creation." Yet I did not want to be simply a nay-sayer. As I saw it from within my new calling, I could appeal to the good and to the goodness in others, and to what I believed to be the common moral sense. After all, whatever our view of heaven or hell, of God or Devil, the plain fact was that we had to find ways of living well together, here and now. To be able to affirm this while avoiding invidious distinctions between believer and heretic that set us apart was an exciting opportunity. I could, in short, go to work in good conscience on current problems that concerned personal and social ethics, without being forced to carry excess baggage or even to dispute matters of religious faith. When asked, I would say that belief in God, heaven, hell, immortality— all the typical issues of religion—were personal matters that did not really concern me, although nothing precluded relaxed informal discussion of such questions.

To be sure, as I became involved in the work, I found that there were places of silence, even deliberate silence. This was so both within the Ethical Society itself and in the many alliances that were built to do things in the community. For the sake of achieving "common ground," I kept my knowledge of what was happening in the sciences apart. I did not argue issues of cosmology with those who seemed to have some remnant of God in their views—a no-longer necessary Deism or a sentimental Theism. I left issues of ideology alone (or tried to) but not always successfully. It was not possible, for example, to silence the debate between Leninism and freedom for the sake of common effort. Stalin was still alive, as was Stalinism, and some American liberals seemed not to know it. Technical questions of philosophy were left to the classroom or the seminar. For example, the limitations of Adler's neo-Kantianism were not so much analyzed as set aside, and the transcendentalism of Emerson—the language of the "over-soul"—was muted in favor of his evident good sense as a critic and popularizer of democratic values.

Nevertheless, I grew more and more ambivalent about whether or not an "ethics without ontology"[8] was possible. Since that was the conceptual center of my stance in Ethical Culture, I grew increasingly more concerned about the adequacy of my position. As the philosophers have it, "ought implies can," which meant, among other things, that the newer scientific information from biology and psychology could not be ignored in developing ethical judgments and ideas. Yet it was the claim of the "independence of ethics"—the Kantian and neo-Kantian claim—that had sanctioned ethical religion. I suppose that I suppressed the notion that this sanction was tied to a historical view of the sciences even as they were changing very rapidly. There were other silences too—not so much deliberate as implicit—silence about the anti-intellectualism of American life that made possible an Emersonian Romanticism and about the Puritanism of American culture that made convincing the call for a "religion of duty." Of course, I talked about these themes—who could not in the 1950s and 1960s when anti-intellectualism and Puritanism gave birth to the grandeur of the new frontier and the disaster of another lost generation. Yet I did not make an explicit connection between these themes and the justifications of my own position. Looking back, an emerging Humanism with naturalistic features that was much more complicated than a univocal attention to the ethics was already visible, but I just did not admit it.

As time passed and the work progressed—within the congregational life of an Ethical Culture Society and the institutional life of a national and international Humanist movement—I was learning that "ethics as a religion"[9] seemed to miss too much of what I was finding in experience. A passion for righteousness did not necessarily develop from ideas of righteousness itself. I worked with many people who "knew" what ought to be done, whose moral arguments and judgments were unflawed, and yet whose commitments took them in different directions. I saw how often in my own life there was a gulf between "good" ideas and "good" actions. Indeed, as Kantians formulated it, action was part of the causal structure of the universe and thus its moral status was at best problematic. The key was the moral will, the exercise of moral judgment, and the rationality of moral law. Passion itself was suspect when the majesty of moral law and the exercise of reason were at stake; "moral passion" was a contradictory notion. Of course, Kant had spoken with "awe" of the "starry heavens above and the moral law within" and Adler exhibited a passion for the good for which his philosophy scarcely accounted. I was learning that the ideas of an ethical religion that I had inherited were simply too austere and inadequate.

Among other things that were forcing me toward a more ragged-edged viewpoint, I was meeting people during those moments when the life of an individual or a family reached a turning point. Visiting the sick in a hospital, counseling a husband and wife in trouble with their marriage, responding to family and friends at times of death . . . a "religion of duty" simply missed too much. Even for social action and reform, motive and commitment needed other sources than reason or the moral law. On the other hand, I was able to respond in times of crisis and help people to meet their needs without resorting to false promises. A basic honesty was available to me—for instance at death or when facing what could not be changed—that was not as available to those with different commitments. I had to confront evils, but I did not have to confront the "problem of evil" and "justify the ways of God to man." I learned that the sources of strength and meaning turned on our love or sympathy for the victims of unrighteousness or on the pains of conscience that make us aware of "things undone that ought to have been done." The idea of duty, in other words, was not a sufficient basis for doing the work of duty. At the same time, doing the work of duty did not require sanction from "on high" or from another world. I found what we needed in our relations with others and in our experience together even if our theory did not embrace that experience.

I also learned that "ethics as a religion" defined a historical neighborhood where the centrality of the good and the good life were touchstones of organization and affirmation.[10] Ethical Culture lived in that neighborhood where a complicated Humanist environment was evolving—to be made explicit in the first decades of the twentieth century. That emerging Humanism provided a new context for the Emersonian inspiration and the Adlerian insight that had stirred my own imagination. It was a fitting successor to the various incarnations of a "religion of humanity" to be found in the late nineteenth century. As my forty years of professional work progressed, that environment became much more visible and connected historically, both for me and for others.[11]

At the same time, as counselor and teacher, husband and father, I learned that human needs were not simply moral needs and that the moral good could not always be placed in the center and above all others at the top of some hierarchy of values. That was simply too abstract. Yes, the good had a certain priority, but not in all circumstances. There were moments when the truthful, the beautiful, the joyful, the tragic, or even the humorous moved to center stage. While these might be "good," they were only derivatively morally good and even that sometimes required stretching the meaning of the good beyond the bounds of intellectual responsibility. The good *life*, in other words, is not the same as the *good* life, and a view that was to be responsive to human experience needed to incorporate much more than a moral dimension. Conduct stimulated and verified this as I attended to ceremony and celebration and sought to give sustenance in moments of personal crisis. But my language, and my consciousness, tried to deny what was happening by subsuming it all under the "ethical" until I came to realize that it was becoming a category without boundaries.

Meanwhile, events beyond my calling were teaching other lessons that the emerging Humanist neighborhood needed to learn. The successes of the sciences, it turned out, did not necessarily lead toward a scientific culture or toward a morally advanced culture. Members of modern societies could be addicted to magic and superstition while using the symbols of the sciences and the advances of technology. The sciences could be effectively encapsulated so that inquiry could proceed freely in the laboratory while tyranny and ignorance could rule everywhere else. Anti-clericalism and the secularized state did not necessarily lead to liberation. The church might be suppressed or religion privatized, as in the struggle for church and state separation, and still new forms of ideological slavery were imposed. More people could be admitted to full citizenship—women and minorities, for example—and yet citizenship itself be emptied of content and become a mere form. Most painful of all, people could enjoy a cushioned tyranny without stirring themselves toward democratic revolution. When to this passivity and acquiescence, particularly among the so-called developed, advanced, and civilized societies, was added the manifest improvement in our ability to destroy each other massively, viciously, and in the name of the good and the true on all sides, Humanist optimism seemed shallow and false. The lessons that challenged the Enlightenment had reached a first crescendo with the "war to end war," and since 1918 they had been repeated with increasing intensity.

Experience—both personal and collective—was losing its Enlightenment boundaries much as classicism had lost its idealist boundaries. The reconstruction of "liberty, equality, and fraternity" now became the point. But these did not appear to be tasks for the academy alone—indeed the academy seemed to have abdicated content and imagination in favor of increasingly abstract exercises in isolated compartments. Yet the need to hold on to the Enlightenment, to democracy and science, was present in the voices and passions of ordinary human beings even if they lacked a language for giving them utterance, content, and connection. Dismay at the difficulties of democracy or the corruption of science was not simply an intellectual matter. And dismay was joined with hope in a confusing amalgam.

Within the Humanist neighborhood, the children of the Enlightenment—for that is what we were and are—were not immune to that confusion either. I saw us experiment with nouns and adjectives in efforts to give voice to our views and clarity to our commitments. We introduced "ethical" Humanism to "ethical" religion, saying, perhaps without knowing it, that Humanism unadorned, religion unadorned, and ethics unadorned somehow confessed their inadequacy. Still others experimented with psychological nostrums, keeping the vocabulary of Humanism but losing its critical edge—its political and even its ethical sources—in a vague sentimentalism. Continental Humanists who observed us found our insistence on the "ethical" a reflection of American pietism and the notion of "religious" Humanism utterly mystifying. At the same time, I watched their own struggles with the need to give voice to Humanism out of a confusing situation. Reflecting their European and British sources, they found other adjectives more congenial, such as "naturalistic" or "scientific" or "evolutionary" or "socialist" or "secular" or "democratic" Humanism. To be sure, some Americans followed suit, leaving the "ethical" behind. In short, the Humanist neighborhood was not immune to the inadequacies of Enlightenment values. Unfortunately this took the form of word games and a sectarian divisiveness reminiscent of nothing so much as the debates among Christian sects about fine points of doctrine or among Talmudists about fine points of law. Effective self-criticism and significant reconstruction were hardly addressed.

Other events pointed to our undone homework. Repeatedly an attack on the modern world was mounted in the name of some eternal truth. The sciences were confronted by "creationism," which in its latest version called itself, with unintended irony "creation science." Equality was eroded by class privilege, which in its modern incarnation appealed to freedom of choice, calling itself "libertarianism" as if liberty could itself be an ideology without becoming illiberal. Everywhere, religious warfare grew more virulent—in Ireland and the Middle East, in Pakistan and India and Tibet, in sub-Saharan Africa and in Latin America. Perhaps the forms of democratic society were more and more visible, but their reality was less and less evident. Humanism was not silent in the face of events, but its voice was easily assimilated into mere humanitarianism or into alliances with other defenders of civil liberty. To be sure, neither humanitarianism nor civil liberty were unworthy commitments, but they were obviously neither uniquely Humanist nor did they derive their inspiration from Humanist values alone. Something was missing and that, too, is a comment on the Humanism that grew out of my biography.

My essay moves from philosophy to biography, and the issues I shall be exploring emerge from a biographical reprise. But I do not think that my experience is only my own. So, if objectivity is elusive, at least I can trust that my inquiry is corroborated in the subjectivity of others and that my reflection evokes recognition in others—and not only among Humanists. If experience does not neatly and easily lend itself to parables and lessons, nevertheless my recollection suggests points of inadequacy and of promise.

Looking back, then, I have found myself moving toward a far more complicated view of what is needed than was envisioned in the Ethical Culture with which I began. I have also moved—or tried to move—beyond the simplicities that are sometimes asserted by other Humanists. Too often, the matter is phrased as simply the need for a victory over the forces of darkness disguised as a given orthodoxy. "Erase the infamy," as Voltaire cried, and then truth will shine forth and goodness long repressed will inevitably arise. But if biography tells me anything, it is that we need a reconstruction of Enlightenment values toward a richer Humanism and a recapturing of classical and Renaissance values in a richer Humanist synthesis. This would be so even if fundamentalism vanished tomorrow and orthodoxy finally surrendered.

At the same time, and this is the unfortunate result of an aggressive fundamentalism, I find Humanism growing more and more defensive. Forced to belligerence—although I admit that many Humanists enjoy the battle—we retreat to a raucous Humanism caught in the trap of rationalism and anti-clericalism. Elsewhere, I find us retreating to mere intimacy and to a communitarianism that seeks, following Candide, to "cultivate your own garden." These two current moves—toward defensive warfare and quiescent intimacies—are troubling enough for Humanists who take their history and tradition seriously. Were this merely the inadequacy of a few souls at the edge of the social galaxy, it might be regrettable, even humorous, but surely irrelevant. Were Humanism only a philosophic and ideological aberration, we could comfortably close the book on it as we have done on other movements that arose, did their work, and vanished.

My argument, however, is of a different sort. Humanism has its part to play in the world—and not solely for Humanists. The record is clear enough. Humanism, emerging out of the Enlightenment, carried the message of democracy and science, whether through specifically Humanist associations like those of "free religion" or as a Humanist accent in the religious and political history of others. Within the movements of our age, it took form as the revolutionary theme of the "rights of man." In our country it gave shape to a Humanist neighborhood that has been a vehicle for reform and liberation. Opportunities for the organized development and defense of liberty and intelligence are too few and too valuable to permit us lightly to dismiss any of them. But that is of the past; the question for this essay, except incidentally, is not about the history of Humanism.

Nor are the issues that emerge from biography merely addressed outward to the reconstruction of society, although social ethics is in such disarray that Humanism could, as it once did, easily justify giving all its attention to it. But that would be to miss the point. For if Humanism was anything and is to be anything, then it is because it served once as a center of meanings, a faith that led now outward toward society, now inward toward intimacy. In a sense, the *polis* was only a theater where a deeper truth about human beings was played out or, more accurately, where human beings played out a deeper truth. With self-consciousness, with memory and language, the human animal everywhere faces a struggle between independence and dependence, between accepting the sufficiency of this world and needing some other . . . and that is not only a political matter. Everywhere, the Gods appeal to and respond to the impulse toward another world, Gods that seem to populate reality with forces and powers we scarcely understand and even less frequently control. Typically, the Gods employ as their agents other human beings, whose sacred authority, unchallenged simply because it is sacred, has been more disastrous than helpful wherever it has been exercised. In response, another impulse appears among us: we are heretics and skeptics too. Finally, working our way into this world and away from some imagined other, we are rightfully proud of our ability to perform and to achieve. So, when the Gods threaten and their agents impose, we need to be Promethean in our rebellions and Socratic in our doubts . . . we need to be Humanists whatever the label.

Humanism is thus a permanent and necessary feature of experience. Even if our present Gods vanish, others will take their place. Some are even more vicious when they appear in secular disguise. If the churches are for a time content to exist peaceably with each other and with us, other powers have taken their place in using human beings for the sake of some one true faith. Where the voice of Humanism is stilled or confused, experience is the loser and not only for Humanists. A needful balance is lost, a tension that gives shape and texture to the healthy rebelliousness of human beings is unfelt.

To capture this perennial sense of a Humanist mission is to go beneath the Enlightenment, beneath the Renaissance, beneath classical skepticism and materialism. Understandably, since the seventeenth and eighteenth centuries, in England and France and elsewhere, Humanism has had to address the politics of oppression. So much modern energy was devoted to economics and politics, the rebellious impulse had to find a home there too. But this forced on modern Humanism a kind of monocular vision, turning it outward toward reform and social action. So much effort was required to attend to these matters that it is unsurprising that Humanism neglected other features of human life. Above all, it yielded to the temptation to activism in the name of the good. When to this political requirement was added the reinforcement of a reductionist modern science whose central metaphor was matter in motion, the nearly monomaniacal interest in a "public" life alone was not only understandable but justifiable. To be sure, this public impulse became particularly problematic as the ideas and metaphors that gave credibility to the Enlightenment deteriorated into mere formulas and as reductive science began to yield to systematic and organic images. Today, Humanist activism is but a shadow of its revolutionary past and shows itself in a popular "pragmatism" that even boasts of its lack of theory and of its attention to "problem solving." Of course, having lost its theory, it has lost its identity as well and is submerged in liberal good works with others who have lost their way too.

Consider, for example, rationality itself. The idea of "reason" emerged in a special way with the coming of modern science. By way of contrast, consider how routine "reason" has become. Losing the connection between reason and imagination, discovery, liberation, and equality—indeed between reason and its work in reshaping the world itself—we have lost the meanings of rationality and become instead mere mechanics relegating reason to technical skill. Indeed, rationality itself gets a bad name because it seems to deprive us of things about which we care like love, and because it seems to lead to the horrors of a technology gone wild. At the same time, Humanists really do not have the luxury of a despair of reason, for without it Humanism loses its inspiration. Reason, after all, was not only the key to the sciences, but was the common human capacity that justified political freedom and moral autonomy. Democratic values were sanctioned precisely because any human being could inquire, observe, think, judge, and decide. An object might legitimately be manipulated and used, a reasoning being could not be. Of course, Humanists have complained often enough about the limitations of reason and are not immune to the same despair of reason that is so ubiquitous. Humanists too know the need for emotion and passion, for poetry and art. And Humanists live full and complicated lives. But modern Humanism, still reflecting its eighteenth century roots, lacks a convincing way of including these in its philosophy and practice. That is a legitimate criticism of the children of the Enlightenment. At the same time, Humanism, like its neighbors, has lost the excitement of reason itself, which is much more problematic for Humanism than for its neighbors. Left unreconstructed it would be fatal.

I have, as is easily seen, many questions and few answers. But then, at its best, Humanism invites explorations. Humanism is not a center of eternal truths to be known and proclaimed. It is but a creature of history and place with its own continuities and turns. It is unsurprising then that it is both many and one. I want to picture that Humanist process—or, better, Humanist processes—and not pretend to some definitive restatement of ideology and belief. Indeed, I am convinced that the latter must fail not because of any inadequacy in the saying—though that is likely enough—but because of inappropriateness in the doing. So, for example, the writing of Humanist Manifestos has been characterized by initial excitement and rapid invisibility.[12] Ironically, it is the "opposition" that takes these Manifestos most seriously—or seems to—and is far more knowledgeable about them than are many Humanists. Often too, apart from a scholarly interest,[13] which is appropriate enough, the Manifestos provide ammunition on all sides for a warfare of believers. That seems to be the present condition of Humanism. To understand it, we need to understand why, instead of fostering a mood of inquiry, the present scene is too often a battleground between self-proclaimed true believers on all sides. We turn thus to the argument that begins with the accusation that Humanism is a creature of the devil and that Humanists are lost souls.

NOTES

1. For example, in his 1969 Christmas Message and in the encyclical *Populorum Porgressio*, Paul VI said, "Some men would organize the earth without God, but without God, they will finally only organize against man himself. Secular humanism is an inhuman humanism . . . a true humanism without Christ is impossible."

2. Branko Horvath, Mihailo Markovic, and Rudi Supek, eds. *Self Governing Socialism—A Reader* (White Plains, NY. International Arts and Sciences Press, 1975).

3. The theme of temptation has been with us for a long time. I am indebted, among others, to Paul Kurtz for calling attention to the idea in his book, *The Transcendental Temptation* (Buffalo, NY: Prometheus, 1986). That which is tempting is both attractive and suspect, a helpful notion which I feel captures the human condition quite accurately.

4. See *Timaeus*, in *The Dialogues of Plato*, vol. 2 Benjamin Jowett (New York: Random House, 1937): 3–68; also Thomas Kuhn, *The Structure of Scientific Revolutions* (Chicago: University of Chicago Press, 1962).

5. The approach to argument that cites opposing arguments and then reasons toward an adjudication between them can be dishonest, a confrontation of straw men. Perhaps, today, this is the way the scholastic method exemplified by St. Thomas appears to us. I suggest, however, that in its own context, that method was a genuine form of inquiry. See *Basic Writings of Saint Thomas Aquinas*, ed. and ann. Anton C. Pegis (New York: Random House, 1945).

6. For a discussion of "dialogue," see Howard B. Radest, *Can We Teach Ethics* (New York: Praeger, 1989), particularly Chapter 7.

7. For a discussion of the history of Ethical Culture, see Howard B. Radest, *Toward Common Ground* (New York: Ungar, 1969).

8. The familiar formulation of this view in the Ethical Culture movement is that ethics is "autonomous," independent of any particular view of the world or what is in it, and that ethics is "central"—its values take priority over all other areas.

9. Typically, David Muzzey developed his view of Ethical Culture under this title. See *Ethics as a Religion* (New York: Simon and Schuster, 1951).

10. The movement toward social reform in nineteenth-century America was in no small measure fueled by ethical religions. The Society of Friends, for example, led the way in the abolitionist movement. Social Gospel Protestantism was developing. Utopian movements were reconstructing communities. For further discussion, see Radest, *Common Ground*, particularly Chapters 1 and 6.

11. For further discussion of this theme, see Howard B. Radest, "Ethical Culture and Humanism: A Cautionary Tale," *Religious Humanism* 16, no. 2: 59–70.

12. The first *Humanist Manifesto* was published in 1933, the second in 1973. Others, immediately dissatisfied, were already working on a third. In 1980, a *Secular Humanist Declaration* was published. Meanwhile, in one guise or another, efforts to arrive at statements of "principle" (some have even said "belief") recur. Interesting as moments for catching one's breath, so to speak, the Manifestos have more often looked backward rather than forward. And that, I suggest, is unsurprising given the view that Humanism is a process evolving within the bounds of history and place.

13. For example, see Louis Dupre, "The Humanist Manifesto," *Commonweal* 99, no. 3 (October 19, 1973): 55–58.

2

The Devil and Secular Humanism: The Fundamentalist Temptation

I am struck by the apparent innocence of Humanists about the powers and practices of the world. We seem to have an inordinate faith in words, as if the ability to say something right and true is sufficient to make reality over. We are an argumentative lot—and this is not surprising given our roots in a pamphleteering tradition. It is seldom indeed that we recognize the demands of political life, let alone go to the barricades. And this is all the more ironic when we consider how intertwined Humanism and politics have been from the outset. There have been, to be sure, moments of high drama and passion. Dutch Humanism developed during the anti-fascist struggle in Nazi-occupied Holland; Norwegian Humanism grew out of the anti-clerical struggle with an established church that tried to force "non-believers" to baptize their children; Indian Humanism grew out of a left-wing challenge to Gandhi's ruralism; and American Humanism grew out of both social reform and the struggle for church and state separation. But when we visit with Humanists today, we usually find them listening to lectures, reading books, writing letters to the editor, and always arguing. There will, of course, be sociable moments when food and drink and song replace debate. And there will be moments of deep feeling when the death of someone beloved reaches beyond intimacy to affect a Humanist community. But our first impression remains of a seminar *manque*, of a group of people more interested in the act of debating a problem than in doing much about its substance. It is as if Humanists were not fully aware of what is at stake in Humanism, of its origins in democratic revolution, of its requirements for committed effort on behalf of its values. But then today, we also find this same lack of seriousness with Christians and Jews toward their faiths.

Of course, there are other realities. The same Humanists whom we find obsessed with the word are active in good causes. But their Humanist identity will typically be submerged into alliances and coalitions built along common interests—mostly liberal interests. So, we will encounter among Humanists a familiar agenda made up of civil liberties and civil rights issues, peace issues, and environmental issues. Given the history of American re-form, it is not surprising that this agenda will often lack an ideological base and will be what is loosely called "pragmatic" or problem solving in ap-proach. Above all, there will be little apparent in these alliances that can be called Humanist as such—but then that would be as true for those members of alliances who have Christian or Jewish affiliation. It is difficult to know whether and how these background commitments play a role in bringing people to these alliances. Faith may have something to do with their mo-tivation, but even that is not clear. It is clear enough, however, that the alliances are not sustained by any common view of the world, of God, of destiny, of heaven, or of hell.

Along with Humanist talk and participation in coalitions, we are also likely to find Humanist projects. Humanists will attend to the moral edu-cation of children—much as traditional groups build Sunday Schools—or to community-serving needs like mental health clinics or "fair housing." In other words, Humanists will show many of the typical features of "con-gregationalism." This is not surprising given the social history and the sociology of American religious groups. Even the recently organized and vigorously secularist Committee for Democratic and Secular Humanism (CODESH) has been moved to organize "friendship groups," which on examination, have nearly all of the features of American congregationalism.[1]

To be sure, some Humanists give the impression that, were they in power, they might, like some modern Torquemada, be willing to put the opposition to an *auto da fe*. Reminiscent of the rationalism of the eighteenth and nine-teenth centuries, they give voice to an antagonistic Humanism that divides people into sheep and goat, that identifies its enemies as superstitious and benighted, and attacks them for their deliberate blindness. But these are voices on the fringes of the Humanist neighborhood and they are as likely to affront as many Humanists as churchgoers. Indeed, I find that most Humanists are embarrassed at the lack of courtesy shown by those on the fringe, much as one is made uncomfortable by a troubling relative.[2] More often than not, I share in this embarrassment. Yet I also admit a certain satisfaction—often, only an observer's satisfaction—at watching the cudgels of controversy used so well by my free-thinking and atheist cousins. Finally, however, they are only a small if noisy piece of the encounter with Hu-manism. When to the addiction to words and arguments, the submersion of Humanists within alliances, and the organization of Humanism into typical American congregations, one adds the fact that Humanists are a very tiny part of the American population,[3] I would have to conclude—at least on the face of it—that Humanism would seem to represent no real threat to anyone.

Then I hear the shrill and angry voices of the enemies of Humanism. I wonder if I have missed something. I meet those for whom the Antichrist is quite real and who find in Humanism the Devil in modern disguise. For example, an extended correspondence between Paul Kurtz, editor of *Free Inquiry*, and Homer Duncan, Executive Director of the Missionary Crusade, Inc., and author of *Secular Humanism: The Most Dangerous Religion in America* [sic], included the following letter:

Dear Paul

For many years, I have preached that Satan always makes his first attack upon the Word of God. In the Garden of Eden, he whispered to Eve, "Hath God said... ?" This is still the method he uses throughout the world to cause people to doubt the integrity of the Word of God. The Bible is the foundation upon which the Christian faith is built and if the foundation can be destroyed the entire superstructure will fall. Of course, this will never happen because the Lord Jesus has given the promise, "Upon this rock I will build my church and the gates of Hell shall not prevail against it...."

I think that it is a tragedy indeed that you and many other Humanists with whom I'm acquainted have allowed yourselves to be deceived by Satan. He is indeed a powerful and subtle being. I know this because I have had dealings with the old boy for over fifty years.... Of your own will, you have chosen to believe in the devil's lie rather than to believe the truth of God.... If you continue to follow the leadings of Satan rather than to listen to the still small voice of the Spirit of God, this letter than I'm writing to you now will haunt you throughout all the countless ages of eternity.[4]

I meet those who believe that, inspired by the Devil or not, a Humanist conspiracy exists. They are convinced that Humanists have taken over the schools, the government, the courts, and indeed nearly all the centers of American culture and power. For them, the small numbers claimed by Humanists are only further evidence of a hidden conspiracy. I have heard it seriously argued that the successful conspiracy must be hidden from view and thus that the tiny size of the self-confessed Humanist population really verifies its effectiveness. We need only look around to see the massive power that is wielded unseen by what is a vicious and dangerous and even Satanic minority. Consider the decay of the American family, the rise of homosexuality, the availability of abortion, the crime rate, etc., etc. All of this is evidence of Humanist success.

It was not accidental that in the 1970s, many of those taking this view united in response to this perception behind the banner of a self-proclaimed "moral majority." The name itself was a commentary on their view of their own status and the status of the enemy.[5] For them, and their successors, the miniscule size of Humanist groups only proved the subversive nature of Humanism. A typical instance of the fear of Humanist power could be found in the recent Alabama textbook case. The issues were summed up as follows:

Is it religion to teach that God is, but not religion to teach that God is not?

The questions lie at the heart of a suit brought by 600 parents against the Board of School Commissioners of Mobile County. The plaintiffs contend that "Secular Humanism" is for all constitutional purposes an establishment of religion. They assert that this religion is being systematically taught through the textbooks and teaching materials used in Mobile schools. They ask a U.S. judge to halt the use of these texts and to order them replaced by others in which God gets a fair shake.

What is "Secular Humanism?" Humanists describe themselves as "non-theists." . . . To the Humanist, science and reason are the be-all and end-all. There is no life after death. Orthodox religious teachings are "sham." . . . Are its precepts embodied in public school curricula? The evidence appears to be overwhelming in support of that view. Plaintiffs in the Mobile case have offered half a dozen expert witnesses who have testified to the literally "godless" nature of teaching materials. Such prominent Humanists as Charles Francis Potter and Paul Blanshard have described education as "a most powerful ally" and "the most important factor moving us toward a secular society."[6]

Ironically, the very term "secular humanism" was not generally used by Humanists at all until the early 1980s and then only after anti-Humanists had seized upon it as a term of reproach. It was introduced almost accidentally in a narrow legal context some twenty years earlier. Thus, in a letter, Joseph L. Blau wrote:

In reply to Morris Earle's question, "Did the expression 'secular humanism' spring fully grown from the head of Mr. Justice Black?" (letter, June 9), I can answer that Associate Justice Hugo L. Black repeated the term as it was used in an *amicus curiae* brief submitted by the American Humanist Association in *Torcaso v. Watkins* (367 U.S. 488, June 19, 1961). . . . A memorandum I wrote for the legal committee of the Ethical Union for an earlier case was used as a basis for this part of the *amicus* brief in Torcaso.[7]

And, Leo Pfeffer, counsel for Torcaso in a companion letter added:

As the attorney who argued Roy Torcaso's case before the Supreme Court, I can perhaps shed some light on the term, "secular humanism."

In my brief to the Court, I urged and the Court agreed that denial of a notary public license to one who refused to take an oath that he believed in the existence of God violated the First Amendment's ban on laws respecting an establishment of religion or prohibiting its free exercise. Mr. Torcaso was an atheist and probably knew no more than I then did what was meant by "secular humanism." . . .

What came out of this was footnote 11 of Justice Black's opinion. "Among religions in this country, however," he wrote, "which do not teach what would generally be considered belief in the existence of God are Buddhism, Taoism, Ethical Culture, Secular Humanism, and others."

Had I anticipated that the term would be used in the Education for Economic Security Act, I would have kept my mouth shut and not urged it in my argument or included it in my brief.[8]

As the King remarks in *Anna and the King of Siam*, "It's a puzzlement." The Humanism we actually find is supported by a nearly invisible minority and the Humanists we meet are busy arguing "fine points of the law" among themselves. At the same time, a much larger number on the Christian Right—also a minority, however—see Humanism as a conspiracy that is capturing the United States. Since the statistical data are clear enough and since a visit with Humanists will reveal their innocence, we might conclude that the Christian Right is simply mistaken or else that its leaders are lying in order to justify their leadership. Needing an enemy now that anti-communism has run its course and that anti-Semitism and anti-Catholicism are no longer respectable, they have found it in Humanism and Humanists:

[Martin] Marty, who is also a Lutheran minister, says that, because it is almost impossible to be a militant heretic in America today, the Christian Right was forced to create secular humanism so that it would have something to attack. "Whenever you wish to organize a group in America, as diverse and pluralistic as we are, you have to focus on a bogeyman. If you have a diffuse enemy, there is no way to hold a group together and motivate it. When the Christian Right organized—remember its outlook tends to be Manichean, a simple world where it's God versus Satan, Christ versus the anti-Christ, modern Christians versus who?—the enemy turned out to be secular humanism."[9]

Were this the full story, we might simply conclude that we have here one more instance of "the paranoid style in American politics."[10] And, were that the case, then we should really spend our time examining the role of the Christian Right or the "new right" or the "moral majority" as the modern development of an old theme in American history. It would be wasteful to pay attention to a conflict between it and some putative Humanist conspiracy except as a diagnostic tool. It is possible to make a good case for this view of the matter. Clearly, Christians and others on the right have felt themselves to be under attack since the end of World War II. They have felt the passing away of what they call traditional values—really nineteenth-century rural values—which reached a climax in the frustrations and angers of the Vietnam war. Starting from their view of things, it is also possible to conclude that the loss of a number of legal battles in the Supreme Court around issues like "religion in the schools," "bible reading in the schools," or the "right to privacy," signals the erosion of so-called Christian values—at least a middle-class American establishment view of these. Given the changes in family life that attend urbanization and industrialization[11] and the variety of "life-styles" that flourished in the 1960s and that show no sign of vanishing, we can understand that a Christian interpretation of family values is threatened by competitors with equal claim to legitimacy. Above all, we can sympathize with the feeling that something is terribly wrong with what is going on in our country and that we face a genuine moral crisis. After all, Fundamentalists are not alone in reciting the litany of drug abuse, crime, abandoned children, poverty in the streets, and corruption in political office.

The defenses against this feeling of violation and dismay have developed in a number of ways, not least by uniting around a national politics where traditional American Protestant values are honored in rhetoric if not in action. Certainly, this was the mood and message of the Reagan administration and it continues, although somewhat muted, in its successor.[12] To be sure, these values are derived from a sentimental view of American history, but they are no less genuinely held for all of that. In the mid–1970s, this religious politics was already achieving electoral success, and it was not only a partisan political matter. President Jimmy Carter, certainly more attuned to civil liberty than his predecessor or successor, nevertheless explicitly traced the roots of his politics to his religious views and had, as he confessed in a moment of suicidal political candor in his 1980 campaign, a "sense of sin." Symptomatically, he justified his achievement of an Egyptian-Israeli détente on near-biblical grounds. Almost vanished was the secularism of John F. Kennedy's appeal to national idealism or the opportunism of Richard Nixon's reliance on expediency. Clearly, much of the support and excitement of the Reagan campaigns in 1980 and 1984 was generated on the Christian Right. The measure of change in the political climate is suggested by Reagan's rejection in the 1960s and his "heroic" stature in the 1980s. Ironically, given Mr. Reagan's family history—divorce and estranged children—substance obviously surrendered to form and reality to rhetoric. The development of media evangelism has also been a phenomenon of the past decade.[13] So I could easily dismiss Humanism as a political convenience for its enemies. I could as easily make the case that Humanists have had little power to produce the situation that so discomforts the religious and political Right.

But, there is more to the story even if the drama of it, the attention paid to it, and the language in which it is told these days is rooted in the vagaries of American politics and the complexities of constitutional law. Behind the manifest changes in modern life and values there is an emerging and triumphant secularity that shows itself everywhere—not just among those who call themselves Humanists.[14] The token of that secularity is the reliance in public and private life, in matters large and not so large, on what is going on here and now. It is fair to say, I think, that few take God or religion seriously in their daily lives and that most judgments that carry weight— judgments in business, politics, the law, schooling, or what have you—are supported by reference to secular values. Of course, secularity as a fact of practice and consciousness is not necessarily secularism,.... that is, not identical at all with an ideological affirmation of worldly values. But this distinction seems to escape both Humanists and their enemies.

Certainly, even in so-called religious ages, sacrilege was not exactly rare and the daily round was lived in its own terms. Yet people knew what sacrilege was. The common sense view was betrayed in its very name, even for those who disdained priests and churches. For most of us, however, reference to the sacred scarcely plays a role today. The daily round in the past was punctuated by sacred moments and was not isolated from them. Today, even religious and patriotic holidays are rearranged to suit the convenience of the three-day weekend. It is true that most Americans still claim a belief in God, and religious institutions show no sign of disappearing. Yet God has grown rather vague, and religious institutions have taken on a decidedly secular appearance. Sociability, counseling, and fund-raising seem much more to the point than the prophet and the pulpit. Moreover, both belief and institution exist, as it were, in a byway of experience or, if that is too harsh, in a separated compartment of experience. Where this is not the case, for example in the influence of churches and church people on political office, the game is essentially political, a give-and-take of compromise where religious values are more likely to be submerged than dominant. The issue is power and not piety. We pay attention to the ability to influence votes, appeal to ethnic and religious blocs, and not to a prophetic voice or a priestly practice.

Conceivably, the controversy over abortion rights might be considered an exception. Symptomatically, it is precisely because it is rooted in what remains of religious values that the controversy gives little sign of resolution.[15] The public passion it arouses reflects a rear-guard religious defense having little to do with the issue as such. At the same time, personal practice departs from the pretensions of public debate so that a substantial minority, if not a majority, of the women communicants of the strongest organized religious opposition to abortion, the Roman Catholic Church, are found to favor "choice" and in fact avail themselves of abortions. It is also predictable that just because of its embeddedness in irreconcilable religious and secular assumptions—about when life begins—ways will be found to return the issue of abortion to secular society for the sake of civil peace. Already this is becoming visible and was dramatically illustrated in the results of the 1989 elections. This is further evidence of the isolation of religion from the arenas where important decisions about life and death are really made these days. Consequently, we may expect the virulence of the controversy to grow and not diminish for some time.

In other words, the Christian Right perceives and responds to a situation where religion has become almost irrelevant even for many who call themselves religious. The battle with Humanism then is at root a battle with the modern world, which is clearly set on a secular course and has been for several centuries. Given that view of things, Humanists are only the symbolic occasion of an attack on modernism and defending them by pointing to their numbers or non-political style is not really to the point. At least as significant as the paranoid course of the Right is the fact that Humanism celebrates the move into a secular world. In other words, a look at Humanism reveals much about where we are and where we are going as a culture and as a society. Even if the religious Right succeeded in making Humanists vanish, they would not succeed in making Humanism vanish. Humanism is a self-conscious statement of our actual conduct in a secular world whether we call ourselves Humanists or not. Putting it even more radically, Humanism is the articulation of the faith that is available to people in a secular world. Without knowing it, the Right is correct in naming its enemy, but it does so for the wrong reasons.

What then is this villainy called Humanism? Humanists are not much help in answering this question. A quick glance over the field shows that there are naturalistic and ethical and scientific and existential and Marxist and evolutionary and secular and religious Humanists. There are, of course, traditional Christian and Catholic Humanists. A movement for Humanistic Judaism has recently emerged within the Humanist neighborhood. There are Humanists who reject the name because of what they see as its misuse by other Humanists. Thus we have atheists, rationalists, and free thinkers on one side and free religionists, liberal religionists, Ethical Culturists, and Unitarians on the other. A less than charitable view—one to which I am sometimes tempted—would find all of this ludicrous and self-defeating, particularly since the numbers involved are so small. It might even seem that each Humanist with his or her jealously guarded Humanist purity intends to wind up in a Humanist society with a membership on one. The comedy is further perfected by the fact that a careful study of the distinctions they all insist on reveals that a great many of the differences are over words, not over meanings. Under a most charitable interpretation, the best I might say about the plethora of adjectival Humanisms is that they reflect a point of origin, a particular tradition, or perhaps a difference in style and emphasis.

I need not write another history, but it is important to be reminded that Humanism has its pre-modern and classical sources.[16] The fifth-century Greek teacher, Protagoras, sounded a Humanist theme when he said, "man is the measure of all things, of things that are that they are, and of things that are not that they are not." The Roman, Seneca, voiced yet another Humanist theme in proclaiming that "nothing human is alien to me." Along the way, in the materialism of Democritus and the naturalism of Epicurus, we find the seeds of a classical Humanism in the West. With the Renaissance, the celebration of human powers sounds a Humanist note as well. Indeed, we would in any age find Humanist echoes, loud or soft.[17] But another such historical excursion will not do. It will not help us grasp the anger and fear that Humanism engenders in those who see themselves as its enemy nor will it provide clues to a secularized world that appears to lack meaning and coherence and for which Humanism is the remedy.

For our purposes, modern Humanism begins with the Enlightenment and reaches explicit formulation only in the twentieth century with the publication of the first *Humanist Manifesto*.[18] Seen against the backdrop of the development of modern science in the seventeenth century and revolutionary democracy in the eighteenth century, Humanism has a radical and critical edge that, among other things, makes the fears of the religious Right understandable. That which appears today so pallid and tame when we visit Humanists at home in their debates or join them in liberal coalitions was not ever thus. If the current quarrel is fought in the courts around so-called religious values in schools or in families, it is nevertheless true that Humanism began in a political and intellectual whirlwind. It developed as a consequence of forces generated by the emergence of modern science, modern economics, and modern politics; it exists as a consequence of the peculiar features of experience that have ripened into today's world. That world was already prefigured, however, in the passions and struggles of two hundred years ago.

I sometimes have the feeling that the very self-consciousness with which today's battle is fought—the pedestrian way both friend and enemy address what they say is a great struggle between the forces of light and the forces of darkness—already suggests that the struggle is over. This is particularly vivid to me when I consider how much of that struggle ignores the gulf between the words of battle and the experience of modernism. So much of the language of the struggle is a replay of yesterday and has a certain tired quality. We have been there before—again and again. Nor is it accidental, to my mind, that the struggle today gives birth to no great literature or song but seems so trite, even boring. Of course, real issues are at stake, but we are not moved by our sense of them to risk their unknown implication. We are—on all sides—looking backward, and the debate is about how far backward we need to look, to the eighteenth century or to the thirteenth century.

Meanwhile, the same American public that tells the pollster that it "believes in God" would, in all probability, find unbelievable and surely inconvenient the appearance of God or of God's messengers. Even if we could be convinced of the event, we would, like Dostoevsky's Grand Inquisitor in *The Brothers Karamazov*, really rather that God did not appear. This is strikingly illustrated by our affinity for cults, for magic, and for trickery. With few exceptions—those that, whatever we may think of them, in fact appeal to the latent idealism of the young—we hardly can find in these a religious passion or a demand for life changes. Instead, we find formulas, easy rewards, and a good deal of financial racketeering. In other words, the view that turns Humanism into villainy and the counter view that the modern world needs Humanism already prefigure the turn we have taken into an Enlightenment world. The use of inherited symbols and arguments may simply be telling us that we do not yet know how to speak of this world. The very appearance and articulation of an independent Humanism in the twentieth century, one that is no longer only an accent in another movement, may itself confess that both the Enlightenment and its enemies are in the midst of an as yet unimagined transformation.

In order to approach that transformation, we must return to the story. The Enlightenment was many things. It signaled a political movement and a change in the way people approached life. As clearly, it was the plaything of a tiny and articulate intellectual minority that spoke a special language within its own circles as in the salons of pre-revolutionary Paris. Yet, in its sloganeering and pamphleteering, it sought to stir popular awareness of new things on the horizon, new hopes that would defeat old enemies. It was simultaneously an elite and a popular movement.

The Enlightenment may be interpreted as the coming together of three notions, each of which is now a commonplace: the notions of rationality, of equality, and of tolerance. Obviously, it would be an intellectualist error to believe that the American revolution or the fall of the Bastille were perpetrated by an idea. It would be an even greater mistake to believe that people suddenly turned rational, became egalitarian, or practiced toleration. Yet, if any movement may be said to have had an explicit ideological platform tied to its actions, it was the Enlightenment. If any movement may be said to have had an identifiable style coordinating its language with its actions, it was the Enlightenment. As it proceeded, it set forth a model that has been echoed in nearly all revolutionary and radical movements since. Of course, we can always find a gulf between ideology and experience. Yet, the words were genuinely prophetic in two senses—as an omen of what was to come and as a standard of what ought to come. Symptomatically, the Enlightenment was a movement of manifestos and speeches, of pamphlets and broadsides that sought to proclaim, to justify, and to mobilize for the sake of freedom and progress. It is not accidental, in consequence of its style, that the children of the Enlightenment were and are given to written law and elaborate explanation . . . often to the despair of those who simply want to get on with it.

I know the dangers of trying to reduce a movement that spread over two continents for more than a century to a few simple ideas. Yet, I think it possible to locate its genius. The key to a grasp of how Enlightenment rationality, equality, and tolerance serve as the source of modern Humanism lies in the changing notion of the person. In this context, these ideas take on more than political or scientific meaning. They signal an interest in the human being as such, the free citizen of modern politics and the autonomous being of modern ethics. No longer is he or she the creature of some other and greater being, whether God or King. Innocent as that may sound to our ears, it marks a shift in attention and self-consciousness of which the radical import should not be understated even today. It is this shift that finds its reality in law and in action, in schools and political parties and laboratories. Taken seriously, it undercuts the intellectual, and ultimately the social, legitimacy of the authority of the Creator and of the earthly powers that act in His name.

Institutions built upon such claims of legitimacy like churches and monarchies understood this quite well as is attested by the bloody round of battle that followed when people took the idea of the person as such seriously. The idea was translated into other than political matters and the person as such appeared as a legitimate holder of wealth, property, and control. It was not merely a changing economics that raised and then answered differently from all past history the question of "ownership." The struggle for private property, whose meaning has been so overshadowed by a deterioration into mere selfishness, was, as Karl Marx correctly perceived, a revolutionary struggle. Of course, the motivation to battle was, as with all motivation, a mix of self-seeking and idealism. But the source and sanction of authority in nearly everything, the possession of authority, and the justifications for the possession were moved from another world to this one, from another being to human being.

Taking the person as such seriously had further import as well. Among other things, it put the center of judgment and choice within the person. This had the double consequence of a morality and a politics without God. Historically, to be sure, we had always been forced to decide whether the voice we heard came from God or Satan. That problem, as we know, went back to the Garden of Eden. But now the locus of responsibility and ultimately of power had shifted. Even the traditionalist was forced to decide alone—as much as he or she might try to deny it. The security of sacred or of secular institutions sanctioned by the sacred vanished. Taking the person as such seriously also meant deciding the legitimacy of those institutions on grounds other than some extra-personal source of authority.[19] Conservatives, in defense, tried to find in history or tradition a source of reliability, but even here they were forced to secularize both. As history became comparative history and as tradition itself became a subject of inquiry, even conservatives found themselves without the guarantees of another world. For those who took the more radical step, morality and society were now conceivable and justifiable in their own terms. The move toward secularity was well advanced.

To be sure, the children of the Enlightenment took the rejection of history to extremes so that the new was inevitably seen as better than the old. Fed by the intellectual success of modern science, progress seemed not only desirable but indeed provable.[20] This led to yet another feature of taking the person as such seriously. Not only was the issue of responsibility and choice given over to the inhabitants of this world, but the very judgment of truth or falsehood no longer resided in privileged places. In principle at least—although a sophisticated experimentalism was still developing—truth was available to any person who opted to consider the evidence. Evidence was to be found in the natural world, not in the sacred volumes of the past or in the sacred utterances of their interpreters. Nor was science only a matter of physics and chemistry. Empirical psychologies and biologies were not far behind nor was it surprising that empirical economics and politics should appear as well. Reason, in other words, was not some abstract human attribute. It took shape in structured inquiry, and the power of inquiry was available to all persons.

Ultimately, of course, inquiry was applied even to intimate and holy things like morality and faith. The Enlightenment move toward Deism and away from the personalism of Judaeo-Christian ethics and metaphysics revealed the attempt to build up a rationalist's religion, a moralist's religion . . . an attempt, still, to hold onto a past that could not ultimately be held. As Thomas Paine wrote:

I believe in one God, and no more; and I hope for happiness beyond this life.

I believe in the equality of man; and I believe that religious duties consist in doing justice, loving mercy, and endeavoring to make our fellow creatures happy.

But lest it be supposed that I believe in many other things in addition to these, I shall in the progress of this work declare the things I do not believe and my reasons for not believing them.[21]

Paine was not alone. Jefferson spoke of "nature and nature's God" and his judicious reduction of the Old and New Testaments to the moralist "Jefferson Bible" was atypical only in reflecting the genius of the man.

Taking the person as such seriously meant, too, taking his or her—not so much her, to be sure—opinions seriously. Tolerance then, was not simply a courtesy or merely a way of securing social peace where issues divided. It was instead a recognition of the intellectual consequence of equality and an implicit statement about the nature of the world. The ability to inquire successfully so clearly demonstrated to the children of the Enlightenment by the sciences meant that the world was unkind to falsehood. If, unlike classical idealism, the Enlightenment did not make Reason the power that moved the universe, although it came close to doing so religiously in Deism and philosophically in Hegelianism, it saw in the workings of natural causal laws a certain hospitality to rationality. The belief that truth would vanquish falsehood that underlay the notion of tolerance, relied on that presumed hospitality. A bit later, it was left for John Stuart Mill to give voice to this view as a politics as well as an epistemology in his classic essay, *On Liberty*.

Summing up this brief excursion into the Enlightenment, we can understand that taking the person as such seriously leads to the typical vocabulary of modern Humanism, a vocabulary of rights and responsibilities, of science and progress, of liberty and individuality, a vocabulary of secular democracy taken, paradoxically, as a religious ideal. Sadly, many Humanists today mute the critical and radical qualities of Enlightenment ideas. Tolerance is often reduced to courtesy, to the unintelligible view that all opinions are equivalent and that the holders of foolish opinions should not be reminded of their foolishness. More seriously, the fact that the rhetoric of individualism, equality, and liberty has become commonplace has masked the corrosive import of these ideas. It is in other places where the Enlightenment and its politics have yet to happen that these ideas are exciting, new, and urgent, places like sub-Saharan Africa or in an Eastern Europe finally escaping the chains of Stalinism.

Yet for Humanism, the Enlightenment remains the source of its language, its values, and its world-view. The most articulate recent statement of this connection may be found in *A Secular Humanist Declaration*, written by Paul Kurtz and circulated in 1981. It reads, in part:

Regrettably, we are today faced with a variety of anti-secularist trends: the reappearance of dogmatic authoritarian religions; fundamentalist, literalist, and doctrinaire Christianity; a rapidly growing and uncompromising Moslem clericalism in the Middle East and Asia; the reassertion of orthodox authority by the Roman Catholic papal hierarchy; nationalistic religious Judaism; and the reversion to obscurantist religions in Asia. New cults of unreason as well as bizarre paranormal and occult beliefs, such as belief in astrology, reincarnation, and the mysterious power of alleged psychics, are growing in many Western societies. . . .

Secular Humanism is not a dogma or a creed. . . . Nevertheless, there is a loose consensus with respect to several propositions. We are apprehensive that modern civilization is threatened by forces antithetical to reason, democracy and freedom.[22]

It is this Humanism growing out of the Enlightenment that threatens those on the Christian Right for whom the person is a dependent, sinful, driven creature that must be saved by some extra-human and extra-natural force. At the same time, it is this Humanism that does not entirely serve to account for or to articulate our situation. Enough has happened and is happening which suggests that the optimism embedded in the notion of progress and confidence in the world's hospitality to rationality needs the corrections of recent events. Enough is going on in our experience to tell us that the reductive style of Enlightenment ideas does not do justice to the richness and complexity of that experience.

In short, there is more than one battle being fought, even though the battlefield, the secularized world, is the same for both. A struggle goes on between those who would fight secularism and those who embrace it. At the same time, another struggle also appears. Variously, it is touted as a "search for meaning," or as an effort to recapture "spirituality" in a materialistic world. These two struggles are often mixed together, resulting in an inevitable confusion. The moralist tone of Enlightenment Humanism misses too much of that second struggle, and yet if Humanism is finally to articulate the possibilities of a secular world, that struggle must also be clarified.

NOTES

1. In 1980, under the leadership of Paul Kurtz, Professor of Philosophy at the State University of New York, Buffalo, a "Secular Humanist Declaration" was published and a new journal, *Free Inquiry*, was issued. By the late 1980s, however, the Committee for Democratic and Secular Humanism had employed a staff member to organize "friendship groups" and was sponsoring annual meetings for members— that is, was moving toward a congregational movement even while denying it.

2. Examples of this minority voice in the Humanist neighborhood are to be found most often among those whose "atheism" and "secularism" have become almost ends in themselves. The clearest model is the Society of American Atheists, founded by Madelyn Murray O'Hair, but she is by no means alone. As an example, I recall a "dialogue" between Roman Catholics and Humanists held in New York City in 1972 (May 5–7 at America House). As *The Washington Post* reported:

Paul Blanshard, the octogenarian author and lecturer who gained a nationwide reputation 20 years ago from his anti-Catholic views. . . . began to read an account of Pope Paul's encyclical issued four years ago, against artificial birth control. . . . "Your idea of the Church is not what we're dealing with," said the Rev. Richard McCormick, a Jesuit theologian from Chicago. . . . "We know what Cardinal Cooke thinks," retorted Madelyn Murray O'Hair, the self proclaimed atheist whose court suits led to the outlawing of prayer in public schools a decade ago. (Marjorie Hyer, "Side Effects of Vatican II," *The Washington Post*, May 13, 1972)

Given a troubling style, it is also true that voices from the fringe have been heard in defense of freedoms where less strident voices have simply been ignored. I should add that Ms. Murray rejects the label Humanism—which she regards as wishy-washy and weak-kneed because it flirts with religion. She prefers to be known as an avowed and uncompromising atheist.

3. Statistical data in dealing with membership and religious organizations are hardly reliable. However, if we add up the claimed memberships of Humanist groups in the United States we would hardly reach 50,000. And even if we included those members of the Unitarian-Universalist Association who identify themselves as Humanists we would still not reach 150,000, that is, less than 1/10 of 1 percent of the population. To be sure, and with some justice, Humanists claim that there are many out there who are unaffiliated but whose values and loyalties are Humanistic. They also point to the thousands who come to Humanist groups for specific purposes— moral education of children, marriages and funerals, counseling—but who never join. Nevertheless, Humanist organizations, no matter how liberally the numbers are interpreted, are clearly a tiny, if not utterly invisible, minority on the American landscape.

4. *Free Inquiry* 6, no. 1 (Winter 1985–86): 42.

5. Recently, it was reported that the "moral majority" had dissolved, no doubt

in response to the scandals attending various media evangelists. Nevertheless, and accurately, the report claimed that its work had been effective, achieving "a terrific maturing process on the right." Peter Steinfels, "Moral Majority to Dissolve; Says Mission Accomplished," *The New York Times* June 12, 1989.

6. James J. Kilpatrick, "Showdown Over Humanism," *Chicago Sun Times*, February 18, 1986. On appeal, the decision of Judge W. Brevard Hand upholding the parent plaintiffs (March 4, 1987) was overturned by a unanimous three-judge panel of the 11th Circuit (September 3, 1987). The issue of "creationism" has also reached the courts and is another point where a "Secular Humanist" conspiracy is said to be at work—for example, see the U.S. Supreme Court decision in *Edwards v. Aguillard* (Case No. 85–1513). On June 19, 1987 the Court ruled seven to two that a Louisiana law requiring public schools to give balanced treatment to theories of "evolution science" and "creation science" violated the First Amendment prohibition against the establishment of religion.

7. Joseph L. Blau, Professor Emeritus of Religion at Columbia University, letter to *The New York Times*, June 19, 1985.

8. Leo Pfeffer, letter to *The New York Times*, June 19, 1985.

9. Wray Herbert, "Fundamentalism vs. Humanism: Cultural Battle Threatens The Humanities," *Humanities Report* 3, no. 9, American Association for the Advancement of The Humanities (September 1981): 6.

10. See Richard Hofstadter, *The Paranoid Style in American Politics* (New York: Knopf, 1965).

11. See, for example, Philip S. Gutis, "Family Redefines Itself, And Now The Law Follows," *The Week in Review, The New York Times*, May 28, 1989, also Arlene S. Skolnick and Jerome H. Skolnick, *Family in Transition* 5th ed. (Boston: Little Brown, 1986), particularly Chapter 1.

12. Domestic policy is more likely than foreign policy to reveal a conservative temper these days, and abortion is one of the telltale issues. While the public is more tolerant, the administration still follows a right-wing line. For example, see Irving Molotsky, "As Expected, Bush Vetoes Bill That Would Pay for Some Abortions," *The New York Times*, October 22, 1989.

13. For a discussion of this theme, see Edward L. Ericson, *American Freedom and the Radical Right* (New York: Ungar, 1982).

14. For a discussion of the evolution of a secular culture in the framework of the development of American religion, see James Turner, *Without God, Without Creed (The Origins of Unbelief in America)* (Baltimore: Johns Hopkins, 1985).

15. The attempt to secularize the abortion issue seemed successful in the Supreme Court's decision in *Roe v. Wade* (410 U.S. 113, 1973), but that "success" is now being challenged in an appeal from the decision in *Webster v. Reproductive Health Services* (Supreme Court, October Term, 1988). The decision of June 1989 upheld Webster, but on narrow and confusing grounds. One of the *amicus* briefs before the Court sums up its argument as follows:

There is no scientific consensus that a human life begins at conception, at a given stage of fetal development or at birth. The question of "when a human life begins" cannot be answered by reference to scientific principles like those with which we predict planetary movement. The answer to that question will depend on each individual's social, religious, philosophical, ethical, and moral beliefs and values. (*Amicus Curiae Brief of 167 Distinguished Scientists and*

Physicians Including 11 Nobel Laureates, in Support of Appellees, Jay Kelly Wright, Counsel of
Record, and David T. Cohen, 1988)

16. For a useful and comprehensive discussion, see Alan Bullock, *The Humanist
Tradition in the West* (New York: W. W. Norton, 1985).

17. For a discussion of the sources of Humanism, see Corlis Lamont, *The Philosophy of Humanism* 6th ed. (New York: Frederick Ungar, 1982) and Harold J.
Blackham, *Humanism* (Middlesex, England: Penguin, 1968).

18. *The Humanist Manifesto* was published in 1933. There were, of course, a
number of nineteenth-century forerunners of Humanism:

For the real deity behind the veil was humanity itself. . . . There were not many Americans
baptized in Auguste Comte's Religion of Humanity. . . . But, like Comte's Positivist religion,
the faith of many unbelievers set Humanity on the altar in place of God. . . . Francis E. Abbot
extended rather than extirpated his Protestant heritage when in 1871 he called his Free Religion
"organized faith in Man." But it was a considerable extension: ultimate meaning resided in
the destiny of the human race, not in anything transcending it. "My doctrine," said Ingersoll,
"is this: All true religion is embraced in the word Humanity." (James Turner, *Without God,
Without Creed,* p. 251)

19. Re-reading the Declaration of Independence in this context is quite revealing.

20. Perhaps the most completely worked out eighteenth-century statement of the
idea of progress can be found in Condorcet's *Esquisse d'un Tableau Historique de
Progres de l'Esprit Humain.* See also J. B. Bury, *The Idea of Progress* (New York:
MacMillan, 1924).

21. Thomas Paine, *The Age of Reason: Being an Investigation of True and Fabulous
Theology,* Paris, 1794. The citation is from the first section and appears on the first
textual page of all available editions.

22. See *Free Inquiry* 1, no. 1 (Winter 1980–81): 3–6.

3

Religions of Humanity: Rationalism, Free Thought, and Ethical Culture

It takes no unusual skill to find Humanist echoes in any culture or any civilization. But the Humanism we meet today is rooted in a particular experience—the arrival of democratic revolutions, modern science and technology, and an urban industrial society. Suddenly, at least as historical time is measured, what was once the possession of a privileged intellectual class became—in its dreams if not in its realities—a popular possibility. Humanism left the salon for the market place. The Humanism that grew from the arts and humanities and the Humanism that had a religious, scientific, and political center grew apart. The former lingered in the academy and among those for whom human powers had an aesthetic and necessarily limited appeal.[1] The latter found its home in those great nineteenth-century arguments concerning heaven and earth, creation and evolution, nature and nurture, and freedom and equality. To be sure, a common tie bound them together; both celebrated human abilities and expected a great deal from human nature. Inevitably, they spoke in different voices and, as they evolved, to different people.

The point of separation was the Enlightenment; the impulse to separation was modern empirical science. An aesthetic Humanism could and did make its peace with God and the Church; indeed some of its greatest achievements were embedded in a sacred vocabulary. The arts of the Renaissance still today provide living testimony to the fact that God's creature was manifestly able to be both creation and creator. Modern Humanism, the Humanism of the market place and the laboratory, set itself upon a different path. Still, whether classical or modern, it was the intellectuals and not popular culture that carried the message. And it was among the intellectuals and their hangers-on that the rationalism and radicalism of an Enlightenment politics developed. Jefferson might address "all men," but it was in the language and style of a Roman republic and not in the popular discourse of the tavern and the field. The "philosophes" in France might attack the Church and the privileged classes and their benighted views of truth and society. Yet it was in the salons of the rich and established and in their active correspondence with each other that the attack was developed and sharpened. Of course, they published the message in the newspapers and pamphlets of the time, even in popular theater and story.[2] But with literacy the possession of a few, the reach of the message was limited. In short, Humanism emerged from the eighteenth century already giving signs of its division—one might even say, a division between the arts and the sciences—but still living within the bounded world of the articulate, educated, and privileged.

As modern Humanism emerged, it took its symbols and fought its battles, quite naturally, within the arena that had given it birth. Nothing typifies this more than Diderot's and D'Alembert's *Encyclopedia*,[3] the effort to capture reason and politics, and to give stature to human creativity not only in the arts but in the sciences and in the work of the world. Not least of all, it signaled the turn of attention to the secular world and the celebration of its virtues and achievements. Still tied to a traditional culture, however, modern Humanism could not make a sharp break with the values and institutions it had inherited. God remained in heaven. However, it was a depersonalized God, a first mover or first cause or, perhaps, a great watchmaker who, having set the works in motion, stepped away from creation leaving it to the operations of natural law. Heaven itself was transformed into the heavens of the astronomer and cosmologist. The Deists may have known their Aristotle (through Rome, to be sure), but more significantly they knew their Newton. God and heaven moved from another reality to this one. Gone was the Dantean image of human destiny . . . to live forever in a glorious paradise or a terrifying hell. Gone, too, was the comforting thought that priest and church would worry about these matters, while taking, of course, their payment in power and possession for doing so.

At the same time, the human scene was changing radically. A new economics—stimulated in part by the notion that human beings could eventually understand everything and thereby control everything—was founding itself in the realities of industrial technology, expansive exploration, and trade. The comfortable tyranny of village life was passing away and the great cities—dirty, soot-covered, and crowded, but also energetic, exciting, and rich—were emerging. Seen from the optimistic heights of modernism, the scene was one of newly released powers and newly acquired wealth. From below, the misery of the past now had fewer comforts and protections to cushion that misery. So, much as the struggle between religion and science excited the intellectual passions, the struggle between property and reform stirred the political passions.

Meanwhile, the sciences themselves did not stand still. What began with a new astronomy and a new physics moved quite naturally toward a new chemistry and eventually, particularly in the nineteenth century, to a new biology and a new psychology. Along the way, a science of society was being born as well although initially, as with physics and chemistry, its home was philosophy and its language was still the language of the educated amateur. Where an earlier Humanism had found its symbols and its values in the arts, a modern Humanism was finding them in the universal impulse to bring everything under the banner of science. Indeed, nothing seemed immune to empirical inquiry and once it was tried, nothing was the same . . . not the heavens, not the earth, not animal life, not politics, not economics, not the soul, and not the church.

No one better caught the possibilities and the problem of the Enlightenment than Immanuel Kant. Uncluttered by the passions of revolution, Kant was the perfect academic, teacher, and thinker.[4] Far from the action, he made the underlying structure of action all the clearer over a lifetime's work that ranged from empirical science to proposals for "perpetual peace." True, his abstractions have confounded students from more than two hundred years. Yet his "critical philosophy" illuminated the Humanism that was to follow, its concern with ethics, the high values it placed upon autonomy and democracy, the centrality of rationality and the sciences, and at the same time its intellectualism and its suspicions of the sensual and the passionate in human experience.

As were nearly all the leading thinkers of the age, Kant was convinced of the truth of Newtonian physics. Unlike most of them, however, he recognized that the world picture drawn by that science left little room for human life as we know and feel it. Before most others had discovered the problem, he identified the dilemma posed by the Newtonian metaphor: that to be accurate and truthful required deserting historical and traditional comforts. Yes, this freed us from the tyrannies of priests and kings, but it left no place for beauty, love, and passion. These were but epiphenomena to be reduced to their underlying basis in atoms in motion and the workings of cause and effect. Above all, such a picture left no philosophic room at all for human freedom.[5] Reality was constructed as a "great chain of being" with no gaps and no unconnected elements. Ironically, the science that was the stimulus for liberty, equality, and fraternity now seemed to deny their possibility, to introduce an even more devastating challenge to freedom by making freedom itself an illusion.

Powerful as science was in its grandeur, and as the acid that eroded the legitimacy of claims of divine authority based on the possibility of divine intervention, this scientific view of things had the strange outcome of utterly dehumanizing nature. The Enlightenment indeed forced liberation from past tyrannies, but it simultaneously impoverished the life for which we were being liberated.

In response, Kant offered a double picture—but of a single universe. He was not a supernaturalist. There were, as the sciences demonstrated, phenomena that we could know and that could be described by arithmetic and the laws of motion. But human knowledge had its limits, not least because it was indeed human and thus the "phenomenal" was but a limited rendition of what is. Consequently, and in order to save a place for human beings, he imagined a "noumenal" world, the world as "it is in itself." Of course, the noumenal was forever closed to human inquiry for we were caught in our senses and had to approach reality through the structures of space, time, and causality. The latter were the ways in which we had to come to the world and, reciprocally, the ways it had to come to us. But we could not know— nor would we ever know—how these structures fit with the world itself, that is, in the world without human beings. When we ask any question, *we* ask it, and of necessity, from within our own limitations. We may speculate, hypothesize, imagine . . . but we cannot *know* the ultimate nature of what is. We can only know reality as given in our experience.

We might be tempted to reduce Kant's view to a standard discussion of "appearance and reality."[6] This simply misses the point. Yes, the phenomenal world is the site of human knowledge, but human beings have other capacities and needs, above all the capacity to make moral choices and to exercise moral and aesthetic judgments. These, however, cannot be accounted for by the Newtonian metaphor and thus cannot be a matter for scientific knowledge. The noumenal, then, is for human beings the locus of purpose and judgment, indeed for history itself—unless we wish to deny any possibility of purpose or judgment and any significance to history.

I think we can best understand what is going on by recognizing that Kant was a superb philosophic strategist making the moves of a chess player or, if I am not too flippant, a bridge player. If the phenomenal is all that is and the determinism of natural law all inclusive, then the game is lost in any case. So, we must play it as if there were more to the game than appears in the sciences since that is the only way that victory is conceivable.

This problem had led, in the past, to the dichotomies of faith and reason and it would again.[7] But Kant understood that to be forced by the implication of the sciences to reintroduce this double vision of the world could invite the worst forms of superstition and the agents of superstition—the priests and kings—back into history. Hence his painful, even tedious invention of special terms and his use of an involuted and complex style in the attempt to avoid misunderstanding. Moreover, were this critical effort to fail, the invitation to the priests and kings would now be issued on the grounds that science itself, because of its limitations, led once again to a doctrine of "two truths." The agents of superstition could make the claim that they were responsive to the modern sciences and to the needs it illuminated. Enlightenment, in other words, could give birth to its worst enemies and, in a way, it did. Indeed, the nineteenth and twentieth-century adventures with political romanticism, with charismatic leadership, and with metaphors of "folk" and "nation" verify the dangers of legitimating "two truths." The ability of leading scientists to put their science into one compartment and their beliefs into another testify to the ever-present temptations of philosophic schizophrenia.

To save the richness of human experience and still remain truthful to modern science, Kant searched for a reliable way of talking about the noumenal, the "world in itself." Not surprisingly, he used that most powerful instrument of Enlightenment, the human capacity for rationality, the very instrument that had generated Newtonian physics. Refusing to resign reason and science in despair, or to escape to faith, Kant invented his "critical philosophy." The generative question for him—the strategy, if you will— was to ask: How are freedom, morality, and beauty possible in a world where everything we can know is reduced to interconnected causes and effects and is an outcome of matter in motion?

Taking his cue from the Newtonian metaphor itself, he saw the same need for lawfulness in the world of freedom, morality, and art that he saw in the world of modern science. So he suggested that the world, being one world, had to have coherence in form. The world of physics could not be lawful while the world of ethics remained chaotic. A moral and aesthetic equivalent for causality was needed. Thus, reason, for Kant, was elevated to ontological status, to a place in the world and not only in human consciousness. Much as science reduced the complexity of phenomena to a few simple rules, so too ethics and other forms of judgment—aesthetic and political—could be reduced to parallel simplicities. In other words, Kant used modern science as a metaphor, a source of insight, for the pattern of the world as it was in itself. Clearly, he did not propose a scientific ethics, a temptation to which others, including later Humanists, succumbed, nor was a scientific ethics even conceivable on his grounds for that would marry the incompatibles of freedom and determinism.

Newtonian physics offered a metaphor for Enlightenment theory everywhere. A secularized politics was built around the idea of a social contract.[8] A historic term of law, contract now became a term for constituting social and political reality. Human beings as rational agents knew their own interests, and interest was a force as direct and as unevadable as gravity. Thus, human beings joined together to achieve a few simple purposes like self-preservation or the protection of property, and the interaction of interests like the interaction of atoms in motion could be described as the outcome of the laws of social motion. But these laws were initiated in an act of choosing, an act of will.

Kant, however, took the Newtonian metaphor well beyond politics and contract. Lawfulness for him became the point of entry into the noumenal world that was inhabited by rational beings, that is, beings capable of giving law to themselves. His reasoning is clear enough: if the noumenal is defined by the presence of "things in themselves," or ethically speaking, "ends in themselves," then the generic definition of such "ends" is their freedom. They are not dependent on the action or authority of other "ends." To be an "end" is not to be a "means"; the association of "ends" with each other is freely chosen and can be as freely rejected. By implication, then, among the defining terms of "ends" is that they give law to themselves and are not the creatures of laws imposed by others. The step from this definition of the population of the noumenal to a theory of democracy is not very great. Human beings are among that population because they are, in part at least, rational beings. They are able to grasp the construction of the noumenal just because consistency, coherence, and the elementary laws of logic are available to them. The best demonstration of this latter fact is the manifest success of Newtonian physics itself.

The aesthetics of the noumenal, the shape and texture of the world, also followed from the notion of lawfulness. Logical propositions were by nature abstract, and logical entities were by nature simple and primitive. So, Kant's ethics, following this pattern, made its centerpiece a single universal and logically simple proposition, the "categorical imperative—Act only on that maxim whereby thou canst at the same time will that it should become a universal law."[9] An ethics of unadorned obligations and duties developed. We arrive at moral judgments by using a rule of universalization and co-herence. At the same time, the moral status of acts and their consequences became problematic since they were also "natural" phenomena to be de-scribed by an empirical science. The only "good" was a "good will." Feelings and loyalties became ethically irrelevant, since as phenomena they were the subject of empirical psychology and political science. The reductive impulse that drove the Newtonian metaphor thus missed the richness and the evocativeness of human experience. The passions, blind and unpre-dictable, were suspect. Sensuality was troubling for it led human beings to deserd reason and to descend to the level of the brute. And faith was to be rejected because it made human beings vulnerable to the false prophets and resigned the power of knowing and ruling to the few.

The price of Enlightenment was very high—but the willingness to pay it was understandable. Passion, sensuality, and faith had indeed been historic instruments of tyranny in politics and in religion. The claim of special truths and powers had indeed been used by the few to oppress the many. Such claims had also been used to deny to most of us the availability and the possibility of knowledge. Nor is that temptation behind us. Elite theories of knowledge and power persist.[10] In short, the Enlightenment was con-cerned with making knowledge and thereby power available to all persons and with legitimating the democratic impulse. In his agenda, and in his philosophic development, Kant, however, took the Enlightenment to new ground, moved beyond polemic, and set the scene for Humanist issues of the nineteenth and twentieth centuries.

More than a century later, in 1933, the first *Humanist Manifesto* was published. It told the tale of the continued struggle for Enlightenment and shows the marks of the battle between faith and reason. As I reread it, I am struck by the effort to bring religion under the banner of nature and to walk a careful line between modernism and negativism. Indeed, the tone of the piece was optimistic—and this is all the more striking given the Great Depression and the rise of Stalinism and Fascism. I cannot help but reflect too on how the 1920s must have seemed to the signers—the deterioration of democracy that marked the notion that the "business of America is business" and the speculative insanity that shaped the American economy. The very notion of a manifesto was not accidental either. It betrayed the double view that things were deeply awry but that powers existed to set things right. The *Manifesto* was, in other words, a statement of self-confidence and a challenge in the name of a naturalistic and religious interpretation of democracy to the materialism and harshness of that other manifesto that drew the loyalty of radicals and reformers. Its mood, above all, was indeed reminiscent of the Enlightenment, the sense that however the present may dismay us, a better future was within our grasp and the way of creating it was known.

The key notions of the *Manifesto* derive from the philosophic naturalism that emerged from the debate around Darwinism and from the social radicalism that emerged from the attempt of nineteenth-century reform to meet both the Marxist and the laissez-faire challenge. In its fifteen points, the signers of the *Manifesto* assert that the "universe is self existing and not created," and that "man is a part of nature and . . . has emerged as the result of a continuous process." The setting of the document is explicitly religious. This is unsurprising given its source among the more radical Unitarian ministers and the stimulus of John Dewey's distinction between "religion" and "the religious."[11] The Fourteenth Point calls for a "socialized and co-operative economic order." Above all, confidence in the sciences is reflected throughout, particularly in the Fifth Point which "asserts that the nature of the universe depicted by modern sciences makes unacceptable any supernatural or cosmic guarantees of human values." Confidently, the *Manifesto* states that "religion must formulate its hopes and plans in the light of the scientific spirit and method."

The road from the Enlightenment to the *Manifesto* takes us through skepticism and atheism, free thought, Ethical Culture, liberal religion, social Darwinism and social gospel, utopianism, and the "religion of humanity." To be sure, in the decades of the nineteenth century there were successful anti-Enlightenment forces at work too. Conservative and traditionalist moves appeared in politics and in religion. Industrialism and imperialism combined to increase the numbers of an underclass and to keep them under control. A new nationalism achieved the shift from divine to secular power, but at the same time was unchecked by anything other than competing nationalisms. This competition was to produce in our time a century of war and destruction. Science, now married to technology, was to become an instrument for the deterioration of life's quality—at least as much as for the liberation of energies and the production of goods. Democracy was to produce its own tyrannies and its own terrorism, populist movements that were as skilled in oppressing minorities and controlling polities as the worst of history's monarchs.

With the advantage of hindsight, it is possible to see the ambivalence and the ambiguities of modern experience, each promise bringing its own defeat, each defeat opening a doorway to some new promise. But as lived, and particularly among those who shaped modern Humanism, it was still a time of progress. Of course, the atheists and skeptics, free thinkers, Ethical Culturists, and utopians were not blind to the horrors of urban industrial life. They knew and recited the litany of political corruption and economic exploitation that was all too visible. They confronted the moral horror of slavery. But, at the same time, they "knew" that they really were on the side of history—not the Marxists and surely not the conservatives—that time and evolution inexorably were on the side of democracy and of liberation. There was work to be done . . . but sooner or later that work would be successful.

Obviously, the story of the struggle for Enlightenment is long and complicated . . . and it has been ably told elsewhere.[12] Just as obviously, a century or more of life and living cannot be summed up in a few brief paragraphs. Yet, we can, I think, catch the mood and spirit of the time by attending to that story's main themes—and they lead us toward Humanism. To begin, we cannot forget that most human beings lived their lives, as they always had, hardly aware of or concerned with the issues and struggles that excited the protagonists of the Enlightenment and their enemies. But people were affected by the outcomes of cultural change as they always were and this, for the democratic inheritors of the Enlightenment, could not be ignored as once it might have been. At the center of an Enlightenment view of history, therefore, we find a reflexive politics, as it were, a self-consciousness that interpreted its very struggles as embedded in the struggle to get people to realize that a struggle existed. Hence, the attention paid to the "word," to pamphleteering and propaganda, to the pulpit and the lecture platform. Despite the appearance of intellectualism, this activity was not an intellectual conceit. A persistent background theme for a nascent Humanism was the need for universal literacy and the urgency of participatory democracy.[13] Politics and pedagogy were thus joined together, as they continue to be for the liberal community generally and for the Humanist community specifically. Thus, history itself would cease to be a story of passivity, of being done to, for the vast majority of people. Condorcet, sounding this note even in the midst of the terror in 1793, called upon the Assembly for universal education in order to achieve the "rights of man." Jefferson asked that his epitaph note two things, that he was the author of the Declaration of Independence and the founder of the University of Virginia. It was not incidental then that the Enlightenment community made schooling a central feature of liberation and of the new society. As the post-Enlightenment era developed, we find—and are not surprised to find—schools and schooling a continuing theme that reached a climatic point in the development of "progressive education" in the early years of the twentieth century.[14]

Another background theme of that post-Enlightenment age led to 1933 and *The Humanist Manifesto*. The politics of terror, tyranny coupled with populism, that followed revolution set the world on a political path that has yet to find its end. Whether organized through the technologically equipped armies of the new nation-state or appearing as guerilla warfare and "liberation" movements, secular politics could not escape an undertone of chaos. The orderly worlds of the City of God and the City of Man, the worlds that admitted limits on what might and might not be done in the name of power, had vanished. The Humanists knew this very well indeed and even rejoiced in it although they sensed that something of value had been lost along the way. Simultaneously, efforts to control chaos marked the history of political life within societies and between them. Among these, the struggle for lawfulness was basic, in conjunction with the search for a legitimate ground on which law might stand—between nations and between warring groups within nations. The appeal to "nature" and to "nature's God" did not do the job nor did the appeal to reason. So on one side, a conservative criticism of Enlightenment was justified on empirical grounds and a conservative reassertion of tradition and history as ways of reintroducing law and order was defensible.[15] But even tradition and history were now secularized. Except for those few who tried, vainly, to restore the divine right of kings, other rulers sought support in constitutionalism or else in the power of conquest and the support of the new bourgeois elites. For the liberals, the struggle for lawfulness turned to constitutional law, to the attempt to constitute society itself by consent. Within that struggle between tradition and contract, a nascent Humanism continued its faith in rationality and progress. Thus, an appeal to the common decency of humankind and to social idealism stimulated reform efforts as diverse as widening the range of popular suffrage, improving the prisons, passing child labor laws, establishing free public education, and emancipating slaves. Where, alternatively, there was an appeal to self-interest, it was to the rational calculator who could look beyond immediate gratification. In place of the conservative's history,

finally, the appeal to fairness set a moral, even moralistic tone, to reform. This moralism as well as a reliance on literacy is still evident in
the Humanism of the late twentieth century.

From the Left, but still showing its Enlightenment roots, Marxism tried
to marry a sense of history with "realpolitik," that is, in yet another way
to move history from passivity to politics, or as Karl Marx remarked, to
"stand Hegel on his feet." *Das Kapital* was clearly a successor to the political
economy of Adam Smith and the *Communist Manifesto* was worthy of the
"philosoph." The Newtonian metaphor revealed itself in the claim to be
"scientific," to deny the role of human choice, and to interpret constitutional
law and morality as class characteristics of the bourgeoisie. Marxism, at the
same time, challenged the Enlightenment confidence in reason and good
will, forcing the children of the Enlightenment to account for their political
views by a reconstruction of democratic ideas. The clear and simple model
of Jeffersonianism needed the corrective of social democracy and of democratic socialism.

The revolutions of 1776 and 1789 had not ended the struggle for a democratic society. This was not simply because the beneficiaries were white,
male, and property owners. Important as the move toward greater inclusiveness was, what was needed as well was a richer view of democratic
possibilities. The austerity of reason, the democratic elitism of Jefferson,
and the economics of a rural society simply did not meet the needs of a
developing urban and industrial culture. Indeed, the notion that democracy
was just a legal and contractual political form that was central to constitutionalism did not touch the problems that were emerging—problems of
human development, of family life under conditions radically different from
farm and countryside, of labor for wage and not for product. Not the least
of the problems was the emergence of increasingly diverse populations who,
over time, were finding their own voices. Ethnic, religious, class, and caste
diversity was a fact of the modern city and, among other issues, posed the
problem of what a later generation was to call "mass man," the threat of
"mass" movements, and the notion of social conformity.[16]

Among the nineteenth-century's voices for democratic reconstruction,
none sounded more clearly than Ralph Waldo Emerson's. Popularizer, es-
sayist, and lecturer, he concerned himself with the essential hopefulness of
Enlightenment democracy and, in particular, the reshaping of the Enlightenment individual in optimistic but more ambivalent terms. For Emerson,
each person was the possessor of a talent—the ability to be uniquely individual and to contribute in some special way to others. This ability could
be discovered in the course of living, could be given expression in the
conduct of life. Never joined with a method or a politics, this Emersonian
theme, and above all, the style in which it was conveyed, influenced a
generation of liberals and reformers in the pulpit, in the academy, and in
the market place:

And since Emerson was the real prophet of the progressive tradition—the Scholar without plan or system, who impressed men of all radical creeds—his polarized attitude toward the individual has a direct bearing on the history of progressivism in America. For the progressives who followed him felt his impatience with men in the mass—this "maudlin agglutination" as Emerson put it. Like him, they held forth the possibility of human development while noting the appalling evidences of human mediocrity. Like him again, they fervently condemned the shortsightedness and selfishness of the middle class at the same time that they cherished its virtues and faith. Emerson was the perfect representative and his ambivalent attitude toward man in the aggregate was shared by the progressives who followed him.[17]

Nothing was more significant for the emergence of modern Humanism than the work of Charles Darwin—the theory of evolution and the political, social, and religious interpretations of evolution that followed. For the Humanist, Darwinism completed the Enlightenment and was the final step in destroying the believability of traditional views of the place of human beings in the course of nature. To be sure, another kind of "social Darwinism" led to a brutal political "realism," taking as its motto the "survival of the fittest" and as its rule the elevation of unlimited competition for power and property. In America, this view was exemplified in the sociology of William Graham Sumner, in Europe by Herbert Spencer:

Sumner concluded that these principles of social evolution negated the traditional American ideology of equality and natural rights. In the evolutionary perspective, equality was ridiculous; and no one knew so well as those who went to school to nature that there are no natural rights in the jungle. "There can be no rights against Nature except to get out of her whatever we can, which is only the fact of the struggle for existence stated over again." In the cold light of evolutionary realism, the eighteenth century idea that men were equal in a state of nature was the opposite of the truth; masses of men starting under conditions of equality could never be anything but hopeless savages. To Sumner rights were simply evolving folkways crystallized in laws. Far from being absolute or antecedent to a specific culture—an illusion of philosophers, reformers, agitators, and anarchists—they are properly understood as "rules of the game of social competition which are current now and here."[18]

For the Humanist, the matter was otherwise. Not only did the account of development offered by evolution challenge Old Testament views of creation, but it offered, more generally, the possibility of a complete and unqualified naturalism. Explanation for all phenomena could now be found without recourse to another world and to supernatural powers and intentions. Copernicus had moved earth and humankind out of the center of the universe and into their own corner of existence. The Newtonian metaphor had permitted, even encouraged, efforts to bring all that was, is, and would be under the single rubric of scientific law. Now, Darwinism closed the door to any exceptions, including the human exception. Typically, toward the end of the century, it was Thomas Huxley, who put the point:

Whether this difference of the fortunes of Naturalism and of Supernaturalism is an indication of the progress or of the regress of humanity; of a fall from, or an advance towards, the higher life; is a matter of opinion. The point to which I wish to direct attention is that the difference exists and is making itself felt. Men are growing to be seriously alive to the fact that the historical evolution of humanity, which is generally, and I venture to think not unreasonably, regarded as progress, has been, and is being, accompanied by a co-ordinate elimination of the supernatural from its originally large occupation of men's thoughts. The question—How far is this process to go?—is, in my apprehension, the Controverted Question of our time.[19]

So the themes were set and the agenda developed—issues of lawfulness and democracy, of naturalism and supernaturalism, of history and schooling. The Enlightenment individual, rational, free, and equal, and the Enlightenment society, progressive and democratic, were now set into a context grown more and more ambivalent. It was not just the conservatives who were skeptical of the benign qualities of human nature, not was it just the realist politicians who understood "war as diplomacy by other means." Emerson was not alone in his despair at man in the mass or at man as we find him. The reformers—whether it was the utopians who turned their backs on the city to found ideal communities or the preachers who took the pulpit into the marketplace—understood that criticism of reform was not simply a ploy of its opponents. They struggled with a reconstruction of the idea of human nature itself, no longer as sanguine about it as their eighteenth-century ancestors had been.[20] Evolution, for them, was converted into the theme of potentiality and progress into the theme of development. Yet they retained a visceral optimism, a sense of the inevitable success of democracy led by an evermore ubiquitous and effective science.

As religion moved into the world of the marketplace, so science too left the laboratory. The former appeared in a fascinating variety of "liberal" religions. Within existing faiths, it was among the Unitarians that the radical call for "free" religion appeared, led by Unitarian ministers like Theodore Parker and William Ellery Channing, and stimulated in no small measure by Emerson himself despite the fact that he had left the pulpit:

Wise on all other, they lose their head the moment they talk of religion. It is the sturdiest prejudice in the public mind that religion is something by itself; a department distinct from all other experiences and to which the tests and judgment men are ready enough to show on other things, do not apply . . . the moment the topic of religion is broached he runs into a childish superstition. . . . When I talked with an ardent missionary, and pointed out to him that his creed found no support in my experience, he replied, "It is not so in your experience, but it is so in the other world." I answer: Other world! There is no other world. God is one and omnipresent; here or nowhere is the whole fact. The one miracle which God works evermore is in Nature.[21]

At the same time, Emerson's transcendentalism, his flirtation with the "over-soul," left the children of the Enlightenment with a deposit of mysticism, or at best sentimentalism, that remained at war with the rationalism and empiricism they had inherited from the eighteenth century. This romantic attachment to some "power not ourselves" and the distinction between "Reason and reason" set the stage for Humanist controversies that linger to this day.

For Protestant Christianity, the move into the marketplace appeared in the "social gospel," while for Judaism it was "Reform" that sounded the note of modernism. At the same time, individual and independent congregations appeared and vanished as their leadership came and went. Among the "free" religious movements that grew and survived was Ethical Culture, founded in New York in 1876.[22] Whatever the different roots and styles, whether Protestant or Jewish or independent, the platform of "free" religion was a mix of accommodation with science and evolution in particular, an appeal and a justification of individual conscience, and a commitment to moral—and, at times, practical—reform.

The sciences too moved into the marketplace. The critic could now begin to see them as an emerging social institution and not simply as the intellectual activity of disparate individuals. Their future was already visible in the disciplinary structure of the graduate university at the newly founded Cornell and at Johns Hopkins. Concretely, the move was the consequence of the marriage of science and technology and the home of that marriage was an emerging industrial system. Transport and product, assembly line and wealth testified to the socialization of science itself. It was symbolic and symptomatic that the Centennial Exhibition in Philadelphia in 1876 celebrated a "century of progress in the arts, sciences and industries."[23] Nor was it merely an aberration for the French sociologist August Comte to read history as the evolutionary development through defined stages to a scientific culture, to "positivism." A bit later he was to preach a "religion of humanity" with the scientist as priest and science as scripture.[24]

Among the voices in America that proclaimed the wedding of science and democracy, secularism and faith was the agnostic, Robert Ingersoll. Typically, he wrote:

Secularism is the religion of humanity . . . it is a declaration of intellectual independence; it means that the pew is superior to the pulpit, that those who bear the burdens shall have the profits. . . . It is a protest against theological oppression . . . against being the serf, subject, or slave of any phantom, or of the priest of any phantom. It is a protest against wasting this life for the sake of one that we know not of. It proposes to let the gods take care of themselves. . . .

Secularism is a religion, a religion that is understood. It has no mysteries, no

mummeries, no priests, no ceremonies, no falsehoods, no miracles, and no perse-
cutions. . . . It says to the whole world, work that you may eat, drink, and be clothed;
work that you may enjoy; work that you may not want; work that you may give
and never need.[25]

The decades between Enlightenment and the 1933 *Manifesto* could easily
have been read as a time of despair. As Dickens put it in the opening of *A
Tale of Two Cities*, "it was the best of times, it was the worst of times."
Slavery had been ended but the exploitation of increasingly large numbers
of people continued. The excesses of imperialism included an American
expansionism that had nearly destroyed Native Americans and their culture
and that by the end of the century was spreading to Latin America, the
Philippines, and the Caribbean. The new city of industry and commerce
was also a city of filth and slum. Yet, the twentieth century opened on
hope, and the nascent Humanist fresh from the triumphs of science could
still feel that same optimism that had shaped the progressivism of the Enlightenment.

But the darker tones could not be ignored and indeed in less than
two decades were revealed in all their terror. For those like myself who
were raised with World War II and the struggle with Nazism as our
reference point, for those coming afterward for whom Korea or Vietnam are "their" wars, World War I seems ancient history. Yet, for the
children of the Enlightenment it was that moment when democracy,
liberation, and science came together to announce their failure on the
battlefield. Here, after all, was a war initiated by a Germany that was
the great representative of science, industry, and philosophy. It was
fought with equal brutality by the homeland of the "mother of parlia-
ments" and by the nation where "liberty, equality, and fraternity" had
been enshrined. When America entered the war to make the world
"safe for democracy," the critic could not help but note that it was the
overwhelming power of industry and technology, not the pretense to
virtue, that carried the day. Woodrow Wilson, echoing Kant's call for
"perpetual peace," might speak of "open covenants, openly arrived at."
The reality was to be found in the struggle for power and property and
in the national interests of the victors.

Never again could progress and optimism be claimed without a certain
twinge of conscience. For the liberal community, as Eric Goldman wrote:

Thousands were like the progressive . . . in Muncie, Indiana. With witch hunters
thrashing through the state, this man was no longer signing petitions or making
speeches at the town meeting. "I just run away from it all to my books," he explained
resignedly. Still other progressives turned to the cushion of cynicism or to expa-
triation which offered the delights of disillusionment on a devaluated franc, or to
the exhilaration of Socialism or Communism.[26]

Humanism now appeared as a minority voice within the liberalism and progressivism that were its historic home. The issue was not retreat but reinterpretation, the effort to move beyond Enlightenment while not deserting it for a new "realism" and "pragmatism."[27] Felix Adler who, while unfriendly to the name "Humanist" nevertheless founded one of the longest-lived modern Humanist movements, put the issue in a Sunday address to the Ethical Society:

How do you manage to support your confidence and belief in humanity, seeing that all civilization has broken down? It is a trifle trying to one's patience to hear these weak meowings that civilization has broken down. No, civilization has not broken down. The war has demonstrated that *what we believed was civilization was not civilization.* . . . And the challenge of the War is that we should now get together and try to build up a real civilization instead of trying to build up a money civilization and power civilization.[28]

In the decade that followed Versailles and the League of Nations, Humanism began to find its own voice through the pages of *The New Humanist.*[29] The themes of Enlightenment, now somewhat muted by more than a century of experience with human nature in a secularized world, were still to be heard. Reason, science, and democracy shaped a Humanist platform and naturalism, a Humanist philosophy. The way to the *Manifesto* was clear.

NOTES

1. For a discussion of this theme and its place in the history of Humanism, see Alan Bullock, *The Humanist Tradition In The West* (New York: W. W. Norton, 1985), particularly Chapters 1 and 3.

2. The great example of the literary turn of the "philosophs" is Voltaire (1694–1778), born in Paris as François-Marie Arouet. His plays, essays, and novels show clearly the programmatic and polemical structure toward which aesthetic forms were directed by Enlightenment figures—another instance of the departure of the two Humanisms from each other. His work also reveals the audience to which it was addressed, essentially a popular audience. See Paul Edwards, "Voltaire," in *The Encyclopedia of Unbelief,* vol. 2, ed. Gordon Stein (Buffalo, NY: Prometheus, 1985), 713–33.

3. *L'Encyclopédie* was published in seventeen volumes, in Paris, between 1751 and 1765. Its subtitle was "a dictionary of the sciences, arts, and vocations."

4. Immanuel Kant was born in 1724 and died in 1804. He was poor, never traveled, and lived his entire life in Konigsberg, Prussia. The poet, Heine, is said to have remarked that no life history of Kant was possible for he had neither life nor history.

5. That this "hard determinism" is still current may be seen in today's behaviorist psychologies, where conduct is reduced to the outcome of bio-neurological and

chemical causes. The idea of consciousness and indeed of self-consciousness is in that view, simply a mistake; freedom of choice is an illusion.

6. The point is clear: Kant was not a Platonist and did not present the view that there was a "heaven beyond the heavens," a reality behind what only appears to us as real. Nor was he a supernaturalist. His analysis applies to one natural universe which for human beings can only be known in a certain limited way, by using notions like time, space, and causality.

7. In another age, St. Thomas struggled, successfully, to accommodate the demands of the Church and the science of Aristotle. In our own, theologians seek to accommodate a different sense of time, or else radically to isolate the natural and the non-natural.

8. Familiar, seventeenth- and eighteenth-century social contract theories are to be found in Thomas Hobbes' *Leviathan*, in John Locke's *Two Treatises of Government*, and in Jean Jacques Rousseau's *The Social Contract*.

9. Immanuel Kant, *Selections*, Theodore Myer Greene, ed. (New York: Charles Scribner's Sons, 1929): 302.

10. As an example, see "Schooling, Culture, and Literacy in the Age of Broken Dreams: A Review of Bloom and Hirsch," *Harvard Educational Review*, 58, no. 2 (May 1988): 172–194. References are to Allan Bloom, *The Closing Of The American Mind* (New York: Simon and Schuster, 1987), and to E. D. Hirsch, Jr., *Cultural Literacy: What Every American Needs to Know* (Boston: Houghton Mifflin, 1987).

11. References are to *Humanist Manifesto I*, 1933 (available from Prometheus Press, Buffalo, NY). Among the signers were Unitarian liberals like Raymond B. Bragg, John H. Dietrich, Llewellen Jones, R. Lester Mondale, Charles Francis Potter, Curtis Reese, and Edwin H. Wilson. Philosophic naturalists who also signed included Edwin Arthur Burtt, A. Eustace Haydon, John Herman Randall Jr., Roy Wood Sellars, and of course, John Dewey. The distinction between "religion" and the "religious" is developed in Dewey's *A Common Faith* (New Haven: Yale University Press, 1934, Chapter 1.

12. There are many sources for that story, not least of all in the biographies and memoirs of people like Jane Addams, Samuel Gompers, Jacob Riis, and Lillian Wald. Dipping into the essays of Ralph Waldo Emerson, Thomas Huxley, or Robert Ingersoll give both a flavor of the time and an insight into its issues. I have found the following helpful: Joseph L. Blau, *Cornerstones of Religious Freedom in America* (Boston: Beacon, 1949); Alan Bullock, *The Humanist Tradition in the West* (New York: W. W. Norton, 1985); Edward L. Ericson, *The Free Mind through the Ages* (New York: Frederick Ungar, 1985); Charles H. Lyttle, *Freedom Moves West: A History of the Western Unitarian Conference, 1852–1952* (Boston: Beacon, 1952); Arthur Mann, *Yankee Reformers in the Urban Age* (Cambridge, MA: Harvard University Press, 1954); Stow Persons, *Free Religion*) New Haven: Yale University Press, 1947); Herbert W. Schneider, *A History of American Philosophy* (New York: Columbia University Press, 1946); James Turner, *Without God, Without Creed* (Baltimore: Johns Hopkins University Press, 1985).

13. It was John Dewey who initially used the term "participatory democracy." In the 1960s, the term became a polemical and, unlike Dewey's usage, its intention was populist and, in its outcome, anti-democratic—that is, it confounded democratic processes by insisting that everyone had to be heard all the time, to be counted on all questions, with resultant noise and paralysis. Such a situation begged for au-

thoritarianism, and so it was not surprising that the same move toward "participation" was simultaneously a move toward leading "personalities" and manipulation.

14. See, for example, John Dewey, *Democracy and Education* (New York: Macmillan, 1916), (reprinted, New York: The Free Press, 1966), particularly Chapters 2, 6, and 8. For a history of the development of progressive education, see Lawrence Cremin, *The Transformation of the School* (New York: Vintage Books, 1961).

15. The central philosophic figure for the reassertion of "history" was G.W.F. Hegel:

> Like Goethe, Hegel concluded that the event was irreversible: the Middle Ages were over. This is the sense of his political reflections at the time (1806), not to mention his later writings, among which the *Philosophy of Right* (1821) is usually mentioned for its qualified defense of authoritarianism. It is true that Hegel was never a democrat, and a liberal only insofar as all his life he adhered to the rationalism of the Enlightenment. It is also true that his almost Burkean worship of continuity and the "organic" did not preclude a sense of the inevitability of catastrophic change. Hegel does not celebrate progress in the liberal manner, but neither does he share the conservative nostalgia for the past. Standing between the Enlightenment and the Romantic reaction, he seeks to synthesize them in a procedure which makes the course of history appear at once necessary and tragic. (George Lichtheim, Introduction to *The Phenomenology of Mind*, by G.W.F. Hegel, J. B. Baillie, trans. [New York: Harper Torchbooks, 1967]: xx)

16. There is, as we know, a rich critical literature on the deterioration of democratic society into mass society. Clearly, this theme was central to John Stuart Mill's *On Liberty*, and his discussion of the "tyranny of the majority." It was to appear in an ironic way in Nietzsche's attack on "mass man" and on Christianity as a slave morality. In a much later discussion, it was the theme of David Riesman's *The Lonely Crowd* (New Haven: Yale University Press, 1950).

17. Daniel Aaron, "Emerson as Democrat," in *Ralph Waldo Emerson, A Profile,* Carl Bode, ed., (New York: Hill and Wang, 1969): 162. For examples of this democratic theme, see also Emerson's "Self Reliance" and "The American Scholar."

18. Richard Hofstadter, *Social Darwinism in American Thought* (Boston: Beacon, 1955): 59. In other words, the position of the conservative social Darwinists combined free-enterprise economics with evolutionary social science and took individualism to what might be called its logical extreme. Thus:

> All animals were regarded as essentially struggling, each for its own existence even within a single species. . . . The struggle was conceived individualistically even by those who were chiefly interested in the theory of the survival of species or "favored races." This was particularly true of the Spencerians, for Spencer's *Sociology*, which appeared in the early seventies, formulated the principles of political and economic individualism in terms of the "survival of the fittest." (Herbert W. Schneider, *A History of American Philosophy*, 381)

19. Thomas H. Huxley, *Science and Christian Tradition* (New York: D. Appleton, 1899): 7.

20. Perhaps one of the clearest examples of this mix of reform, hope, and realism about human nature "as we find it" was Felix Adler, founder of the Ethical Culture movement. At the same time, he persisted in seeking for new intellectual and theoretical ground and was particularly sarcastic about "mere" reform—that is, reform without a basis in theory. Inspired by Kant and by Emerson, Adler never-

theless knew the realities of urban society and the problems of industrial organization. His work took him variously into political and housing reform, the settlement
house movement, progressive education, and indeed nearly all of the projects of the
period. See Howard B. Radest, *Toward Common Ground* (New York: Ungar, 1969),
particularly Chapters 4 and 12. See also Eric F. Goldman, *Rendezvous With Destiny*
(New York: Vintage Books, 1956). The essays and biographies of the reformers
themselves—Jane Addams and Jacob Riis, for example—give ample evidence that
a much more complicated and mixed picture of human nature was emerging.

21. Ralph Waldo Emerson, "The Sovereignty of Ethics" (1878), *Lectures and
Biographical Sketches, Emerson's Complete Works* vol. 10 (Boston: Houghton, Mifflin
and Company, 1887): 191–192.

22. See Radest, *Common Ground*, Chapters 1 and 6; also Stow Persons, *Free
Religion* (New Haven: Yale University Press, 1947).

23. See Lally Weymouth, *America in 1876, The Way We Were* (New York: Vintage,
1976): 13.

24. See, for example, Walter M. Simon, *European Positivism in the Nineteenth
Century. An Essay in Intellectual History* (Ithaca, NY: Cornell University Press, 1963).

25. Robert Ingersoll, "Secularism," *The Independent Pulpit*, Waco, Texas, 1887
(reprinted in *International Humanist*, September, 1987, p. 13).

26. Eric Goldman, *Rendezvous with Destiny,* (New York: Vintage, 1956): 223.

27. By the mid-twentieth century, liberalism had lost its philosophic voice and
had become instead a motley political collection is disparate views including the
"thought-less" reform of the "New Deal," the neo-orthodoxy of Rheinhold Nie-
buhr, and the international "realism" of anti-communism. "Liberal" became an
umbrella term for "good" causes and for humanitarianism in political and social
life.

28. Felix Adler, *Ethical Prerequisites of Personal Peace* (unpublished address), December 16, 1917, p. 16.

29. Begun in the 1920s as a mimeographed paper *The New Humanist* was edited
by Edwin H. Wilson, a Unitarian Minister and later Executive Director of the
American Humanist Association. It was in its pages that the 1933 *Manifesto* was first
published, and it was through its pages that Humanists found each other, leading
in 1941 to the formal organization of the American Humanist Association. For an
informal recollection of the beginnings of Humanism in the United States, see Edwin
H. Wilson, "The History of American Humanism: What Worked; What Didn't
Work," *Humanism Today* 2 (1986): 41–53.

4

Humanism Against Itself: The Religious Debate

'Tis but thy name that is my enemy,
Thou art thyself, though not a Montague.
What's Montague? it is nor hand nor foot,
Nor arm nor face, O be some other name
Belonging to a man.
What's in a name? that which we call a rose
By any other word would smell as sweet.
So Romeo would, were he not Romeo call'd,
Retain that dear perfection which he owes
Without that title. Romeo, doff thy name,
And for thy name, which is no part of thee,
Take all myself.[1]

In 1933, the Humanists who joined in *Manifesto I* set out to reconstruct faith in a modern world. Without apology, they described their enterprise as "religious humanism." In 1980, a number of Humanists led by Paul Kurtz issued *A Secular Humanist Declaration* and explicitly rejected the idea of a "religious" Humanism. They accused those who retained the adjective of intellectual confusion, sentimentality, and even opportunism. The 1980 *Declaration* identified religion with:

The reappearance of dogmatic authoritarian religions; fundamentalist, literalist, and doctrinaire Christianity; a rapidly growing and uncompromising Moslem clericalism in the Middle East and Asia; the re-assertion of orthodox authority by the Roman

Catholic papal hierarchy; nationalistic religious Judaism; and the reversion to obscurantist religions in Asia.[2]

Religion was the enemy and Humanist flirtation with it ensured confusion
at best and surrender at worst. Clearly, the climate of the Humanist neighborhood had changed. The style of attack was reminiscent of the pamphleteering spirit that had animated the Enlightenment. The secularist
broadsides had a familiar ring. Echoes of the "philosophe" could be heard
and nineteenth-century battles over atheism and agnosticism were again
replayed. Sadly, however, the views that had animated the attacks of earlier
centuries now seemed only trite. The polemic and the anger were, however,
addressed to the enemy within. Humanism seemed intent on destroying
itself.

The 1980s found Humanists—or at least many of them—as antagonistic
toward their fellow Humanists as to Fundamentalists and right-wing Christians. The terms of the internal quarrel were not new but the tone of disdain
was. I recall that in the 1950s, the question, "are we religious," would also
evoke debate in Humanist circles. I recall, too, that efforts to distinguish
Ethical Culture from the American Humanist Association on one side and
from Unitarianism on the other circled around the "religious" issue and
the "God" issue. For Ethical Culture, the Humanists were just too "secular," while the Unitarians were just too "pious." In turn, Unitarians and
Humanists found Ethical Culture too straitlaced in its ethicism and just out-
of-date in its neo-Kantianism. But these were arguments with a certain
friendliness of spirit; by 1980 that seemed to be gone.

The assurance with which the authors and signers of *Manifesto I* had taken
to the task of religious reconstruction was unsurprising. In the late nineteenth century, religion on the Left in America had developed a moralistic
tone and center. The pulpit addressed itself to social criticism as much as
it did to salvation. Its efforts were often to be found in the secular world,
and its energies were devoted to social reform. As biblical scholarship, the
"higher criticism," and archaeology revealed the mundane sources of cult
and text, and as science held sway not just in the academy but in the
marketplace, the need to bring religion into the modern world was felt by
many in church and synagogue and not just by secular critics. At the same
time, ordinary life came to be focused on this world and its demands. To
be sure, the sacred was given its due with typical American piety in the
patriotic rhetoric of "God and Country." In the twentieth century, religion
was assigned to a Sunday "ghetto," to the occasional "revival" meeting,
or to the rhetoric of a political campaign. By contrast, the new immigrants
and ethnic minorities still held on to their religion as a defense against the
assaults of the new world. But, they too were pushed and were pushing
toward Americanization, toward assimilation and toward secularization.

All of this invited the reconstruction of faith from the left and reformulation from the Right. The "old time religion" really would not do.

This cultural pattern of secularization was an appropriate home for the appearance of a self-conscious and organized Humanism. Much of the stimulus for its emergence came from the Western Unitarian Conference, informal successor to the Free Religious Association of the nineteenth century. As Edwin Wilson recalled:

Religious Humanism as a movement had no one source, but it first came to self awareness as a movement among Unitarians. In 1917 at a meeting of the Western Unitarian Conference at Des Moines, Iowa, the Reverend John Dietrich and the Reverend Curtis W. Reese compared notes. They decided that what Reese had been presenting as a "revolution in religion: from theocracy to humanism, from autocracy to democracy" was precisely what Dietrich was preaching at Minneapolis. In a sense, the Humanist movement, as such, was born at that moment.[3]

Of course, a Humanist point of view did not go unchallenged in Unitarian circles, and two other ministers, Drs. George R. Dodson and William Lawrence Sullivan, argued that the issue for the denomination was between "the God-men and the No-God men."

Another stimulus to organized Humanism, albeit not without controversy either, came from within Ethical Culture:

Felix Adler . . . was himself scornful of naturalism as a basis for ethics and religion. Though he invited humanists into membership . . . he made it clear that they did not yet share the full "religious" vision which he identified with the transcendental or "supersensible" to distinguish it from crude supernaturalism. He did not knowingly admit the humanist or non-religious members into positions of leadership. . . . The news that two of the professional leaders. V. T. Thayer, Director of the Ethical Culture Schools and Frank Swift, a young Associate in Philadelphia, had signed the Humanist Manifesto of 1933 was kept from Dr. Adler in his final illness.[4]

In the academy, the third source of modern Humanism, the argument appeared on philosophic grounds, the issue of naturalism, and on institutional grounds, the proper role of scholarship. Led by John Dewey, the academy was challenged to put its ideas to work, to avoid mere academicism. We might even think of it as a controversy between an older Humanism and a new one. The former held itself aloof from the world of action, harking back to an aestheticism and a putative notion of scholarly purity, of art for art's sake, of truth for truth's sake. For this Humanism, the humanities and humanistic study were sufficient. The latter took its cue from the Baconian notion that "knowledge is power." Interpreting modern science as "organized inquiry" and "inquiry" caught in the realities of activity, it insisted on the political and social basis of ideas as well as on the utility of ideas for politics and society. In schooling, this controversy showed itself as the argument between the "old education" and the "new"—as Dewey called it; and the "new" flew the banner of "learning by doing."[5] In politics, it was to appear in the mobilization of scholars as policy advisors as in Franklin Roosevelt's "brain trust."

Humanism continued to be the object of attack from "neo-orthodox" and traditional religious points of view. But it was also shaped by the fact that modern Humanism itself became a matter of controversy within its own neighborhood. Among the symptoms was the appearance—after the end of World War II and repeatedly since—of Humanist departures and Humanist fragments. The American Humanist Association was organized in 1941 to bring together Unitarian ministers who could not turn to their own denomination, Ethical Culture leaders who could not overcome the neo-Kantian idealism of their founder, and academics who sought a place to locate their philosophic commitments. Efforts were made to arrive at common projects with other Humanists but these were few and, with two exceptions—joint activity on behalf of the separation of church and state, and the Conference on Science and Democracy (1944–1945)—relatively minor. Two decades later, the American Humanist Association was caught up in an internal leadership struggle. The Fellowship of Religious Humanists was organized in 1963 "by a group of liberal religious leaders, mainly Unitarians and Ethical Culturalists, and is principally concerned with the practice and philosophy of Humanism as a religion."[6] In 1968, a Society for Humanistic Judaism was established in Birmingham, Michigan by Rabbi Sherwin Wine. He moved toward an explicit Humanism while not departing from a secular Jewish point of view. In 1981, following the publication of A Secular Humanist Declaration, the Committee for Democratic and Secular Humanism was organized by Paul Kurtz. Meanwhile, within Unitarian-Universalism and within Ethical Culture, the Humanist strain grew or faltered depending on the leadership and the climate of the moment. Despairing of ever uniting these disparate organizations that seemed to appear with increasing frequency, a North American Committee for Humanism was established in 1980 to bring individual Humanists together. This was met with suspicion as yet another fragment, another competition. Meanwhile, rationalism, free thought, and atheism went their separate ways. Implicitly or explicitly, each of these fragments claimed to represent the best, or the most adequate, or the most comprehensive of Humanism.

I confess that the vicissitudes of these organizational ventures are not really of any great interest in themselves. There was little originality in each "new" platform and each "new" effort only revealed a familiar pattern and told a familiar story. But the fragmented and even sectarian development of Humanist organizations since 1933 can be used to trace the struggle of Humanism with its own ideas. The organizations, while often the result of the temperamental and idiosyncratic Humanism of individuals or reflective of particular histories, also serve as markers of Humanist efforts at self-definition. They offer clues to the evolving meanings attaching to modern Humanism. Whereas the nineteenth century witnessed the struggle of Humanism to appear, the twentieth century witnessed the struggle of Humanism to know itself.

The message of these organizational ventures is that modern Humanism does not exist yet. The checkered career of Humanist efforts to state and restate themselves in organization, program, and language since the 1933 *Manifesto* are symptoms of that fact. Indeed, the arguments between "god men and no-god men," between philosophic naturalists and philosophic idealists, between activists and contemplatives, between socialists and libertarians, and above all between religionists and secularists remain points of polarization within the Humanist neighborhood. At a distance, many of these points seem increasingly less worth the divisions they encourage. Yet they are real enough to the protagonists. Symptomatic of these unresolved issues was *Manifesto II* published in 1973.[7] It was signed by Humanists from nearly all points of the Humanist compass. At the same time, gone was the clarity, directness, and assuredness of the 1933 document. *Manifesto II* is a long and puzzling essay, giving with one hand and taking away with the other. In its discussion of religion, for example, it says:

FIRST: In the best sense, religion may inspire dedication to the highest ethical ideals. The cultivation of moral devotion and creative imagination is an expression of genuine "spiritual" experience and aspiration.

We believe, however, that traditional dogmatic or authoritarian religions that place revelation, God, ritual, or creed above human needs and experience do a disservice to the human species. . . .

Some Humanists believe we should reinterpret traditional religions and reinvest them with meanings appropriate to the current situation. Such redefinitions, however, often perpetuate old dependencies and escapisms; they easily become obscurantist, impeding the free use of intellect.

In speaking of science it notes:

The controlled use of scientific methods, which have transformed the natural and social sciences since the Renaissance, must be extended further in the solution of human problems. But reason must be tempered by humility. . . . Nor is there any guarantee that all problems can be solved or all questions answered.

Perhaps, most revealing of all is the following from the *Manifesto* 's introduction,

Many kinds of humanism exist in the contemporary world. The varieties and emphases of naturalistic humanism include "scientific," "ethical," "democratic," "religious," and "Marxist" humanism. Free thought, atheism, agnosticism, skepticism, deism, rationalism, ethical culture, and liberal religion all claim to be heir to the humanist tradition.[8]

I do not want to overstate the differences, although within the Humanist neighborhood an exaggerated importance attaches to them. On all sides, there is agreement on the values of rationality, on the moral responsibility of human beings, and on the importance of living socially and in the present. On all sides, there is agreement on freedom of conscience and the urgency of free inquiry. On all sides, there is agreement on the moral and political priority of democracy. On all sides, there is a commitment to nurture human capabilities for good and an essential hopefulness about human beings.

At the same time, these agreements often mask deeply felt disagreements. The proponents of democracy separate into libertarians and social democrats, and the confidence in human potentiality founders on issues of practical policy, of how to give political and social reality to that potentiality. The commitment to human responsibility divides in the argument about the appropriate role for Humanists and for Humanist organizations in social action. Indeed, Humanists seem to rehearse in their own terms the same kinds of quarrels that have divided churches and fragmented political parties. I might be tempted to leave it that Humanists have turned out to be human, after all. But that does not solve the problem: what, really, is Humanism up to?

It seems to me that the fragmentation, even sectarianism, that has emerged in Humanism since 1933 is only partly explained by the differing sources from which Humanists and Humanist organizations came. Instead, fragmentation is a consequence of the quarrel over faith, and in particular, of the way in which that quarrel has been framed in the argument with Fundamentalist Christians. Given to dogmatic assertion, they invite equally dogmatic contradiction. And given that they, often for their own opportunistic reasons, insist that Secular Humanism itself is a religion,[9] it is understandable that they evoke denials that it is a "religion." But Fundamentalism is only the current occasion for Humanist argument. Were the quarrel over the nature of faith resolved, a quarrel that is really about the nature and function of Humanism itself, the other differences would vanish in a constructive diversity.[10]

At one level, the religious argument is really only over words. For example, the leading proponent of "secularism," Paul Kurtz, has struggled painfully with the issue and has even gone so far as to coin the term *eupraxophy* to describe Humanism:

If humanism is not a religion, what is it? Unfortunately, there is no word in the English language adequate to describe it fully. . . . Accordingly, I think we will have to coin a new term in order to distinguish nontheistic beliefs and practices from other systems of beliefs and practices, a term that could be used in many languages.

The best approach is to combine Greek roots. I have come up with the term *eupraxophy* which means "good practical wisdom."[11]

I sympathize with Kurtz's impatience and I understand his concern over the confusions of religious language and the political uses to which those confusions are put. In our world, a religious temperament prevails that, in its current anger, is often viciously anti-intellectual and anti-democratic. The identification of religion with Fundamentalist dogmatism and anger tends to monopolize public consciousness and compromises all others who would use the term. Indeed, liberal and centrist religions like mainstream Protestantism and Reform Judaism have moved to the right in response to this Fundamentalist climate. Like Paul Tillich, who once called for a moratorium on "God language," it might be worthwhile to call for a moratorium on "religion language". At least the dust might settle and we could all get on to more substantive matters.

At the same time, there is a historical and intellectual truthfulness in the effort at religious reconstruction that was evident in *Manifesto I*. It recognized that "religious" values were among the persistent features of human experience everywhere. In seeking to capture the point, Dewey remarked:

It is pertinent to note that the unification of the self through the ceaseless flux of what it does, suffers, and achieves cannot be attained in terms of itself. The self is always directed toward something beyond and so its own unification depends upon the idea of the integration of the shifting scenes of the world into that imaginative totality we call the Universe.[12]

Paul Kurtz, himself a naturalist, is not unaware of the needs of human experience. When he shared the draft of his text on "eupraxophy" with me, I wrote in reply:

I think the matter (of religion) is a "non-issue" on the evidence of your own text. Thus, when you describe what humanism should be up to, i.e. a method of inquiry, a cosmic world view, a life stance, and a set of social values (p.13ff), you're talking about what others call "religion." Furthermore, when you talk about "humanist centers" or other institutional forms, you're really describing Ethical Culture Societies, Unitarian Fellowships, etc. I don't think you've developed a new form but only have given a new name to an existing one.[13]

But the argument is not simply over words and the quarrels are not merely semantic. Although we might be successful at inventing new vocabularies as Kurtz and others have tried to do,[14] we would still face the question of modern Humanism's lack of coherence, and its deterioration into polar positions since 1933. This lack of coherence might find a more hopeful resolution were polarization over religion settled. These days, sadly, we avoid working on the question, "what is Humanism up to," and instead play a game of "either/or." All of us are infected by the features of right-wing politicized religion, here and abroad.

Our thinking is distorted by the fact that we love to choose sides. Humanists, more than most, are given to an argumentative game by temperament and by history. Often, however, what begins as an intellectual exercise takes on a life of its own and drives us toward separations that were unimagined when the argument began. I have seen this happen repeatedly, and never more than in the past decade. We lose ourselves in the joys or argument and forget that it is only argument. The game of either/or itself becomes our reality. So it is with many of the polarities that afflict Humanism. In the heat of argument it is easy to turn "faith" into a caricature of itself and then to identify all faith with superstition. When such a mood seizes us, we embrace its complement, a simple-minded secularism that denies any value to a move beyond the immediate. In saner moments, we know that experience is too rich with possibilities to be reduced to abusive labeling and that we are ill served by the mentality of the arena. Yet it is all too human to invest ourselves in our arguments and then to be unable to retreat. Losing the argument comes to feel like a loss of self.

I do not mean to trivialize what occurs as a result of debate although its origins and issues are often trivial. The consequences of argument appear in realities of relationship. We come to like, associate with, and support some, whereas we reject others. These separations are then often reflected in our conduct so that the next debate is not only about words but about these realities too. Our arguments become weapons of internal warfare rather than tools of understanding and social criticism. We lose sight of the problem. Fundamentalist religious movements here and abroad have succeeded in constricting freedom, influencing public policy, and corrupting education. These political realities cannot be ignored and there is a legitimate need for a responsive Humanist politics.[15] This would seem to require unity rather than fragmentation, but that is the opposite of what happens.

At the same time, we are stubborn and contrary. We convince ourselves of the correctness of our own views and proceed to act on that conviction. So I ponder the Humanist adjectives that have emerged in the less than sixty years that have passed since *Manifesto I*—scientific, naturalistic, religious, evolutionary, Marxist, existential, secular, rationalist, and ethical. It is, I confess, ironic, perhaps even sadly comic. Humanism set out to be inclusive. Its method, from classic times to ours, has been dialogic, the effort to catch the partial truths on all sides and to erect transcending truths that would move us beyond the present encounter. Yet today, Humanism retreats into secularism and surrenders to its own Fundamentalist temptation. It allows the non-Humanist to set the terms, the style, even the content of the argument. It hereby becomes ineffective and loses itself.

I think that we are given to the game of "either/or" precisely because the ambiguities of experience have become nearly intolerable. The authors of *Manifesto I* could speak with confidence about the world to come. They had not yet seen science perverted into holocaust and nuclear destruction. They had not yet watched democracy turn into populist conformism. To be sure, they warned of these possibilities, but these warnings seemed merely conceptual. Given the events of the decades since 1933, it is understandable that Humanist confidence should be eroded and that Humanism should lose its way. In the midst of chaos, it is much more satisfying to separate into sheep and goat, saved and damned. To confess the truthfulness and the humanity in the other is never easy; to admit the falsehood and inhumanity in ourselves is even more difficult. But then that is the permanent difficulty of all human relationships. Today, as we lose our moorings, that difficulty nears impossibility.

Humanists, like all other human beings, are caught in the terrors of our age and have difficulty holding onto the genius of their position. Like everyone else, they tend to revert to a mythic past where matters were simpler, clearer, more assured. So it is that when Humanism meets Fundamentalism, it responds in Fundamentalist style with a "raucous Humanism." The world we live in seems to justify the Humanist in his or her defensive aggression. Surely the twentieth century has taught us through the horrors of genocide and the possibilities of global destruction that we are not God's special creatures. It is an affront to be told that these horrors are, after all, just punishment for evil or unknowable features of a divine plan. Too much has happened for us to be beguiled any longer by promises of eternal elevation. As we grow increasingly more sensitive to other natural beings, indeed to nature itself, we also learn how arrogant "speciesism" is, whether advanced by the story of creation or by the "religion of humanity." So the pretentions and pretentiousness of traditions that single us out as "lords of creation" stir us to a noisy Humanism as if we could shout down the enemy. But the noise deafens us too and blocks the effort to reconsider the place of human beings in a reconceived nature.

This game of either/or, of absolute meeting absolute, encourages other instances of Humanism's loss of itself, like meeting the foolishness of "creation science" by polemicizing evolution theory. We play out, once again, the post-Darwinian battle. Or else, we argue God and No-God, moving as if choreographed for and against the arguments from "design," "first cause," "final cause," and so on. We are quite comfortable with these moves, we know them in advance and know that the outcome is predictable. They are, in fact, an indulgence and an escape. Neither side convinces the other, can convince the other, or expects to convince the other. As Corliss Lamont commented recently, "I'm bored with it."[16] Wisdom, then, would search for ways to move beyond the battle . . . but wisdom is surrendered to the joys and protections of battle itself.

Yet something serious is at stake. To be sure, the stories of creation and the promises of providence are poor physics, poor biology, and poor history. Humanism cannot, however, simply dismiss the matter by patronizing diagnosis and thereby betray itself by resigning most of humanity to superstition. If human beings mistakenly "people the darkness beyond the stars with harps and habitations," as Robinson Jeffers put it, a Humanist must ask why and find a better response to the unspoken question for which spirits, demons, saints, and devils are answers. In other words, as the world grows incomprehensibly large and as we learn that it simply does not pay attention to us, we need all the more to attend to questions of meaning and security in experience.

These questions have not yet been answered. The notions of Enlightenment will not do—they addressed a more manageable world. The angers of Fundamentalism and the confusion of sects confess to a widely shared anxiety of spirit. In that sense, both Fundamentalism and raucous Humanism are only symptomatic, and the game of either/or attends only to the symptoms. When we are lost we shout more and more loudly in panic; we mask our desperation with busyness; we seek out a villain. Thus, within the debates that produce a noisy humanism is hidden the question: How shall human life be purposeful and joyful in a universe where human life seems only a chemical and biological incident?

A Humanist can cite the evidence that shows we are indeed living in a secular culture. The powers of the Gods are invisible to nearly all of us—not just to Humanists. They grow increasingly more invisible as time passes. We conduct ourselves as if the Gods, even if they existed, were indifferent. The believer—with the exception of those few who separate themselves from the world—reveals that he or she does not seriously hold to the notions of judgment and resurrection. Eternity is denied in practice no matter how loudly proclaimed in rhetoric. The game of either/or invites the Humanist to take pleasure in the fact, while the Fundamentalist rages against the rule of Satan. The Humanist proclaims that we are already living in the "Humanist century" as the authors of *Manifesto II* put it, echoing the optimism of their eighteenth-century ancestors. That great numbers of people do not hear or respond to that proclamation should give the Humanist pause . . . but it does not.

Reacting against the animation of nature with mysterious deities—there is indeed a renewed spiritualism, a confidence in magic, even a so-called "new age" philosophy—a prosaic Humanism joins a raucous Humanism and calls on the "facts" to witness the falsehood of its enemies. The Humanist forgets, however, that "facts" do not convince and that their interpretation, their meaning, is always at issue. "Facts" need their stories and it is stories that have vanished. Certainly it is important to expose the foolishness of astrology or the trickery of religious charlatans.[17] This has merit as a type of social mental health. But, despite repeated exposure, the followers of astrology persist and the charlatans continue to find their victims. Argument does not work because it does not reach to the depths that move us toward gullibility. At the same time, the naive empiricism that sometimes afflicts Humanism—a consequence of playing the debating game—leads it to an aesthetically impoverished and psychologically inadequate outcome. Thus, Humanism fails to address the depths, and the resort to argument becomes a double defeat.

Nowhere is the need for psychological and aesthetic adequacy more evident than in the utterly personal fact of death and dying. Here Humanists are better in their practices than in their theories—responsive in their relationships and ceremonies while still narrowly rationalistic in their arguments. Of course, Humanism does not, cannot, promise immortality, but the issue is not about immortality although the debate pretends that it is. The believer weeps the same tears the Humanist does, feels the same losses, and the same regrets. Humanist and non-Humanist alike know that their lives do not play out fittingly with a beginning, middle, and end. We are interrupted, repeatedly interrupted, and finally interrupted by death. For our experience, the game of denials on all sides is simply inadequate, the debate pointless . . . and I may add, the promises of tradition not only unbelievable but irrelevant. The hidden question is again a question of meaning and security, how shall we live with the consciousness—and not just the fact—of mortality. As Harold Blackham put it once:

The loved detail of a landscape is annihilated by distance, but one can return and find it. There is no return in time but what was once somewhere had no less reality than what is elsewhere. . . . By the criterion of eventual oblivion, there are no distinctions nor standards, no virtues nor values nor joys nor sorrows: nothing is. This is the true nihilism, to take oblivion as the measure of all things because oblivion is the destiny of all things.

To accept and respect the temporal condition of all things is the beginning of wisdom. . . . To appeal against the temporal terms of the human condition, the ephemeral character of our life, to aspire to an eternal unconditioned existence is not really to look for salvation, for it is to reject and forfeit life. This earnest refusal of life is the profoundest thoughtlessness, the tragic misunderstanding not merely of the terms of human existence but mainly of its very character, what there is there to love and care for, and how it is as it is.[18]

Not only does the debating game force Humanism to respond raucously, noisily, and prosaically, but it leads Humanism to continue to repeat naive views of reason, science, and progress as if the mere repetition would overwhelm the opposition. To be sure, I understand the need to deny the claims of the supernatural; I too find those claims not merely unbelievable but degrading. After all, we are told by the supernaturalist that another reality is necessary for the intelligibility and worthiness of this one. The world that is my home thus becomes the object of a sneer, as it were, even a cosmic sneer: an extra-natural invasion of nature is needed if my life is to have any meaning. We are told that we must lose the world in order to gain it . . . and so on.

The rationalist has little difficulty in demonstrating the contradictions of this extra-naturalism.[19] However, in his or her anxiety to win the battle, the rationalist ignores the absurd features of existence, the non-rational, the intuitive, and the responsive features of our experience, the contradictions and false starts, that should prevent us from attributing a rationalist's structure to nature itself. Science, which is where Humanism embeds rationalism, is not merely reason working itself out in some Hegelian world-historical drama. It is a skeptic's enterprise, but it is a poet's enterprise as well, a fascinating scene of intuitions, guesses, and inventions. A reasonable Humanism, even a scientific Humanism, is not merely a rationalist's Humanism. It understands that we meet the world long before we assemble it in art and science. We meet mysteries, always new mysteries, in a present encounter—just as we think we have dismissed the old one. Of course, that is not the same as elevating the encounter to a meeting with "the mysterious," as the believer would have it. But it does not permit us to deny mysteries as if sooner or later the world will become entirely transparent.

Just as the game of either/or tempts reason toward rationalism and science toward scientism, so too it tempts hope to foolishness. We all hear the promises of salvation. We know enough of sadness, pain, and disappointment to want to believe that somehow, somewhere, it all fits together and that what was sadness, pain, and disappointment had some meaning and purpose. Thus Humanism once secularized salvation with the notion of progress. Our Promethean energies would make things right later, if not now. Ironically, with this belief in inevitable progress, Humanist freedom surrendered to destiny as presented in Comte's positivism or the paradoxes of Marxist determinism, although it was a good destiny, for history was on our side. A selective reading of events, a history that even posed as scientific, outfitted this sentiment for salvation with evidence.

But false promises turn out cynics on all sides. Just as salvation demands blind belief, so progress cannot survive an honest reading of events. The game of either/or does not, however, permit the Humanist to confess the inadequacy of the Enlightenment's idea of progress, nor to reconstruct it. Were it possible to escape the playing field, we might acquire a sense of tragedy, a certain humility, and finally reach a notion of progress as a setting for future action and not as a description of past achievement. Thus, Jean-Paul Sartre from within his Humanism imagines us leaning forward into time not yet:

But there is another meaning to humanism. Fundamentally, it is this: man is constantly outside of himself; in projecting himself, in losing himself outside of himself, he makes for man's existing; and on the other hand, it is by pursuing transcendent goals that he is able to exist; man being this state of passing-beyond, and seizing upon things only as they bear upon this passing-beyond, is at the heart, at the center of this passing-beyond. . . . This connection between transcendency as a constituent element of man . . . and subjectivity in the sense that man is not closed in on himself but is always present in a human universe is what we call existentialist humanism.[20]

There are many instances where Humanism has been betrayed by its compulsion to fight its enemies with inappropriate weapons; I have named but a few of them. The game of either/or, wherever we find it, induces a recurring pattern of simplification confronting simplification, absolute confronting absolute. As in all games, there are winners and losers, points to be scored, and cheers to be heard. Sadly, the game of either/or is played most viciously when faith is the playing field . . . and this is not surprising. For whatever the point of view, faith, unlike politics, business, or sports, addresses itself to those deepest issues of human experience, issues of life and death and meaning. It is these issues, not the name given to them, that stir the passions and call for attention. For Humanism, which is neither simple nor absolute, the game of either/or forces a loss of integrity, a loss of its own character.

The argument over whether or not Humanism is religious or secular needs to be reconceived. Perhaps there is some wisdom, given today's environment, to minimizing religious description and language. We might avoid the worst dangers of the game of either/or. Humanism might then illustrate the virtues of dialogue in a world of partisans. But dialogue is not merely toleration—the final temptation of the game of either/or. It is almost inevitable that those Humanists who find the noisiness of their fellows an affront suppress criticism for the sake of peaceableness, confuse courtesy with clarity, and dialogue with the exchange of opinions. Dialogue, however, transcends opinions in the continuous renewal of knowledge and meaning. That is the genius of the sciences that are dialogues between persons mediated by events and that offer reliability through the constructive uses of uncertainty. In place of the game of either/or, Humanism, in its commitment to the sciences, intended to substitute an inquirer's biography for the "man of faith." For Humanism, discoveries, reasonings, and arguments were always in the process of acceptance, rejection, and transformation. Moments of organization were indeed found in experience, but they were moments. The universe was not organized once and forever.

By contrast, the religious climate today is indeed sectarian and absolutist. Diversity is taken as a sign of sin. Humanism, if it could avoid the Fundamentalist temptation, might preach an appreciation of diversity from within its own genius for inclusiveness. It would not then simply take its identity from its opposition as seems to be the current fashion. Ironically, it is the secular Humanist who is most likely to enter the lists of religious warfare as a protagonist and often with relish. While always denying it, he or she still fights the religious/anti-religious war—often confusing it with the clerical/anti-clerical war—on the same ideological, even theological, territory as his or her opponent.

Humanism is worldly and secular. The qualities of experience to which Humanism must address itself, however, are those that have legitimately been called religious. The authors of *Manifesto I* knew this very well and knew the need for a reconstruction of faith. Since then the religious question has not been faced adequately in Humanist terms—in secular terms. Here, the game of either/or blocks the reconstruction of the terms of its faith— progress and hope—by driving Humanism to a mere echo of its past or to inane simplifications. Not the least of these simplifications may be found in the confusions surrounding the notion of the "secular" itself. In one sense, the term only describes a location. For example, "secular priests" in the Roman Catholic Church exercise their vocation in the world. In another sense, the "secular" is contrasted or even opposed to the "sacred." Thus, St. Augustine's City of God and City of Man, or Jesus' advice to "render unto Caesar the things that are Caesar's and unto God the things that are God's." But neither of these meanings conveys the intention of secularity for Humanism. It is where the action is, all of the action, including that which has historically been religious action. For the Humanist, the "sacred," the name given to that which is untouchably precious, departs from its separate universe to inform this one, the only one we have. Thus both sacred and secular are transformed under the aegis of a Humanist naturalism.

The story of twentieth-century Humanism in the period after *Manifesto I* is a story of departing from that notion of the interpenetration of sacred and secular in the natural world, and is instead a story of attack and defense. This contrasts starkly with the revolutionary excitement of the Enlightenment which enshrined its secular saints in its own pantheon. It contrasts as well with the intellectual and cultural excitement of the nineteenth century when Emerson could embed the transcendent within experience and nature, and Ingersoll could call for a "secular religion." It contrasts finally with the philosophic confidence of that religious naturalism that inspired *Manifesto I*.

Some of the differences within Humanism may be traced to differences of origin, for example, as Unitarian Humanism arose within a Christian framework or as Ethical Culture arose within a Reform Jewish context. Each of these, as we have seen, experienced an internal lack of clarity at the outset. By and large, their legacy of controversy over Humanism has been muted. It is regarded as a legitimate possibility in Unitarian-Universalist circles even by non-Humanists, and naturalism, if not Humanism, has replaced neo-Kantian idealism in Ethical Culture. In other words, Humanist fragmentation can no longer be attributed to its pluralist sources. To be sure, varieties still show themselves in differences of organization, practice, and language. Yet, important as these are, they no longer in themselves require fragmentation. Still, Humanism is not yet. This arises from the fact that the game of either/or and not the accidents of history blocks the reconstruction the signers of *Manifesto I* proposed.

NOTES

1. William Shakespeare, *Romeo and Juliet*, act 2 sc. 1, lines 80–90.

2. Paul Kurtz, founder and editor of *Free Inquiry* and of Prometheus Press in Buffalo, NY, was the author of *A Secular Humanist Declaration* (1980), which was signed by hundreds of Humanists who were almost relieved to confess their secularism.

3. Edwin H. Wilson, "Religious Humanism in America," *The Standard*, 38, no. 6 (April 1951): 307.

4. James F. Hornback, "Naturalism Is a Humanism." *The Humanist*, 35, no. 5 (September/October 1975): 23.

5. See among other texts, John Dewey, *Democracy and Education* (New York: The Free Press, 1966).

6. See statement of purpose, republished on the inside back cover of the Fellowship's quarterly journal, *Religious Humanism*, Yellow Springs, Ohio.

7. *The Humanist* (September/October 1973): 33, no. 5, pp. 4–9.

8. References are to the First and Fourth Articles of *Manifesto II* and to the Introduction. The *Manifesto* was written by Paul Kurtz and Edwin Wilson, who shared preliminary drafts with a number of us and who responded to criticisms, amendments, and suggestions.

9.

A federal judge in Mobile, Alabama, last week ordered 44 textbooks removed from the Alabama public schools because, he said, they unconstitutionally promote the 'religious belief system' of secular humanism. . . . The landmark 172 page ruling was widely viewed as a major victory for fundamentalist Christians, many of whom have long contended that secular humanism is a religion that places man's values above any divine authority and that its tenets pervade the public schools. ("Federal Court Finds Secular Humanism a Religion," *Education Week*, 6 no. 24, March 11, 1987)

Judge Hand's decision was later overruled on appeal.

10. A recent doctoral dissertation by Beverly Earles of Wellington, New Zealand defends the distinction between "faith" and "religion" and identifies Humanism with the former. Dr. Earles carefully reviews the "secular" wing of Humanism, for example, Kurtz, Lamont, and Russell, and concludes that secular Humanism like the rest of Humanism meets the criteria of faith. See Beverly Earles, *The Faith Dimension of Humanism* (Wellington, New Zealand: Victoria University: 1989).

11. Paul Kurtz *Eupraxophy, Living without Religion* (Buffalo, NY: Prometheus, 1989): 13–14.

12. John Dewey, *A Common Faith* (New Haven: Yale University Press, 1934: 19).

13. Letter from Howard Radest to Paul Kurtz, January 3, 1989.

14. A recent example can be found in a resolution proposed to the International Humanist and Ethical Union (Utrecht, The Netherlands), on "The Identity of Humanism." It reads, in part:

Being concerned about the confusion and contention sometimes caused by the words "religion" and "religious," this Board wishes to place on record the following points which can be agreed by all Humanists:

(a) Some Humanists use the word "religion" as roughly equivalent to "life stance;" others take it to imply some theistic or non-naturalistic reality.

(b) Those Humanists who use the word "religious" to describe themselves or their organizations do not imply that their Humanism accepts any theistic or non-naturalistic realities.

(c) In the sense of "religion" which implies "accepting a god," Humanism is not a religion; in the sense of "religion" meaning "life stance," Humanism is a religion (Minutes, Board of Director's Meeting, International Humanist and Ethical Union, June 28–29, 1989).

15. On June 11, 1989, the Reverend Jerry Falwell announced that the Moral Majority would dissolve (*The New York Times*, June 12, 1989). He, and many others, claimed—with a good deal of accuracy—that their "mission" had been accomplished. On June 13, the Southern Baptist Convention, the largest Protestant denomination in the United States, once again elected a conservative and literalist as its head (*The New York Times*, June 14, 1989). During the same weeks in June 1989, the Supreme Court of the United States narrowed civil rights and civil liberties protections in a series of five to four decisions. The conservative agenda that was at the heart of Fundamentalist politics has been largely achieved over the past decade. The Humanist/Fundamentalist debate is not confined to politics, however. Instead, it spreads to issues of faith and truth, that is, to religious, and not simply political, issues where confrontation, and therefore winners and losers, may be appropriate.

16. Lamont spoke to the Congress of The International Humanist and Ethical Union, Buffalo, NY, August 3, 1988.

17. Under the leadership of Paul Kurtz, the Committee for Democratic and Secular Humanism has developed a number of projects intended to reveal the trickery of much that goes by the name of modern religion. Among these are the Committee for the Scientific Examination of Religion and the Faith Healing Investigation Project. Among the publications that describe the results of their work are *The Skeptical Inquirer* and *Free Inquiry*, both published in Buffalo, NY.

18. Harold J. Blackham, *Humanism* (Middlesex, England: Penguin, 1968): 210.

19. For a classic example of this exercise, see David Hume's chapter on "miracles" in his *An Inquiry Concerning Human Understanding*, 1748.

20. Jean-Paul Sartre, "Existentialism Is A Humanism" in *Existentialism from Dostevsky to Sartre*. Walter Kaufmann, ed., (New York: Meridian, 1956): 310.

5

Illusions of Spirituality: The Sentimental Temptation

Those for whom reason is the essence of Humanism find spirituality an affront. Others insist that Humanism must somehow accommodate transcendent matters. Unfortunately, they have no language of their own for giving a Humanist account of it. At the same time, they know that feelings, responses, and intuitions give texture and thickness to human experience. Reason, freedom, and duty are just too fleshless for them. So while remaining within a naturalistic framework, many Humanists find more in their experience than can be grasped by their Enlightenment language and idea. Borrowing from their neighbors, they try to naturalize the spirit. But the borrowing also invites misunderstanding.

Acts of appropriation are by no means new. Jefferson, Paine, and Madison could not do without "natural religion" and a creator God. However, theirs became the depersonalized God of Deism, a God who was really a stranger to both Christian and Jew. Unitarian reformers like Theodore Parker and William Ellery Channing moved from Calvinist Christianity toward a more merciful and moral view of the "spirit."[1] For religious liberals, Emerson set the tone with his notion of the "over-soul." In various ways, transcendentalism fed the need of reformers for resources other than those to be found in reason and science. As Stow Persons writes:

By introducing and familiarizing literate Americans with transcendentalist schools of Germany, France, and England, as well as with the mystic religions of the East, American transcendentalism was preparing the way for important new developments in religious thought. . . . the transcendentalists welcomed the latest contributions to scientific and social thought with, if anything, a too glib assurance that their intuitive faith would be only further confirmed by the accumulation of natural knowledge.... A more tangible contribution of transcendentalism growing out of the same cosmopolitan awareness of contemporary European and Asiatic thought was the awakening of interest in the comparative study of religions.[2]

Felix Adler joined spirituality with practical reform in the new industrial society by interpreting Kant's "kingdom of ends" democratically as a "supersensible" community of unique ethical persons. One of Adler's colleagues, Stanton Coit, who was to establish Ethical Culture overseas, built the "Ethical Church" in London. Among his projects, he rewrote the *Book of Common Prayer* into *Social Worship*, eliminating all supernatural references while retaining worship itself. Another of Adler's associates, Alfred W. Martin, was deeply involved in spiritualism as well as in the study of comparative religion and the higher criticism of the Bible. Meanwhile, the interest in religious matters and in comparative religions brought visitors from Asia and the Middle East to address the liberal and academic community. Typically, *The Index*, journal of the Free Religious Association, reported that Wong Chin Foo had lectured at the Philadelphia Concert Hall on "The Great Religions of China and Japan."[3]

Philosophically and psychologically, the nature of belief was undergoing reexamination too, particularly in the work and thought of William James. In his classic *The Varieties of Religious Experience*,[4] James made the case for a psychological study of religious phenomena and for their personal efficacy, if not metaphysical validity. In a recent discussion of the theme, the late Joseph L. Blau wrote:

The unprovable God of faith may yet seem to be a living force in the life of the believer. Events in the world of space-time may be deeply affected by the force of the belief. Yet, we must be careful not to confuse the act of faith, the believing, with that which is believed. It is the act of belief that is efficacious, not its content, although for the believer himself, the nature of the act may be shaped by its presumptive content. The content of a belief is an attempt to state in public terms a purely private sense of certainty. It is an attempt to translate into communicable symbols—words or pictures or idols, creeds or rituals or liturgies—the unutterable and essentially incommunicable essence of a meaning discovered, a wonder experienced in life.[5]

Such borrowings are understandable but risky. Language and symbol are never only what they seem. They carry connotations and histories that cannot be ignored no matter how hard we try. Thus, the task of seeking to enrich Humanism is as much hindered as helped by adopting the spiritual talk of others. In the post-World War II environment this task invites another distortion as Humanism yields to what I call the sentimental temptation, the misuse and abuse of the notion of spirituality.

An anxiety-driven world tempts us toward strategies of simplification and security. Simultaneously, it blinds us to the uses and limitations of intelligence and reason. So, while we derogate rationality, we deify science and technology. The sciences become "science" and acquire an authority they neither need or deserve. Yet, oppressed by events that seem always to escape our control and by surprises that often do not turn out well, we find the tentativeness of rationality just another burden of modern experience. We do not want to be told to doubt; we do not want to admit that we may have to confess error. In short, we do not want to be reasonable because of how it feels to be reasonable. John Dewey called this feeling the "quest for certainty," Erich Fromm identified it as the "escape from freedom," and Jean-Paul Sartre named it the "awful burden of freedom." It is not surprising that we convert reasonableness into rationalism and that we turn elsewhere for security. Humanists are not immune and turn elsewhere too—although uncomfortably. Hence, we can understand their flirtation with spirituality, with the language and terms of Humanism's opponents.

Spirituality enters Humanist circles ambiguously. It is symptomatic of the need to "thicken" Humanism, to find a legitimate and comprehensible place for affections and feelings, for hunches and intuitions, for responsiveness and meditation. For more than a century, Humanists have tried, unsuccessfully, to complete the science and politics of the Enlightenment, to find a place for beauty and love, and to give the life of reason personal, as well as public, meanings. As a consequence of the world today, however, spirituality enters Humanism illegitimately, perhaps even as a "failure of nerve." The Humanist flirtation with spirituality seems to confess Humanism's inadequacy—which is quite different from confessing Humanism's incompleteness.

As you may gather, I am leery of the confusions with which spirituality is surrounded. As Felix Adler, no stranger to spiritual talk himself, warned:

In the region of mental activity which is called the spiritual life, vagueness is apt to prevail, the outlines of thought are apt to be blurred, the feelings aroused are apt to be indistinct and transitory. The word, spiritual, becomes a synonym of muddy thought and misty emotionalism.[6]

It seems to me that a turn to spirituality comes much too conveniently to us when we confess our perplexity and our despair. It is particularly problematic for the children of the Enlightenment who, before all others, know the record of spirituality, its history of otherworldliness. Our ordinary language echoes that record. So we separate spirit from flesh, soul from body. Spirituality licenses us to populate the world with good and evil spirits; the conduct of the spiritually minded consists in placating the latter while inviting the former. Not the least of our inheritance of spiritually is the hope of another and better world where the pains of our earthly existence will be eased in an "immortality of the spirit." And finally, spirituality has, more often than not, sanctioned those who have a special entry to the other world, the priests, shamans, and elders who exercise divine power. Given these uses, spirituality would seem alien territory for Humanism.

It is not possible for Humanists to claim that these meanings of spirituality are ancient history. Today's newspapers carry astrology columns which are avidly consumed. Even in literate and intellectual circles, it is not unusual to be asked, "What is your sign (of the zodiac)?" The question—unheard a couple of decades ago—is quite commonplace. Perhaps it is innocent, perhaps it is only a fad, but I detect an edge of belief, as if we were hedging our bets. More revealing is the fact that most of us are able to answer the question and think nothing of doing so. Not long ago, in the late 1970s, stories of demonic possession and calls for exorcism were not uncommon either. Spiritual racketeering and trickery in the guise of faith healing are common too. Religious fads abound. New thought and "out-of-body" experiences have succeeded the table-rapping seances of the 1920s or the drug-induced "mysticism" of the 1960s. The message of "another reality" is still quite current. So it is peculiar to find Humanists adopting the language of spirituality as a way of completing their point of view.

Both traditionalists and Humanists, however, can claim that these latter-day flirtations are but distortions of spirituality, superstitious remnants of the past, and that the proper use of spiritual talk is really innocent of them. After all, church and temple have as little use for superstition and spiritual racketeering as do Humanists. Moreover, Humanism, it is argued, must address itself to the "human spirit" and the ability of human beings to create, convey, and live by meanings that transcend the facts. Unfortunately, that simply will not do, and not only because of the history of spirituality nor only because of its current manifestations. Spiritual talk conceals confusions about the relationships of mind and body and the sufficiency of the world. It seems to communicate—when in fact it does not.

It is no accident that spirituality is caught in muddy ideas and expressed in oracular tones. After all, its source is a world that is hidden from human knowledge and ordinary human beings. Mood replaces meaning, and mood is comforting when meaning is lost or frightening. To be sure, Humanist activism and intellectualism need the corrective of silence and contemplation. But this is not enough to overcome the weight of spirituality's other intentions, nor are appreciation and response, which might better be called aesthetic, the paradigmatic expressions of a spiritual view of life.

Even where it is not a racket, spirituality appeals to direct experience of some non-natural "other" through revivalism, drugs, worship, or special disciplines. In its most explicit form as mysticism, it is absorption into that "other" that resides elsewhere. Even if the "spirit" is said to "dwell within," it is separated from our ordinary lives. Unity with the "other" is earned at the price of self-annihilation or self-surrender. Ego is a block to spirituality whether in its Christian or Buddhist forms. There is something essentially alien to the naturalistic and self-confident world of Humanism in this otherworldliness and self-deprecation.

My skepticism about spirituality is further increased by its non-moral stance. It addresses the individual; it pictures the person alone with the universe.[7] Even the notion of spiritual community conveys an essentially private, or at best exclusive, relationship. This antisocial implication of spirituality is a problem that is not unique to Humanism. Prophetic criticism of spirituality led to the "social gospel" in Christianity as it led Felix Adler out of the Reform Temple. In Latin America today, it sanctions that fascinating anomaly, the Marxist priest and liberation theology. Something of this concern must have animated Gunnar Myrdal, the Swedish sociologist who addressed his fellow Christians with the words:

First, in the present extremely perilous situation of America and the world, the servants of the church cannot afford to turn their interest merely to the salvation of the individual, forgetting that society must be radically transformed. The church must stand up for human ideals and their realization through politics by government, local, state, and federal, for which they share responsibility. People must be taught to understand that their actions as citizens and members of other organized groups— for instance trade unions—must be judged from a moral point of view. . . . Questions about dogma or even faith shrink to insignificance in a world where there is uncertainty whether any human beings will be left at the turn of the century.[8]

Finally, there is something pallid and unconvincing in the efforts of some Humanists to give a psychological "spin" to spirituality, to see in it a typical therapy[9] and thus to deprive spirituality of its object. Humanists, in this instance, reflect and respond to the malaise of culture. We seem to have lost confidence in ourselves and in each other, in our own institutions and historical resources—indeed we might better term spirituality the normal pathology of our age. Perhaps that is why, since we live in a culture so deeply doubtful of its values, spirituality in a variety of forms is so attractive to so many.

Humanism's efforts to achieve what spirituality is said to achieve have, as we have seen, historical roots within Humanism itself, in the natural religion and Deism of the Enlightenment, the transcendentalism of Unitarianism and Ethical Culture, the philosophic psychology of William James, and the pragmatic naturalism of John Dewey and the signers of *Manifesto I*. However, much that goes by the name of spirituality is at best confusing and at worst fraudulent. Spirituality, moreover, is not a single thing, and thus Humanism's adventure with it is not a single thing either. To be sure, there are careless, confused, and opportunistic uses of the core values of spirituality. Humanists might argue, however, that there are other uses as well that might be legitimate if separated from other worldliness and resignation.

I can think of three types of spirituality: innocent, apocalyptic, and exploitive. With each, there are appropriate things for Humanists to say and do. Innocent spirituality responds to a cry for help, perhaps in an inarticulate but still convincing way—this is its appeal. It conveys the message that something good and permanent is present for us, entering our universe from another as God, Saint, or Mediator. To be sure, the theologian and the philosopher try to articulate the shape and character of this spirit world, so we get endless debates about whether the "Son" is "of" or "like" the "Father," whether God is one or three persons, whether we may or may not speak the name of Jahveh, or whether the communion wafer is a symbol, a miracle, or an idol. Yet we are told finally that these are divine mysteries that must elude human knowledge. We get fruitless arguments about the "problem of evil" and unconvincing theodicies that seek to "justify the ways of God to man." But the experience of the spirit finally remains inarticulate. It is to be given and kept but it cannot be analyzed. Innocent spirituality is, of course, found in traditional faiths, West and East. Otherworldliness in a variety of forms is the mark of its presence.

When traditions fail us, the search for spirituality turns desperate. Then we find those fascinating historic moments of which nineteenth-century America was one, when new faiths are born and old faiths reshaped. This is also the present situation. Traditional religions, here and abroad, are faulted by communicant and non-churchgoer alike. Those that give signs of vitality, like Evangelical and Fundamentalist Christianity or Islam promise safety and purpose, and with these the intensification of personal experience. The excitement is on the edges, among the fads, the new faiths, and the esoteric. Within the traditions themselves, it is found among things like "kitchen communions" in Roman Catholicism or the struggle to feminize language and person in the Jewish-Christian Bible. The traditions accommodate themselves, although not necessarily admitting that they do. In a dialogue held in Amsterdam in 1988, one of a series between representatives of the International Humanist and Ethical Union and the Vatican, Father Herve Carrier, Secretary of the Pontifical Council for Culture, argued that:

Religion is a universal and permanent category of all cultures." He observed that modernization has been accompanied by secularist efforts to "reduce the role of traditional religious institutions. . . . " But, he said secularization has not succeeded in eclipsing the sacred, nor has it led to an extinction of religion as Marx and others at the end of the nineteenth century believed it would. . . . Religion, Carrier maintained, provides society with a "coherent view of reality" and provides "supernatural legitimation" for celebrating the rites of passage, a sense of the transcendent permeates society.

Carrier granted that the secularization and pluralism of modern life have reduced the influence of the traditional religions in all aspects of social life . . . but the religious tendency is nonetheless expressed instead in the form of cults and New Age religions—or "a religion of trivia" exploited by the media. Thus, he said, efforts to privatize religion have failed, and an "invisible religion" persists in the West.[10]

The keynote of a convincing spirituality is the promise of salvation, the rejection of the world, and the damnation of an identifiable enemy. The truly religious life is the life of the spirit and so salvationism is often linked with moral indifference. After all, the world and all that is in it are irrelevant to eternity. Our earthly home is only a temporary dwelling place. As the old hymn has it, we are just "passing through." Insofar as social reform tempts us to use our energies to change the world, we misplace our attention, so an ethical life, strangely, may even lead to sacrilege. In that sense, spirituality is innocent of the world and puzzled by those who seem so taken with it. In its disdain for the secular, it can lead to a radical separation between temporal and eternal powers. That separation, in turn, can lead to secular freedom or to the worst forms of political barbarism. In this life, innocent spirituality counsels us to accept this "veil of tears." Essentially, then, innocent spirituality is socially and politically conservative no matter how radical it may occasionally be theologically.

Humanism has a dialogic relationship with innocent spirituality, for they mirror each other. Their alienation from each other arises, paradoxically, from within an essential similarity of attention. Spirituality teaches the Humanist perspectives on what is possible in the natural world while the Humanist calls spirituality back from amorality. When clear about their difference from each other, their encounter stimulates efforts at change for both while sustaining the identity of both. A special feature of the encounter between innocent spirituality and Humanism appears when Humanists are found within the traditions as internal reformers and radicals. These voices within demand moral accountability for God's creatures and for God's creations; a prophetic demand is joined to spirituality in criticizing priest and paraphernalia as deserters of a "true" spirituality. Humanists outside, however, do not understand the internal nature of these demands, do not understand that the Humanists-within are still Catholics or Jews or Muslims and intend to remain so. They mistakenly accuse the Humanists-within of intellectual confusion or moral cowardice. At the same time, recognizing kindred spirits, they find themselves able to communicate—hence the dialogic possibility is even attractive.

Meanwhile, the Humanists-within cannot see the need the modern humanist feels to step out and stand apart. Indeed, they confront the Humanist-without in puzzlement for they genuinely believe that tradition can be reconstructed and need not be deserted. They point to a long history of reform, even radical reform, within even the most conservative of traditions. They therefore force Humanism to explain itself and its intentions. At the same time, they force Humanism to admit its need to account for features of experience effectively met within tradition and almost ignored within Humanism—hence, again, the dialogic possibility.

I can think of several instances of the encounter between innocent spirituality and Humanism. Many of us greeted Pope John XXIII and his struggle for peace and pluralism as a Humanist. In an earlier time, Felix Adler's appeal in 1876 for "common ground" may be taken as paradigmatic of this encounter:

We propose to entirely exclude prayer and every form of ritual . . . freely do I own to this purpose of reconciliation and candidly do I confess that it is my dearest object to exalt the present movement above the strife of contending sects and parties, and at once to occupy that common ground where we may all meet, believers and unbelievers, for purposes in themselves lofty and unquestioned by any. Believe or disbelieve as you list . . . but be one with us where there is nothing to divide—in action. Diversity in the creed, unanimity in the deed. . . . This is that common ground where we may all grasp hands as brothers united in mankind's common cause.[11]

Within Reform, leading rabbis expressed puzzlement and anger about what Adler was up to and, above all, about why he needed to leave the temple to do it. As Rabbi Felsenthal of Chicago remarked:

If Professor Adler and the Society for Ethical Culture spurn the idea of separating definitely from the Jewish Church and if they really and honestly have the intention to remain Israelites, they may become the fathers of a great reformation within Judaism. . . . Otherwise, they will leave but faint traces behind themselves. As Israelites, they will probably be harbingers of a new birth of a Jewish religion emancipated from a Jewish nationality.[12]

Manifesto I and the signers' view of themselves as "religious" can be interpreted as the outcome of a dialogue between Humanists-within and Humanists-without. I can also recall students of mine in the Humanist Institute[13] whose loyalty and location was Unitarianism or Humanistic Judaism and who could not see the need to depart their places in order to be Humanists. At the same time, other students accused them of a failure to follow through on their Humanism and of what they saw as a fatal compromise.

Prophetic voices break into the stoicism and salvationism of innocent spirituality and call for attention to and action in this world. But prophecy is also of and from another world. It is sentimentality to read the prophets as secular moral critics. No matter how intense the dialogue with the traditionalist, the Humanist cannot succeed in changing prophecy into social ethics. Hence, the ambiguous morality of Jesus, alternately advising rebellion and obedience, or the unresolved struggle between tribalism and universalism in the Israelite prophets. There is, in short, always a reference elsewhere and backward in the prophetic utterance. In a more recent instance, Alexander Solzhenitsyn addressed a Harvard commencement as follows:

The mistake (of the West) must be at the root. . . . I refer to the prevailing Western view of the world which was first born during the Renaissance and found its political expression from the period of the Enlightenment.

It became the basis for government and social science and could be defined as rationalistic humanism or humanist autonomy; they proclaimed and enforced autonomy of man from any higher force above him . . . with Man seen as the center of everything that exists. We [have] turned our backs upon the spirit and embraced all that is material with excessive and unwarranted zeal. This new way of thinking which had imposed on us its guidance did not admit the existence of intrinsic evil in Man nor did it see any higher task than the attainment of happiness on earth. . . . As humanism in its development became more and more materialistic, it made itself increasingly accessible to speculation and manipulation at first by socialism and then by communism. One does see the same stones in the foundations of a de-spiritualized humanism and of any type of socialism; endless materialism; freedom from religion and religious responsibility, which under Communist regimes reach the stage of anti-religious dictatorship; concentration on social structures with a seemingly scientific approach.[14]

Prophets, ancient or modern, are alike ambiguous in their moral intentions and in their moral consistency. Ghandi led India to freedom but he also supported repressive sexuality and regressive economic policies. Pope John XXIII liberated his Church by "bringing it into the twentieth century," but he remained a traditionalist in faith and morals.

It is this ambiguity, a consequence of the other worldly root and reference for the moral position of prophecy, which helps to give birth to a second type of spirituality, an apocalyptic spirituality. When a culture loses its nerve, innocence rapidly deteriorates and dialogue becomes a luxury. A complex religious task, to work out the life of the spirit and to encounter in good faith Humanists for whom that life is empty, takes a dangerous turn. Dialogue is interpreted as trafficking with the enemy and spirituality is politicized. With the sanction of eternity, a culture of insiders and outsiders evolves. The insiders exhibit an arrogance of spirit because of the exalted nature of their source. A vast gulf opens between them and those who are damned. For the leaders of this apocalyptic spirituality, mass manipulation is justified by "Divine" Right, God, or History, or *Volk*, or what have you. In form, apocalyptic spirituality is always totalitarian. The more extreme examples are not hard to find whether in the Crusades or in the Ayatollah Khomeini.

Spiritual leaders come into this world, all the while denying its importance, even its reality. They pose as the servants of some great and transcending reality. They justify allegiance, wealth, and power by dedicating themselves to another world. In practice, however, allegiance, wealth, and power are politically useful in this world. A privileged spiritual elite emerges and sooner or later—usually after an initial charismatic generation—this elite contends with other elites for power. Their argument is, to be sure, still carried on in the language of spirituality, but now it is the followers who believe while the leaders simply maneuver. In a pluralist society like ours, where no single spiritual elite emerges, followers are taught to find security within communities of the "saved" and parochial values come to dominate public values. Social life becomes a series of treaties between communities of the faithful, to be broken when one side feels strongly enough. Those who have not entered one or another community are pushed to do so. Failing that, they may find themselves excluded from any social life. In response they become variously anomic or angry, passive or aggressive.

This picture of apocalyptic spirituality may seem exaggerated. Yet a deteriorated and politicized spirituality here and abroad already makes for a fragmented society and a threatened civilization. Neighborliness has vanished, politics is mass politics, and irrationality is epidemic. It was not long ago that totalitarian movements nearly swallowed the world. Today, we find a prevalence of sects, small in numbers but so confident of their truths that they will kill for them. We are still living in a world of unreason and terror. Hitler's "thousand-year Reich" was a spiritual ideal—but then so is every holy war. And it is quite consistent with the intentions of apocalyptic spirituality for Solzhenitsyn to call for holy war too.

For Humanism, this turn from innocence to apocalypse forces a move from dialogue to social action, to a Humanist politics and a critical ethics. Mere toleration will not do, for Humanism is a public philosophy as the Enlightenment was a public philosophy, and apocalyptic spirituality in a pluralist society results in privatism. Alliances against apocalypse are formed with those who are troubled by this turn of the spirit. Within the traditions, apocalypse stirs responses of dismay too. Even those who are not Humanists-within join the effort for they are appalled by what they interpret as a betrayal of faith and innocent spirituality. Thus, traditionalists distinguish themselves from "sectarians" and make common cause with Humanists around issues of pluralism in civil society and for the sake of civil liberty.

Humanism in the United States since World War II moved into an unsatisfying duality of alliance and silence. The latter was felt to be necessary because the critical discourse of dialogue would have disrupted alliance, which must always be superficial and must not dig too deeply into motives and differences. Even within the Humanist neighborhood, and for the same reasons, the record of alliance is a sometime thing.[15] Humanists and others periodically interpret the silences as weakness and the alliances as opportunistic compromise. They turn on other Humanists as traitors and so, in conjunction with the game of either/or and the religious question, another difficulty emerges. Humanists come to imitate the sectarians with their own claims of purity, internality, and even "saved" communities. Those who seek alliances, meanwhile, have a guilty conscience about their silences. The typical response, then, is self-critical: Humanists see themselves and are seen by others merely as political liberals. Apocalyptic spirituality, then, is most dangerous to Humanism, for it forces Humanism into a position where it cannot explain itself to itself. Apocalypse induces a crisis of identity.

The least complicated of spiritualities for Humanism to deal with is faddism. It is difficult to see anything more in it than racketeering and it is easy to dismiss it as "media religion." Unfortunately, fads are not merely amusing. They have implication for the health of individuals and in "faith healing"—life itself is at stake.[16] Modern culture is at stake as well. Religious faddism is another way of institutionalizing false promises and thus threatens to deteriorate culture itself. Faddist claims and values fragment democratic society and undermine scientific inquiry. Faddism is not merely a harmless avocation, as it sometimes seems when sophisticates dabble in astrology. Nor is it only a way of fattening the bank accounts of its practitioners.

A special phenomenon of our age has been the emergence of media evangelism, successor to the tent meetings of an earlier America. The sexual and economic scandals that have brought about the downfall of Jim and Tammy Bakker and of Jimmy Swaggert, and the much publicized family quarrel between Herbert W. Armstrong and his son, Garner Ted Armstrong, about the financial activities of the television program "The World Tomorrow," do not seem to have significantly affected the appeal of this form of faddist spirituality. Tens of thousands continue to take their spirituality through radio and television. The message is simple and convincing. Despite the apparent variety of media religion, it reduces to a single promise: that saving grace is achievable by symbolic acts available to everyone like reading "scripture" and "accepting Christ," and by the practical act of sending money.

As I drive southward on holiday, my car radio delivers media evangelism to me. But it is delusional to think that easy salvation is only a feature of bible-belt religion. Liberal culture too has its spiritual fads. They are found on the campus, in the board room, and in suburban living rooms. Compulsive "honesty" and "encounter" strategies have become the bourgeois technique of salvation as legitimate therapeutic methods are turned into illegitimate faiths. I can still recall that refusal to reveal oneself in a group, usually a liberal group—to "let it all hang out"—in the late 1960s was taken as an affront and was met with aggressive response. Silence was a challenge to some deeply held belief about the sacred quality of exposure; salvation was taking a therapeutic turn. Thus, from est to Dianetics to New Age to Transcendental Meditation, the middle class exhibits faddist spirituality too.[17] For it, not surprisingly, psychological strategies are more comfortable than revival meetings. The spiritual intrudes upon the temporal and, no doubt, is an opportunistic way for the temporal to exploit the spiritual.

When evangelism and psychologism are successful, neither science nor reason can be centering values of the world we live in. Modern faddism thus departs from an earlier spirituality which was—and this for the modern Humanist is perhaps difficult to grasp—convinced that science and reason supported it. As Lewis Feuer writes:

> By contrast, the spiritualist movement in the nineteenth century was not anti-scientific. The year 1848 was indeed a year in which men saw visions, both political and spiritual. A new social order seemed to be in gestation; everything seemed possible; and terrestrial bonds were evidently being sundered as were the social. The prestige of science was high and undimmed in the mid-nineteenth century, and spiritualism, far from counterposing itself to science, itself claimed to conform to the canons of scientific method. Spiritualists felt themselves "adamant champions of empiricism" who were extending the scientific method to a new set of phenomena. They claimed to have received encouraging communications from the spirit of Francis Bacon himself. Their theory seemed to them not less mysterious or intelligible than those of electricity and the ether. Unlike contemporary anti-scientists, the spiritualists were "totally committed to the idea of progress." They accepted American technology, its mores and its promises, and were often skilled technologists themselves. They saw no war between science and religion, for they felt both confluent from their empiricist standpoint. They were indeed thorough-going materialists, for they believed that spirit was a higher, more perfect form of matter.[18]

All of us share a common despair of experience and of the values that gave birth to the modern world. We become victims not only because we give money and time to some racketeer but because we have given up the hope of sociability for the sake of salvation. We turn away from the world in what has been called a "new narcissism"—the anxiety that leads to a pathological focus on the self alone and on the virtues of "self- fulfillment." It is this elevation of ego in isolation that represents the more serious import of faddist spirituality. We are thereby confirmed in our loneliness, grow ever more lonely, and literally subvert culture and society.

Finally, a narrow and yet influential instance of faddist spirituality seems to return spirituality to its earlier alliance with science and so might seem compatible with Humanism—but it really is not. It is still tainted by the narcissism that afflicts the rest of spirituality. Indeed, ego is literally taken to be world-creating. Fascinated by the puzzles of quantum physics and the new astronomy, spirituality takes on the clothing of the sciences in a non-scientific, even anti-scientific way. Thus, we are told of the "tao" of physics, and of the claim that the scientific study of the natural world offers a sure path to God.[19] A mixture of mysticism, science, and natural religion, the ways of the sciences are sacrificed and the puzzles of the sciences are converted into justifications of faith. For example:

For the scientists who discovered the underlying reality of quantum mechanics, the quantum leap was also an uncertain and risky affair. The uncertainty was literal. A quantum leap for an atomic particle is not a guaranteed business. There is no way to know with absolute certainty the movements of such tiny particles of matter. This in fact led to a new law of physics called the Principle of Indeterminism. But such new laws were risky, and the risk was to the scientists' sanity and self respect. The new physics uncovered a bizarre and magical underworld. It showed physicists a new meaning for the word *order*. This new order, the basis for the new physics, was not found in the particles of matter. Rather, it was found in the minds of the physicists.[20]

If innocent spirituality calls for dialogue and apocalyptic spirituality calls for alliance, faddist spirituality calls for exposure. Yet that is not enough, for beneath the fad is the anxiety and despair that leads people to turn inward and to accept promises, even promises that they know are false. The growth of faddist spirituality, then, can be used as a diagnostic tool. By examining its various incarnations we are in position to locate the questions that afflict human beings. Faddism tells us that hope and sociability are nearly lost and that the feeling of being manipulated by non-personal, non-caring forces prevails. In that sense, faddist spirituality describes in yet another way the demands Humanism must make upon itself as it seeks to reconstruct the Enlightenment.

At the same time, the exploitations of faddist spirituality in conjunction with the terrorism of apocalyptic spirituality mask the differences among those who, unlike Humanists, adopt the double world of spirituality. In our anger at spiritual racketeering, and in our obligation to expose it, we lose sight of the powers of dialogue with others not like us and of the urgency of alliances for the sake of political effectiveness. This, indeed, has been the case with those Humanist fundamentalists who play the game of either/or and for those Humanist sentimentalists who flirt with spirituality. Dangerously imitative as both are in their separate ways, neither satisfies the need for reconstruction. While retaining its integrity, Humanism, by meeting spirituality in its three different forms, can learn what it needs in order to do its work in the modern world.

Spirituality as such is incompatible with Humanism except where the term is used elliptically. At the same time, the attractiveness of spirituality tells us of the urgency of constructing a new and more inclusive naturalism, of the need to recapture and enlarge the domain of rationality, of the importance of sociability, of the search for hopefulness. These problems are, of course, not unknown among Humanists. As one observer noted:

But the lack of fellowship is truly bothersome to many humanists. . . . The only way I can think to describe this is through a discovery I made several years ago. At that time I loved to watch Monday night football but I disliked Howard Cosell. So I got in the habit of watching the game with the sound turned off. It worked well—for a while. The relief at not having to hear Cosell pontificate was satisfying. But eventually I realized that the drama of the game was significantly reduced. Not only the announcers, but the crowd noise and, most of all, the dramatic music played behind introductions and highlights really did add to the emotional impact of the game.

In a similar way, IHEU [International Humanist and Ethical Union] seemed to lack any background music. There was no melody to hold the meeting together, and no emotional dimensions to the presentations. Perhaps this is intentional—part of the package of relying on rational thought alone. But it seemed a minus to me. I heard humanists themselves speak of a desire for a little more "background music" in their movement.[21]

The "background music" needed to move beyond the eighteenth century calls for a reconstruction of Enlightenment values. It is this reconstruction that is made necessary by the disarray of the Humanist neighborhood.

NOTES

1. For a useful discussion of the evolution of Unitarianism in the United States, see Conrad Wright, ed., *A Stream of Light* (Boston: Unitarian Universalist Association, 1975).

2. Stow Persons, *Free Religion* (New Haven, CT: Yale, 1947): 22–23.

3. The report appears in *The Index*, December 1875. This journal was published in Boston by the Free Religious Association, which had been founded in 1867 by Francis Ellingwood Abbot and O. B. Frothingham. It drew together liberal Unitarians, Universalists, progressive Quakers, Reform Jews, and leading independent reformers. Included in its membership was Emerson, as well as Lucretia Mott, Wendell Phillips, and Julia Ward Howe.

4. William James, *The Varieties of Religious Experience* (New York: Macmillan, 1961). In "The Will to Believe." James wrote:

The thesis I defend is, briefly stated, this: Our passional nature not only lawfully may, but must decide an option between propositions, whenever it is a genuine option that cannot by its nature be decided on intellectual grounds; for to say, under such circumstances, "Do not decide, but leave the question open," is itself a passional decision,—just like deciding yes or no,— and is attended with the same risk of losing the truth. (William James, *Essays on Faith and Morals*, p. 42).

5. Joseph L. Blau, "God And The Philosophers," in *The Idea of God: Philosophical Perspectives* ed. E. H. Madden; R. Handy; and M. Farber (Springfield, IL: Charles C. Thomas, 1968): 142.

6. Felix Adler, *The Essentials of Spirituality* (New York: James Pott and Company, 1905): 2.

7. Soren Kierkegaard, more than any other modern thinker, may be said to

have captured this utterly individualistic—some would say alienated—import of spirituality. For example, see his discussion of the story of Abraham:

Now the story of Abraham contains such a teleological suspension of the ethical. . . . Abraham's relation to Isaac, ethically speaking, is quite simply expressed by saying that a father shall love his son more dearly than himself. Yet, within its own compass, the ethical has various gradations. Let us see whether in this story there is to be found any higher expression for the ethical such as would ethically explain his conduct [i.e. his willingness to sacrifice his son], ethically justify him in suspending the ethical obligation toward his son, without in this search going beyond the teleology of the ethical. (Robert Bretall, ed., "Fear and Trembling," in *A Kierkegaard Anthology* [Princeton, NJ: Princeton University Press, 1947]: 131).

8. Gunnar Myrdal, "A Worried America," *The Christian Century*, December 14, 1977, pp. 1161–1166.

9. It is striking that in *Habits of the Heart*, a major category deals with "the significance of therapy as a general outlook on life that has spread over the past few decades from a relatively small educated elite to the middle-class mainstream of American life." (Robert N. Bellah, Richard Madsen, William M. Sullivan, Ann Swidler, and Steven M. Tipton, *Habits of the Heart* [New York: Harper & Row, 1985]: 113).

10. Paul Kurtz, "The Church Under Siege: Reflections on the Vatican/Humanist Dialogue," *Free Inquiry* 9, no. 1 (Winter 1988/89): 47.

11. Felix Adler, Address of May 15, 1876, Ethical Culture Archive, Standard Hall, New York, NY.

12. *The Index* 10 (1878): 85.

13. The Humanist Institute, begun in 1983 and sponsored by the North American Committee for Humanism, is intended to train professional leadership for the Humanist movement in America and includes participants from all of the Humanist organizations on the continent.

14. Alexander Solzhenitsyn, "A Failure of Spirit and Will," commencement address, Harvard University, June 8, 1978.

15. For a discussion of the relationship of Ethical Culture and Humanism, an example of the complexity and wavering quality of the alliance, see Howard B. Radest, "Ethical Culture and Humanism: A Cautionary Tale," *Religious Humanism* 16, no. 2, pp. 59–70.

16. Many examples may be found in an article by Lowell D. Streiker, "Ultrafundamentalist Sects and Child-Abuse," *Free Inquiry* 4, no. 2 (Spring 1984): 10.

On July 2, 1983, Faith Aliano, age ten, died in Woodbury, New Jersey, of complications from untreated juvenile diabetes. Her parents, members of "an unorganized religious sect," hid her body and held daily worship services, praying for her resurrection. On September 12, the body, now partially decomposed, with skin as tough as leather, was discovered by the police. A local superior court judge, gave the parents three days to arrange for burial for the child. . . . Three days later, the couple appeared in court and informed the judge that they refused to comply with his wishes. Mr. Aliano explained: "God said she will come back and that is what I believe."

In Knoxville, Tennessee, a state appeals court delayed its decision on whether twelve-year old Pamela Hamilton should be forced to undergo medical treatment for Ewing's sarcoma. . . . Her father, Larry Hamilton, pastor of the thirty-eight member Church of God of the Union Assembly . . . said that he would go all the way to the Supreme Court to keep his daughter from receiving medical care. . . .

According to an Associated Press story:

Wearing a blue gingham dress and walking with crutches, the girl gave her testimony Saturday from a couch in the judge's chambers. . . .

"I believe that I can be healed without taking treatments. . . . I don't care what the doctors say." Asked by a state lawyer if she was ready to die, she replied, "When the Lord gets ready for me."

For the past decade, the magazine *Free Inquiry*, edited by Paul Kurtz, has exercised a unique and important public function by publishing the record of faith healing and its consequences.

17. Robert Urquart created est, a form of confrontational training promising personal security and success which has been very popular in the business world. Dianetics was the creation in the 1940s of L. Ron Hubbard, a science fiction writer. It became a significant "spiritual" movement as the Church of Scientology in the 1970's and 1980's, both here and abroad. New Age, stimulated by the writing of actress Shirley MacLaine, builds around a modified notion of spiritual reincarnation. However, it is almost impossible to keep track of the number of "movements" that reflect faddist spirituality.

18. Lewis Feuer, "Anti-Science, The Irrationalist Vogue of the 1970s," *Free Inquiry* 4, no. 1 (Winter 1983/84): 38.

19. See F. Capra, *The Tao of Physics* (Berkeley: Shambhala, 1975) or Paul Davies, *God and the New Physics* (London: J. M. Dent and Sons, 1983).

20. Fred Alan Wolf, *Taking the Quantum Leap* (San Francisco: Harper, 1981): 1.

21. Terry C. Muck in "God and Man In Buffalo," reported on the Congress of the International Humanist and Ethical Union in the summer of 1988, which was meeting in Buffalo, New York, at the same time as a Billy Graham Crusade (*Christianity Today*, January 13, 1989, p. 26).

6

Doing Good: The Liberal Temptation

Humanists are for the "right" causes. We defend peace, argue for disarmament, and oppose nuclear proliferation. Our agenda includes population control and environmental protection, fair housing, and civil rights. We attack censorship and fight for civil liberties. Separation of church and state and religious freedom stand high among our priorities as do "pro-choice" and public schooling. With some exceptions—like the "freedom marches" during the 1960s in the South—Humanists are more likely to petition than to demonstrate, to lobby than to march, to proclaim rather than to analyze.[1] We are still confident in democratic government and, reflecting our eighteenth-century origins, we still believe in schooling as its method.[2]

Most of the time, we just assume the correctness of our views. Most of the time, too, we talk to ourselves, although I suppose this is not only true of Humanists. When we meet others we want to score points rather than find truths, as they do. We are tolerant, of course, but more likely as a matter of courtesy. But we rarely really listen to each other.

There is a certain predictability to Humanist points of view. Like others, we find greater comfort in the habits of the past than in the risks of the future. But, since Humanism is, in principle, a position of risk, such comfort is problematic for us in a way that it need not be for others. So, when Humanists rehearse the clichés of liberalism, they do so with a guilty conscience. This poses two questions: Is Humanism reducible to the social ethics of nineteenth- and twentieth-century liberal reform and is it fair to characterize liberalism as a cliché?

Humanists have participated actively in forming the liberal agenda. This much is clearly on the record. But liberalism has become a shadow of itself.

Events have undermined reform since the 1930s and have threatened civility since World War I. Even as we are given to what is disdainfully called "knee-jerk" liberalism, we are insecure about what were once reliable moral ideas and social programs. Our faith in schooling has been undermined by its inability to overcome the burden of new urban populations. Our confidence in government-sponsored reform has been shaken by the failure of projects like slum clearance and low-cost housing to improve significantly the quality of life for the underclass—an underclass that stubbornly continues to grow. Our reliance on the social sciences has been subverted by the inability of rehabilitation strategies to do much about crime and criminals. Our faith in the growth of intelligence is shaken by the reappearance of a Fundamentalism that challenges scientific knowledge, and by the resort to violence to meet social crisis.

We always seem beset by crisis. New problems or new forms of old problems appear with appalling frequency and in appalling dimensions. The presence on the streets of homeless men, women, and children in growing numbers cannot help but challenge the effectiveness of decades of reform. An epidemic of drug addiction and its attendant criminality seems to elude all efforts at control, let alone cure. The ubiquity of thievery in the marketplace and in government are the subject of daily headlines. To make matters worse, it would seem that the crime most condemned these days is getting caught. Nearly surrendering hope of meeting these problems, most people turn backward in anger to dogmatism; liberals apologize for their liberalism and admit their helplessness.

Yet, liberal habits persist. Certain people are still "good" and others are "not good" or "less good." Liberalism was tutored in the notion that minorities, children, and workers were, by definition, on the side of the angels. At the same time, corporate America, the military, and the national Republican Party were, again, by definition, on the wrong side and needed to be confronted by the forces of virtue. To be sure, these habits reflected a history of repression by those who elevated property and privilege to civilizing values. The liberation of ethnic and religious minorities and the defense of the rights of labor, of women, and of children were and are legitimate causes. Reform efforts were rooted in a realistic analysis of social needs and social powers. But in our time, much of this analysis is outdated. Minorities are not monolithic; there is a black middle class and a black underclass. Labor is not always saintly; labor racketeering and union self-interest have been typical modern phenomena. Liberals have simply not known how to cope. At the same time, they have lost their own history. Republican progressivism, for example, is an old tradition, too—Tammany was a Democratic phenomenon.

When accused of reacting with old habits or, worse, of being "unrealistic," we have been embarrassed and guilty. Caught in the ambiguities of post-World War II Stalinism and its mirror image, anti-communism, liberalism fractured into polar opposites, and gave rise to the blindness of left-wing sentimentalism and right-wing chauvinism. Failing to know their own history, liberals have not been ready temperamentally or psychologically to reconstruct their ideas. Indeed, liberalism itself has become a term of reproach even among liberals—as in the 1988 presidential election campaign. New generations, finding the habits of the liberal past irrelevant, simply do not come to liberal causes.

Liberalism thus gave birth to its own attackers from within, an opposition quite distinct from the conservatism that looked back to an earlier time. A so-called new conservatism emerged out of the anti-communism of the 1950s and the chaos of the 1960s. It seemed as if liberal values were to be turned on their head and as if the ability to do so with a certain literary flair—the so- called New York intellectual establishment—was a sign of intellectual and political respectability. We saw a new nationalism, a new defense of free enterprise, a new "toughness" in economic and military affairs, and a new "realism" about race. Ironically, this "new conservatism"—"new" or a Latinized "neo" were the words to conjure with—was as clichéd as the liberalism which gave it birth. It was possible, is possible, to predict its direction as easily as the direction of its fraternal opposition. Both gave little evidence of seriousness about the kind of dialectic that brought liberalism to birth in the interval between Enlightenment and the New Deal. In a penetrating essay on the subject, Benjamin DeMott stated:

The work to be done now is . . . essentially that of recovering the standard of discourse capable of breaking those habits of condescension. Guided by the standard in question, we can begin to search out respectable living arrangements for shared yet competing values, developing in the process broad philosophical agreements about proper government roles, keeping the contrarieties alive within us throughout the negotiations. The key to the undertaking does not lie in the contrivance of neoliberalisms to match (and cancel) neoconservatisms. . . . It lies, instead, in scrupulosity about intellectual methods—in the recovery of feeling for what Lionel Trilling called "the right conduct of mind."

In the great Jefferson Lecture he delivered in Washington in 1972 . . . Trilling pressed the point that the way a nation thinks determines in the end the quality of its governance. We've come, he said, to "judge societies and their governments by the same criteria we use in estimating the rightness of the conduct of mind," and we're correct to do so; we can find "the paradigm of a just society in the right conduct of mind." Nor are the fundamental principles of this right conduct obscure or mysterious. We locate them in the very act of trusting the energy of mind—trusting the mind's "intentionality, its impulse toward inclusiveness and completeness, its search for coherence with due regard for the integrity of the elements which it brings into relation with each other, its power of looking before and after."[3]

If the "old" liberalism and the "new" conservatism are clichés, it is nevertheless the case that liberalism once reflected an abiding commitment to issues of human freedom and human possibility. It was precisely on this ground that Humanism grew and that liberalism evolved from the Humanist values of the Enlightenment. They evolved together and expressed themselves in the practice of forming coalitions to meet social problems. So liberalism appeared in two ways, as an embodiment of Humanist social and philosophic values leading, among other things, to reform, and as the gathering ground for coalition politics. Both might be described as "pragmatic," except that we tended to confuse the two meanings of pragmatism. As a philosophy, it asked for attention to actual events and situations and measured truth as well as effectiveness by consequences.[4] As a name for problem solving, pragmatism often deteriorated into opportunism, now liberal opportunism.

Liberalism also reflected the need for building alliances against apocalyptic spirituality—religious and political. Often it was the Humanist within non-Humanist organizations or the Humanist organization itself that led in the formation of such alliances. The willingness of persons to come together on the "common ground" that Felix Adler spoke of in 1876 led him and others to decades of reform in politics, housing, schooling, health, and legal services. A liberal alliance seemed at the time to be merely common sense. Exemplifying the mixture of the two liberalisms, Adler himself, however, was also trying to erect a movement around the generic notion of "common ground," which was not the intent of other parties to the alliance. These alliances were instead issue-oriented and anti-ideological. They emerged from the need to confront specific problems of social justice and did not reflect a self-conscious institutional strategy; there was little effort to build a permanent liberal party. The alliances tended to come into being and to pass away as problems like child labor or women's suffrage rose and seemed to be solved. Thus, liberalism had a flickering quality to it. Nothing illustrated this more clearly than the strange career of American national politics with its four-year cycle of unity and disunity.

Each item on the liberal agenda attracted its own coalition of "regulars"—on abolition, on child labor, on minimum wage, on civil rights, on women's rights. A look at reform organizations in various communities to this day shows the predictable presence of the same roster of individuals and sponsoring groups. For Humanism, however, the identification with liberalism was not incidental. It was, in fact, a consequence of a history and an ideology that based social ethics and social reform in the Enlightenment, as well as of the habit of coalition politics. Consequently, Humanism benefited from liberal success but it also suffered the flickering quality of liberalism's periodicity.

Reform alliances, to be politically effective, cannot penetrate to the diverse motives, epistemologies, and metaphysics that lead Humanists, Quakers, Baptists, Methodists, Catholics, Jews, secularists, and free thinkers to join together around liberal causes. Indeed, to raise the issue of "why" and "on what ground" is to risk the fracture of alliances and to invite debilitating and distracting debate. I can recall how clearly this showed itself when Marxists tried to make common cause with the rest of us in a "united front." They could not escape their penchant for ideological clarification and exaggerated rhetoric. This led to endless and frustrating debate—most often late into the night and to everyone's exhaustion. Misusing the deliberate refusal of coalition members to deal with ideological questions, they could not play by the rules of the alliance game because it was so alien to their temperament. Anxious for power, they abused the courtesies of alliance politics to the point where both communism and anti-communism took on a common shape and style in the post-World War II period. Liberalism fractured into rigid polarities and lost its quality of effective ambiguity.

Mixing the two forms of liberalism—as the embodiment of Humanist philosophy and as coalition politics—reduced the force of its ideas and often turned coalition politics into another power play. In other words, the career of liberalism contained within itself the source of its destruction in the deliberately mindless nature of alliances. Humanism participated in that process and suffered the same confusion of acts with values. It shared with the other members of liberal alliances democratic values, confidence in intelligence, the pragmatics of problem solving, and the use of government to meet the needs of individuals. The need for effective action, however, led the Humanist to mute the underlying sanction for such values so that the liberal agenda appeared without articulating the philosophy natural to it.

Humanism became merely a particularity within the liberalism of alliances. Unlike the other participants, however, it was uniquely rooted in the philosophic ideas that emerged from the Enlightenment and had a specific duty to articulate them. This it abdicated and in its cosmopolitanism and inclusiveness it welcomed the formation of alliances as ends in themselves. Humanist values were thus often hidden within liberal practice. This hidden quality was also reinforced in the United States. Here, Humanist ideas were even more difficult to isolate because they were embedded in a democratic social structure. Ironically, Humanism as a liberal ideology emerged most clearly in non-democratic environments like Titoist Yugoslavia or when confronting an established church as in the struggle for the rights of non- believers. Typically, and especially in the United States, Humanism was easily confounded with humanitarianism, with good works, and with coalition politics. In other words, Humanists were not sufficiently attentive to Humanism as the philosophic center of liberalism. And, in a certain sense, we dared not be.

It is possible to be a Theist and a liberal, a Roman Catholic and a liberal, a Calvinist and a liberal, or an orthodox Jew and a liberal. Each of these brings to the liberalism of alliances its own accent, its own quality of participation. Because, however, so much of Humanism emerges from the same inspiration that gives rise to modern democratic politics, the Humanist voice is merged within a general voice for good things. Humanists, however, come to politics for purposes of giving reality to a secular, naturalistic, and rationalist ethic. These Humanist values are congruent with our society because they share the same eighteenth-century roots. These same values stand out starkly in other places, such as traditional, tribal, and authoritarian societies. In short, Humanists in democratic societies yield to the liberal temptation, losing their philosophy for the sake of achieving its purposes.

A Humanist ethic is distinguishable from the ethics of others. Its center is the unchallengeable value of the human being as such, autonomous and not the creature of some "higher" power. By contrast, giving preeminence to love for God's creature leads the traditionalist to the liberalism of alliances from a different point of departure and with other ultimate ends in view. The liberalism of Roman Catholics or Jews is surely genuine but is, in principle, only instrumental and procedural. Liberalism is surrendered or radically compromised when "pro-choice" issues push civil liberty to the edge, or when the welfare of Israel is threatened. However, even where Humanists claim that they are Marxists or libertarians, they are still philosophic liberals and give voice to those same naturalist and rationalist values that Humanism brings to the liberalism of alliances in this country.[5] Indeed these boundary groups within Humanism occupy the same universe of discourse as the other children of the Enlightenment.

To grasp the features of Humanism as a philosophy of liberalism, we turn again to the fact that its modern career begins with the Enlightenment. From the outset, Humanism had a secular and political center and reform has been its theme. As Humanism developed, its attention turned outward to the natural and social world. This was marked by the shift from eternal salvation to social ethics and from otherworldliness to the "pursuit of happiness." In this public character of its attentiveness—Humanist ethics even when trying to deal with the personal was always a social ethics—and in its secularity, we find both the historical strength and the current confusions of Humanism. As increasingly greater segments of the world turn to secular interests and to an instrumental interpretation of state power, the distinctiveness of Humanism within the dual career of liberalism has become problematic.

The liberalism of alliances agreed on the urgency of defending the individual from the unwarranted invasion of persons by tribe, church, or state which made it all the more difficult to distinguish Humanism. If the old regime had been overthrown, the new had its own oppressions. The lessons of the "terror," of the emerging powers of the secular state, and of the incursions of social conformity could not be ignored.[6] Non-Humanist liberals might respond to these on the grounds of the sacredness of God's creatures or some other trans-natural view. In its own defense of persons as such, Humanism took over the philosophic assumptions of social contract theory, often without quite realizing its consequences. This reliance on a metaphor of contracts narrowed the meaning of the person by isolating him or her from others, and by treating him or her merely as a being with rational interests, primarily property interests—as in *homo economicus* or *homo politicus*. In order to legitimate limiting state power, this same view also narrowed its meaning by interpreting society as an arena of competitions. A legitimate society, in other words, was the outcome of an accommodation of self-interested individuals to each other for the sake of those self-interests. The state was not a community but only a social instrument. It had the limited task of ensuring a fair struggle. Its responsibility was to provide a "level playing field" so that social competition would produce the best possible outcome.[7]

Understandable as these moves were, given the long and painful history of tyranny, they nurtured a Humanism that seemed to ignore all but the public values of fairness and liberty. By contrast, the others that joined the liberalism of alliances continued to maintain traditional values as well—the values of family, community, authority, and intimacy within theologically or philosophically conservative frames of reference. For them, liberalism and traditionalism often generated tensions and contradictions between modern needs and inherited values. Modernism and traditionalism still continue to generate conflict for the Roman Catholic church or Jewish nationalism.

Humanism had a different problem. It could not account for intimacy, for family and community, although conscious of the need. Hence, it welcomed, for want of anything better, the development of modern psychology and other social sciences—often converting these from empirical disciplines into prescriptive disciplines.[8] These touched upon limited manifestations of human relationship, focusing on behavioral evidence and measurable conduct.[9] The post-*Manifesto I* debates within Humanism—between the religious and the non-religious—may be understood, in part at least, as an implicit confession that science alone would not do and that Humanism had not done its homework—had not said what it was, particularly when attempting to come to terms with the experiences of intimacy.

The Enlightenment also helped give birth to a Humanist style. Its basic document was the "Rights of Man" which proclaimed the new social ethics; its successors have followed that lead.[10] Humanism, thus, is shaped by a public philosophy.[11] As a consequence of its contractual assumptions, it speaks in the language of law and lawfulness, and "self-evident" truths. Given these roots, it is not surprising that the themes of Humanist ethics are directly or derivatively notions of rights and justice. Nor is it surprising that extended variations on the idea of "due process" become ends in themselves. Jefferson's "pursuit of happiness," which together with "life" and "liberty" form a democratic trinity, says nothing about the nature of the happiness to be pursued. To be sure, he presumed a good life, the life of "honest farmers,' but that is not to be found in the moral utterance itself. It was the latter that became central for Humanism. The features of the "good life" were left to a so-called common sense. As such, the good life is still today seldom described or carefully analyzed. A biographical literature where its patterns might be drawn is almost absent from Humanism. Thus, many Humanists are living examples of Humanist values as the "imitation of Christ" is of Christian values or the life of a scholar of Torah is of Jewish values. For Humanism, however, these personal lives are hardly attended to—except ceremonially at memorial services—and indeed the very notion of doing so would be felt as alien, even embarrassing. The Humanist habit, after all, is to convert events into abstractions.

We have become so accustomed to focusing on the processes of morality that we scarcely notice the radical departure we have made from other moments in ethical and religious history. The attention to process makes moral ideas increasingly abstract. Ironically, the very belief in moral common sense that led to the elevation of due process and its derivatives, alienates ethics from common experience. Moral substance was once the central fact of moral value. Plato's *Republic*, Aristotle's *Nicomachean Ethics*, and the Old Testament exhibit competing images of the "good" life. Ethics was substantiated in chronicles, biographies, and autobiographies. The procedures of morality were only instrumental to its substance. They did not have a life of their own as they do today.[12]

This, in turn, points again to the underlying moral reality assumed by the Enlightenment—its distinctive view of persons. From its point of view, all human beings are like all others. Genuinely concerned with individual rights, the Humanist, paradoxically, exhibits little principled sensitivity to individuality as such. All human beings are rational and therefore, competent to consult their own interests. Indeed, they are the only ones competent to do so. It would be a violation of the moral order for you to substitute your judgment of what is in my interest for my judgment of what is in my interest. It would be even more of a violation for you to join your judgment with others and use collective power, the state, to impose it upon me. On this basis, a notion of privacy appears and even, as in the more recent debates about sexuality and abortion, a right to privacy.[13] Individuality, in other words, is hidden behind a veil of deliberate ignorance—to adapt John Rawl's phrase.[14] This, to be sure, has the virtue of defending the person against the invasion of others but it also has the vice of inviting moral ignorance. And, once again, it makes problematic the moral status of family members and their relationship to each other. It is silent on the great classical theme of friendship. Insofar as community is distinguished from society—as in neighborhoods, congregations, and clans—it leaves us with moral silence on the relationships of the various participants that are neither only interpersonal nor only public.

An Enlightenment doctrine of human rights came to constitute the substance of human relationships. A legalistic ethics was legitimately allowed to pay attention to public matters of give and get. There were, of course, echoes of an earlier ethics in the obligation to grant each other mutual personal dignity. Yet even this tradition took a distinctively modern turn. Essentially, the move was negative—we were directed to keep hands off, to adopt an ethic of noninterference. Neither human dignity nor human worth required the guarantee of a Creator, nor did they need theological justification. "Natural law" as in Jefferson's "nature and nature's God" did provide a bridge from past to future during the transition. Ultimately, however, the notion of the rational being itself led to human rights. But this was not only a matter of theory. People are naturally stubborn, resist authority, resent being pushed around, prefer to "do their own thing," and enjoy an argument. In other words, ordinary experience points to human equality and freedom. A person is the judge of what is best for him or her even where the judgment is faulty in someone else's eyes. Above all, people have a right to be given good reasons if equality or freedom are to be limited for some public end. This was, to be sure, a common sense interpretation of reason, a reason quite literally available to everyman. Putting this more formally, as Immanuel Kant did two hundred years ago, human beings are subjects and not objects.[15] They are self-determining and not to be used or manipulated as things are used and manipulated.

Humanism was rooted thus in a revolutionary ethical environment. As a result, the ethical thinking of Humanism was turned outward and the focus of moral attention was on the interactions of social life. This gave Humanism its moral energy as it took the Humanist into the arena of liberal social action and social criticism. It motivated Humanist organizations to become instruments of reform. It is no accident that whatever the differences we find within modern Humanism, we find agreement on the fact that, as the 1952 *Declaration of the International Humanist and Ethical Union* put it:

The fundamentals of modern ethical Humanism are as follows:

1. It is democratic. It aims at the fullest possible development of every human being. It holds that this is a matter of right. The democratic principles can be applied to all human relationships and is not restricted to methods of government. . . .

3. Humanism is ethical. It affirms the dignity of persons and the right of the individual to the greatest possible freedom of development compatible with the rights of others.[16]

This legalistic environment has often blinded Humanism to the inarticulate qualities of human relationship, those that do not lend themselves to an ethics of rights, responsibilities, and due process. Indeed, the public bias of Humanism sets the intimate aside, reduces it to the "private," and protects it as nearly untouchable. So, as it were, it excludes intimacy from the moral scrutiny of others who, on Humanist grounds, are strangers.[17] Privacy itself becomes a legal category as in the laws governing marriage, the obligations of parenthood, and the notion of property. Humanism has not developed a distinction between private property and personal properties. Its legalist bias makes it difficult from Humanism to account for intuitive and experience-based moral categories like love, concern, care, and sacrifice.[18]

A symptom of that difficulty is the fact that, contrary to the accusations of Fundamentalists, most Humanists are neither anarchists nor libertines but take on the personal values of the society around them and look very much like their neighbors. Ironically, we even seem to take ordinary morality more seriously than our neighbors. We are given to moralism and are much more likely to be offended by, and be much less tolerant of, moral deviation. We are quite conventional when it comes to the typical virtues of middle-class Western society. It is true that Humanists genuinely support the rights of women, the rights of homosexuals, and the rights of "nontraditional" families. But we tend to focus on rights, on "non-discrimination," and equity rather than on the emotionally charged features of radically different ways of living. While giving a rather benevolent "spin" to this fact, Alasdair MacIntyre makes the same point when he notes that:

Almost all the great skeptics and atheists of the modern western world have been morally conservative, often intensely so, in their lives as well as in their teachings. To Freud and Marx, for example, who took many of the traditional virtues for granted, the unorthodox moral behavior and attitudes of many Marxists and Freudians would have been highly distasteful. On the other hand, many Christian theists have played their part in the great crimes of the age: devout Catholics were among the guards of the Nazi concentration camps; and believing Protestants participated in the bombings of Hiroshima and Dresden. In view of these facts, the Dostoyevskian contention that if God does not exist everything is permitted must necessarily appear difficult to maintain.[19]

Humanism's tradition is also scientific and technological. For those given to the idea of progress, all limitations can be turned into problems and all problems eventually have solutions. Morally, this entails the thought that evil is the outcome of the workings of an imperfect society, a society that has not been democratized. Or it is the symptom of a poorly developed person, a person who has not been educated. In more recent forms, therapy has been substituted for schooling and maturity has been substituted for morality. But the point remains the same: evil is not sin but inadequacy or, latterly, illness.[20] It follows that evil is always remediable and that all persons are redeemable. Therefore, we need to find out what must be done and there is always something that can be done. So Humanist ethics takes a decidedly technocratic turn and its activism takes on the features of social engineering. Gone from Enlightenment ethics was the idea of "original sin"—the idea that human nature was inevitably tainted and that the conquest of evil needed the intervention of some trans-natural and trans-human force.

The Humanist did not regret the loss. Indeed, he or she rejoiced in it. While dispensing with the theological trappings of the notion of evil, however, Humanism lacked an awareness of moral limitations which is still a feature of Humanism's moral psychology. Humanists cannot account for and often seem helpless in an encounter with those who are, as it were, morally impenetrable. That makes Humanism seem naive indeed given the intractable features of moral experience in the twentieth century.

Optimism is distinctively Humanist. To be sure, read through the lens of the idea of progress, it had a certain justification when the modern world was new, when revolution was successful, and when age-old tyrannies were in retreat. Even then it was met with a certain skepticism, as in Voltaire's *Candide*, and even then there was a sense that only the future would bring progress to its ultimate achievement in universal enlightenment. A trust in potentiality was thus embedded in the eighteenth century, and the technocratic impulse gave to potentiality an optimistic turn. Indeed, echoing the eighteenth century but now on psychological grounds, a "human potentials" movement in the 1950s and 1960s offered assurance and techniques for a move toward the better. This optimism is by no means gone and contributes to the appearance of a certain naiveté in the face of experience. Sometimes it gives almost a Pollyanna quality to Humanist moral utterance. Interpreting it a wishful thinking, the Humanist is met by those—even in Humanist circles—who speak in orotund tones of a "profound pessimism." Logically, then, optimism must be superficial.

Often enough, I have heard the view that associates profundity with despair. Hidden behind it, however, is a view of the world as inhospitable to human beings and of experience as necessarily frustrating to human hope. Hidden too is the assumption that the possibility of the better relies on forces outside ourselves. The alleged profundity of pessimism is only the surface of a theology that has not confessed itself. At the same time, it is a covert invitation to return power to those better attuned to the extra-natural and extra-human forces of salvation.

But Humanists are not fools, at least not more so than most other human beings. The horrific public events of the twentieth century have not escaped us. We know personal failure, frustration, and pain as often as others do. So, we might interpret Humanist optimism as an article of faith, a modernist version of *credo quia absurdam est* or belief "in spite of. . . . " But that will not do. For the Humanist, faith must appeal to reasonableness. Once this was achieved by the idea of progress. Today, given that Humanists are still optimists, we need to account for experiences where progress is not assured. We cure disease only to foster new diseases resistant to our cure; we prolong life only to face "problems of aging"; we provide welfare only to discover that we are encouraging dependency.

Optimism is really a feature of the Humanist's temperament and decreasingly of the Humanist's philosophy of history. It tells us about the way Humanists feel about themselves and the world. At the same time, optimism is not only a feeling; it takes the Humanist out into the world. It is axiomatic for Humanists to believe that their activity can make a difference in the world, although we are no longer convinced, as we once were, that we can always make a difference for the better. Humanism still holds that human agency can be effective, but it is a chastened activity. Unlike their associates in the liberal alliance, however, Humanists hold that human agency is the only agency available, or as Sartre stated, because man is free he is responsible for the world.

Human beings cannot rely on a cosmic partnership with God or with History. This claim of independence was overstated as in nineteenth-century views that replaced God with Man.[21] More modestly, a modern Humanist's optimism reflects the fact that failure is not given ultimate status in the world. Nor is failure taken as a sign of an ineradicable moral imperfection in human beings. Humanism does not take an apocalyptic view of history nor does it make a place for original sin. Indeed, the Humanist might reasonably argue the case for a "profound optimism."

The idea of an evil human nature has been a justification for tyranny—the need to control the vicious impulses of human beings. In reaction, Humanism has difficulty with the idea of evil itself and has not yet developed a view of evil-doing on secular grounds. Of course, Humanists talk about good and bad, right and wrong. But experience offers too many examples where "bad" is simply inadequate to the event. It is a puzzling ethics that places genocide and murder in the same general moral category even where a system of degrees of wrongness or badness is established. They simply do not feel like the same kind of thing. Evil carries an emotional and even cosmic burden that badness simply does not.[22]

Of course, it may be that human action is a dance of fools or that we are acting out a script authored elsewhere. If we are not to be puppets—not even glorious puppets—then the only choice available is to act as if our actions make a difference. This has been overinterpreted to mean that the universe insures our intentions, purposes, and ends, and guarantees their outcome. It is surely troubling to live with the knowledge that accidents, limitations, and ignorance always cast a shadow over the best of our efforts. For the Humanist, however, risk is not only a negative quality. He or she knows that organized inquiry has grown all the more fruitful in the modern world precisely because error is the pathway to knowledge and action. With a certain paradoxical security, we make discoveries only when things go wrong. It is, in other words, possible to find an empirical justification for elevating risk to a virtue precisely by looking at the career of the sciences once uncertainty was placed at the center of discovery. This is the justification for the permanent place of rationality among Humanist values. Reason is an activity in the world, not just a feature of our mental anatomy. By contrast, the classical view of human beings as "rational animals" missed this transactional quality of reason.

To conclude from the lack of insurance of human intentions in the world that human activity must be surrendered is to over-interpret from the other side. This is the temptation to which non-Humanists succumb. Similarly, to conclude from the fact of risk that the world is necessarily alien and hostile is another way of succumbing to the same temptation. Pessimism, in other words, is not so much profound as illiterate. Unlike those who would turn the world into an alien place and human beings into intruders, the Humanist is at home in the world, although at times somewhat uneasily. Human beings are not merely "passing through." Unlike St. Paul, Humanists are both in the world and of it.

Humanism is participatory in a serious, not merely a ceremonial, fashion. For participation to have significance, however, it must entail something other than a game of universal tiddlywinks and something more than personal revery or aesthetic responsiveness. That involves us in figuring out the part we play or can play in the world. Thereby, moral values acquire objectivity precisely because they are the outcome of an interaction between persons, and between persons and the world. We can talk intelligibly about values because they are found at work in the variety of transactions we enter into with self, others and the world. We develop reliable information and judgments about moral consequences. What we do not find are permanent and unchanging values. This is disturbing to those nurtured on a diet of absolutism. To be sure, as Aristotle reminded us, the degree of certainty varies with the complexity and character of the subject matter. Moral judgments cannot achieve the certainty of mathematics or physics. But to live with uncertainty is not to descend into moral chaos.

I do not minimize the difficulty of demonstrating the validity of some values over others and the difficulty of changing each other's minds about values. But then, all of us—Humanist and non-Humanist alike—have the same problem. Values cut close to home and so are never without an emotional charge. They give rise to our moral assumptions and lead us to differing moral outcomes—although we do not find as much moral variety around us as we sometimes pretend to when we're looking for an argument. The variety of moral values and their resistance to change do not, however, force us to convert the problem of moral clarity and the presence of moral dilemma into a metaphysical conclusion. As experience demonstrates in the sciences or in business—indeed in nearly all of modern life—neither permanence nor ultimacy are necessary requirements of objectivity or effectiveness.

Humanists are often accused not so much of relativism, however, as of subjectivism. To make values "subjective"—"merely subjective" is the way we tend to put it—is to rely on a distinction between "in here" and "out there," a distinction characteristic of traditional dualism but not of Humanist naturalism. Moreover, such a distinction makes participation either unintelligible or pointless—unintelligible because participation would have no arena and pointless because participation would have no consequence. For a Humanist, values are neither whimsical nor hidden away within the personal preferences of the individual. At the same time, to make values absolute would be to isolate values from all other experience, which is never absolutely and forever one thing. At that point, we quite literally are alienated from our values. It is little wonder, then, that an absolutist move quickly converts values into trans-natural or non-natural events. When to this is added a traditional metaphor, valuing ceases to be a human activity and human beings are resigned to obedience and disobedience to powers beyond ourselves. At best, our moral activity is reduced to interpretation and application.

Optimism is the key to Humanism and tracing its course from the idea of progress to the present opens up the theme of Humanist ethics, telling us why it is central to modern Humanism. At the same time a profound optimism has yet to be developed. This is the task of Humanism today, just as it once was for those who risked their lives for Enlightenment and its values. In its place, the clichés of the liberalism of alliances all too often are simply taken as Humanist ethics. This reduction of the two forms of liberalism to one is another instance of the fact that Humanism since *Manifesto I* has not dealt adequately with itself.

NOTES

1. A revealing example of Humanist style and of its continued reliance on rationality and the categories of the Enlightenment may be found—in all their strength and with all their problems—in the recently issued, "A Declaration of Interdependence: A New Global Ethics." Paul Kurtz, *Free Inquiry* 8, no. 4 (Fall 1988): 4–7, and signed by a number of leading Humanists. The Declaration calls for a "global moral consensus," repeats with some modification a list of "human rights," and relies on science and education and democracy. It asks the "citizens of each nation . . . to add the following affirmation to their pledges of loyalty:"

 I pledge allegiance to the world community, of which we are all a part.
 I recognize that all persons are equal in dignity and value.
 I defend human rights and cherish human freedom.
 I vow to honor and protect the global ecology for ourselves and for generations yet unborn.

2. Typically, as corruption in business and insider scandals on Wall Street surface, the solution is to teach ethics in business schools. This reminds me of the brief period when the recommendation was to teach ethics in law schools after the Watergate scandal, which revealed the moral insensitivity of many lawyers in the Nixon administration. Conservative skepticism of this near-formula approach to schooling as a solution to social immorality was exemplified by Irving Kristol who attacked, in exaggerated form, the moral relativism and academic amoralism of much of

ethical inquiry. Basically, he challenged the notion that schooling was the appropriate method of achieving moral change—or at least schooling as we know it:

Not that business ethics cannot stand improvement. Indeed, most major corporations are keenly aware of this and have drawn up codes of acceptable corporate behavior. What is interesting about these codes is not their contents, which are pretty uniform, but the fact that there is so little controversy in specifying those acceptable rules of behavior. Apparently, most corporate executives know without prior instruction, the fundamentals of what is right and what is wrong in the conduct of their affairs. Getting people to do what is right, and to refrain from doing what is wrong, is another matter, of course. But then, it always is. ("Ethics, Anyone? Or Morals?" *The Wall Street Journal*. September 15, 1987)

3. "Rediscovering Complexity." *The Atlantic Monthly*. 162, no. 3 (September 1988): 67–74.

4. Pragmatism was and is one of America's great contributions to philosophic thought. Developed in the work of Charles Peirce, William James, and John Dewey, it does not deserve the superficial and morally dubious interpretation given to the term "pragmatic" in ordinary usage. At the same time, the style and language used by the pragmatists—particularly by William James—lent themselves to the current abuse of meaning. Aware of this possibility, Dewey used the term "instrumentalism" and Peirce, much earlier, tried out the clumsy word, "pragmaticisim."

5. I can recall a series of Marxist/non-Marxist Humanist dialogues—for example, Boston, 1970, Dubrovnik, 1979. The key references for the Marxist participants were to the "Economic and Philosophic Manuscripts," (1844) and interpretations of later documents such as *Das Kapital*—offered with regard to notions of "human value" and the "alienating" consequences of capitalism. See for example, Erich Fromm, *Marx's Concept of Man*, (New York: Ungar, 1961). Stalinism, with its violation of human rights and democratic values, was the villain. Libertarian Humanists, or those who, like Sidney Hook and Paul Kurtz, move toward greater emphasis on liberty in light of state power these days, nevertheless strongly support human rights, defend civil liberty, and urge support for democratic schooling.

6. Social conformity is not a post–World War II phenomenon, nor is it an issue only for commentators and critics of the latter half of the twentieth century. John Stuart Mill in *On Liberty* had already warned of it and de Tocqueville saw social conformity, particularly through community organization, to be a peculiarly American trait.

7. Despite all that has occurred since he wrote, Adam Smith's description of the role of the state still is reflected in contemporary liberal and Humanist ethics:

Every man, as long as he does not violate the laws of justice, is left perfectly free to pursue his own interest his own way. . . . According to the system of natural liberty, the sovereign has only three duties to attend to . . . first the duty of protecting the society from the violence and invasion of other independent societies; secondly the duty of protecting, as far as possible, every member of the society from the injustice and oppression of every other member of it, or the duty of establishing an exact administration of justice; and thirdly, the duty of erecting and maintaining public works and certain public institutions which it can never be for the interest of any individual, or small number of individuals, to erect and maintain. (*The Wealth of Nations*, Book IV, Chapter 9 [New York: The Modern Library, 1937])

8. I can recall the gratification with which many Humanists greeted the development of "person-centered" psychologies and what was called the "human potentials" movement. For examples, consider works by Abraham H. Maslow (such

as *Motivation and Personality* (New York: Harper, 1954) and works by Carl Rogers such as *On Becoming a Person* (Boston: Houghton Mifflin, 1961). Both Maslow and Rogers were identified as Humanists and tried to extend their technical and professional insights into general philosophies of human conduct.

9. Among those few who very early in the development of Humanism foresaw this problem was Felix Adler. While his suspicion of Humanism was partly the outcome of institutional differences, it was more basically a concern with what Adler saw as the limitations of naturalism and the dangers of reducing transcending ideals to scientific hypotheses. See Felix Adler, *An Ethical Philosophy of Life*, (New York: D. Appleton Century, 1918), particularly Book 2, Chapter 3, "Preliminary Remarks on Worth and on the Reasons Why the Method Employed by Ethics Must Be the Opposite of That Employed by the Physical Sciences."

10. Contemporaneous with the Rights of Man was the Bill of Rights, the first ten amendments of the United States Constitution. More recent was the publication of the United Nations Declaration of Human Rights in 1948. It is legitimate, as well, to interpret much of the "manifesto" literature, whether Marxist or Humanist, of the interval as inspired by a "public philosophy" and by a concern for social ethics.

11. On the more conservative side of liberalism, the notion of a "public philosophy" is discussed by Walter Lippmann, *The Public Philosophy* (New York: New American Library, 1955) and on the more radical side of liberalism by John Dewey, *The Public and Its Problems* (1927), reprinted in *The Later Works of John Dewey, 1925–1953*, Vol. 2, *1925–1927*, ed. James Gouinlock, (Carbondale, IL: Southern Illinois University Press, 1984).

12. An interesting example of this autonomy of the process can be found in liberal debates around affirmative action. Proponents put this in process language by asking that everyone be given a "fair" start and by noting the debilitating effects of past discrimination. Opponents rely upon the notion of due process, where distinctions of race or gender are inappropriate. Both, however, underplay the potential outcomes, except to rely on their habitual confidence that fairness, liberty, and equality—all process ideas—will ensure the best possible long-run moral substance.

13.

Prior to nearly all other political question is one that rang out around the country after the Supreme Court's decision in the Missouri abortion case: Who decides? The abortion decision provided no definitive answer but it did give a sense of what the Rehnquist Court believes. It believes that on many issues the state legislatures should decide. By choosing not to overturn the *Roe v. Wade* decision, which legalized abortion, the Court still left it to the individual woman to decide whether she will have an abortion or not. But the 5-to-4 majority expanded the power of the states to impose conditions on how, when, and where abortions are performed. (E. J. Dionne, Jr., "On Abortion, Can Democracy Do the Right Thing?" *The New York Times* [The Week in Review]. July 9, 1989, Section 4).

14. See John Rawls, *A Theory of Justice* (Cambridge, MA: Harvard, 1971) particularly Chapter 3, "The Original Position," 24. "The Veil of Ignorance," pp. 136–142.

15. For a brief discussion of this theme, see Immanuel Kant, *The Fundamental Principles of the Metaphysics of Ethics*, Otto Manthey-Zorn, trans. (New York: D. Appleton Century, 1938). There are many available editions.

16. Declaration of the founding congress in Amsterdam, August 26, 1952.

17. For a discussion of the distinction between the "intimate" and the "private,"

see Howard B. Radest, "The Public and the Private: An American Fairy Tale," *Ethics* 89, no. 3 (April 1979): 280–91.

18. A recent debate on this issue has emerged from criticism of Lawrence Kohlberg's studies of moral development. Kohlberg's theoretical base, with its deliberately Kantian view of ethics, is the work of John Rawls, *A Theory of Justice* (Cambridge, MA: Harvard, 1971). Among others, one of Kohlberg's students and colleagues, Carol Gilligan, has raised the question in the context of feminism, of the need to add "caring" to "justice" as a central theme of ethics, see Carol Gilligan, *In a Different Voice* (Cambridge, MA: Harvard, 1982). For a discussion of this debate, see Howard B. Radest, *Can We Teach Ethics* (New York: Praeger, 1989): 100–103.

19. Alasdair MacIntyre and Paul Ricoeur, *The Religious Significance of Atheism* (New York: Columbia University Press, 1969): 31.

20. For an incisive discussion of this development, see Philip Rieff, *The Triumph of the Therapeutic* (New York: Harper and Row, 1966).

21. A reading of history as stages of progress was, as we have seen, not unusual in the eighteenth and nineteenth centuries. The most elaborated development of this view could be found in the work of the French sociologist, August Comte, who envisioned a time inevitably to come, when a "positive" stage would be reached with science replacing theology and scientists as a new priesthood. The notion of a "Religion of Humanity" was typical for those who saw religion evolving as the rest of history was evolving. For example, O. B. Frothingham, one of the founders of the Free Religious Association, in an effort to take over the idea from the rather specialized use to which the followers of August Comte had put the term, published a book with the title, *The Religion of Humanity*. The initial development of modern Humanism also seemed to deify humanity and to interpret theologies at their best as projections of human ideals. For an instance of the latter, see John Dewey, *A Common Faith* (New Haven, CT: Yale, 1934). An excellent discussion of this general theme can be found in Edward L. Ericson, *The Humanist Way* (New York: Continuum, 1988): Chapter 4. Characteristically, the notion of stages has shifted from history to developmental psychology today.

22. I am indebted to Judith Stecher, a member of the Ethics Department of The Ethical Culture/Fieldston Schools and of the University Seminar on Moral Education (Columbia University), for the development of this insight in an informal paper presented in May, 1988.

7

The Humanist at Home:
Naturalism Revisited

I have moments of doubt and pain, of regret and anger—just as we all do. There are times when I am tempted to look for help from on high and envy my traditionalist neighbors. Yet, I return to the world. It is my home and I am at home in it. Perhaps I was just lucky. I grew up cared for, loved, and befriended and no doubt I extended that love and friendliness outward. Certainly, the public events of my growing up did not promise security. I was born just before the Great Depression. My childhood was simultaneous with the rise of Fascism abroad and the continuation of anti-Semitism and racism at home. Adolescence was accompanied by World War II and young adulthood by McCarthyism, the Cold War, and the Korean "police action." The middle years of family and career were shaped by the Kennedy assassination, race violence, riots in the cities, and Vietnam. Yet, here I am at home with and in the world.

I was not insulated economically or politically or personally from these events. Indeed, I was—as my existentialist friends might put it—*engagé*, involved even in high school with causes and issues. Nor was I protected from experiences of death, disappointment, and frustration. These I knew in my own life and in the lives of my family and friends, sometimes all too well. I took my chances, just as we all did, and sometimes things worked out and sometimes they did not.

The community I grew up in extolled the conventional virtues and the beliefs of church and synagogue. Yes, my friends and I flirted with atheism as an intellectual possibility. As teen-agers, we had our share of night-long bull sessions dabbling in philosophy. In science, history, or literature class, we argued the merits and demerits of belief. Yet, atheism and non-religion were not really, as William James might have put it, "live options" for us. I went through the expected motions of Hebrew School and bar mitzvah but these were more social than religious practices. My experience, in other words, was quite like the experience of many others in middle-class Jewish and Christian white America.

I should have turned out conventionally "religious" as did so many others, or, as did a few, I could have taken it seriously. Yet for me, the world and all that is in it was enough, more than enough. Nothing has happened since to subvert that root feeling, a feeling that is really the center of Humanism. I know, from what others tell me, that there are many roads to Humanism, but I also know that this feeling is where those roads lead. Clearly, what was happening around me could have led to despair, to other-worldliness, or, as it did for most, to indifference. Of course, I had my ambitions, my own immediacies, but I also had a frame of reference that was real and not abstract. Humanism, for me, was not the outcome of an argument, the result of considering alternatives and making a rational choice. Unlike Paul on the road to Damascus, I did not suddenly see the light. Humanism emerged from within my biography.

I do not pretend that I am unique. Others have arrived at the same point and felt the same comfort. I have heard from those who come upon a Humanist group for the first time—an Ethical Culture Society, a Unitarian Fellowship, or a Humanist Chapter—the comments, "Where have you been"' and "that's what I've been thinking all my life." Like Moliere's bourgeois gentleman, they had been speaking Humanism all their lives without knowing it—now they had discovered its name. Finding Humanism is, typically, not a matter of family ties, as it is for many Jews, and not a matter of taking communion, being "born again," or conversion, as it is for many Christians. Paradoxically, becoming a Humanist is not really a matter of reasoning either as rationalism might lead us to expect. It is, instead, an outcome of personal development which is at the same time a typically human development. As William James put it:

Nevertheless, if we look . . . on the life of men that lies in them apart from their learning and science . . . we have to confess that the part of it of which rationalism can give an account is relatively superficial. It is the part that has the *prestige* undoubtedly, for it has the loquacity, it can challenge you for proofs, and chop logic, and put you down with words. But it will fail to convince or convert you all the same, if your dumb intuitions are opposed to its conclusions. . . . Your whole subconscious life, your impulses, your faiths, your needs, your divinations, have prepared the premises, of which your consciousness now feels the weight of the result.[1]

I want to reflect on where this feeling of being at home in the world might come from. Perhaps, I can find a clue to how it happened and how it happens. I know that this feeling—and it is first a feeling and only later a conclusion—is often neglected in Humanist rhetoric with its focus on issues, arguments, and polemics. The experience is not sufficiently captured by the terms often used to set us apart from others, an experience described by words like "secular" and "naturalistic." These have an angular and abstract quality that set a certain distance between what is felt and what is said. They lack the organicism of the feeling, a feeling which, no doubt, is not unfriendly to the experience of the poet or mystic, although for the latter, reports of that experience take on other-worldly pretentions and linguistic baggage that only mask what is felt.

The experience of being at home in the world is not derived from an argument and is not a debating point. I know I am not an alien when I am reminded of my response to a sunset or seascape—or all the other clichés of aesthetic sentimentality. The recollection is of an experience which in the moment was, however, not a cliché. The colors, sounds, and smells shaped and moved, strengthened and faded. As eye and ear and nose— indeed all the tactile and tangible senses—and mind as well, took these in, I responded. In the moment of response, I was entirely within the experience, unreflective, simply present. In the next moment, it fades. I glance backward seeing myself seeing, hearing myself hearing. I linger in that next moment, enjoying the memory itself, replaying the memory. Even as I do, it grows faint. The descriptions grow more and more elaborate as I add detail upon detail in the effort to recapture what cannot be recaptured. The memory renews itself and even acquires a life of its own—I rehearse it to myself and speak of it to others. Expression, when adequate, turns to poetry, song, and dance, to story and anecdote. I do not yet give it meaning—it just is—but meanings creep in.

I realize that while the moment is being experienced doubt and certainty are irrelevant. More important, in the moment I am not an observer of the event but very much part of it, as it is part of me. If someone interrupts— with a comment even of appreciation—I lose something irrecoverable, the moment too soon broken, and I am annoyed. At the same time, the moment is not prolonged, cannot be prolonged, even if I would wish it so. The sun sets; the sea changes with wind and light; I move on. My annoyance, then, is in a certain sense unwarranted.[2] But even the wish to preserve comes after the fact only as the moment fades and I become aware it is fading. In the having, the passage of time is neither short nor long, is itself unnoticed. At the same time, too, the moment reminds me of other moments, is also a recollection. Even in the midst of having, there is a background where I am naming, associating, and comparing, for my mind as well as my senses are caught in the event. Try as I do to suppress that background, I never quite succeed. Finally, I want to share the moment, to speak of it to others, to recall it with others, as we do when we tell stories. I notice that they

understand, they have had their moments, and cannot really understand—
my moment is mine, not theirs.

Looking backward from a greater distance, the experience takes on dimensions and interpretations that it did not have for me while it was happening. Above all, in the happening itself, the unification, the connection
of self and event, is impressive. By contrast, what happens in the daily
round is often routine and mechanical—not really happening to me at all,
in a sense. The notion of subject and object is defined only after the fact of
a connection that itself cannot be parsed. In the moment I am genuinely a
subject, while in the daily round I am more like an object, thing. In the
former, the resentment at interruption and the sense of loss when interrupted
tell the valuableness of the connection. Routines, on the other hand, are
gratefully interrupted.

Reflection tells me that the moment is also a reminder, an echo of other
events. That is how I know that it will be repeated, differently and yet
similarly, for that too is my experience. The moment is not only an isolated
moment. I anticipate others. At the same time, I know that I will die, that
there will be a final moment—although I cannot ever know which of them
will in fact be final. This experience is the pathway to confidence in nature,
to really being at home in the world.

On further reflection, I know that the moment is touched by anticipated
finality. Each moment could be the last and its texture is richer for it. A
background shadow highlights its colors, as it were, makes them stand out
all the more vividly in the contrast between the timelessness of the having
and the temporariness of what is had. Confidence is built on the thought
that the moment, while transient, is a herald of other moments that can
happen, indeed will happen. Yet given the moment's transience and my
own, confidence does not turn into *hubris*. The moment teaches me that I
am capable of entering the world and that it invites my entry. In sharing
its memory with others, there is the sense of giving to others and of being
with others. We move beyond mere functionalism to community.[3]

I do not want to overburden the moment. It is, after all, a commonplace
thing. Yet I think I am not inaccurate when I find in it, in the way it reminds
me of other moments experienced and promises future moments to come,
the nub of meaning that Humanism attaches to nature as felt. It is in the
experience, utterly personal and yet manifestly transpersonal, that I find the
source of Humanist naturalism. At the moment, thought of its causes and
purposes do not enter—these are later importations as when we take in the
meanings of the natural sciences or confront the contradictions of extra-
naturalism. After all, we were naturalists before Galileo, Newton, and Copernicus, and we were Humanists before the Enlightenment. In short—and
not only for Humanists—the moment has its own integrity although a
subsequent physics or metaphysics or theology will try to fit it into some
scheme of things. In that, the Humanist is closer to common experience,

and ironically, Humanism can be seen as more primitive than other views for all its intellectual and rationalist pretenses.

The moment is an occasion for feelings. Sense is always joined with emotion. It is only during the most abstract thought that we can sever "sense data" from "affective responses" as if we were neutral and distant.[4] I feel warmth or rejection, happiness or awe, laughter or tears. Above all, I am grateful to be alive in a world where such moments are possible. Like other feelings, that gratitude is within the event itself and only much later is it abstracted, attached to an object, and given expression as in prayers of thanksgiving. Indeed, if a Humanist were to have a notion of sacrilege, it would have its source in the belief that somehow natural events cannot be appreciated in and for themselves. Taking the moment for what it is as felt and had, the Humanist finds no need to subvert it with extra-natural explanation. The moment stands in all its integrity.

Clearly, the moment is also a metaphor for the actual relations of person and nature. There are many reminders of our primitive naturalism, not just sunsets and seascapes. There are moments of human relation too that have the same quality of immediacy, integration, connection and self-sufficiency. Language can only point to these in words such as love, loyalty, care, and concern. Again, although these may be clichés in the reference, they are original in the having. There are moments, too, of perspective, when sense, feeling, and mind are caught in the experience of space and time itself— space and time as perceived and not as quantified. As I floated through the fjords of Norway and Alaska, I was responding to the immediacy of sea and mountain. But there were other moments too when I was party to the shaping of sea and mountain—not as a geologist studying natural history but as a person connected to them in experience. I saw the heavens late at night from within the darkness of the Australian outback and the feeling of space itself was tangible, unmathematical. Neither duration nor measurement, the rationalities of quantity, were involved at all. I was within an experience of time and space. The experience stood for itself, not for something else.

All of us have experienced many moments in this way. The arts in all cultures tell us that this is so, and it is in the arts that a genuine Humanist language will be found. This the Greek and the Renaissance knew better than the Enlightenment.[5] As Julian Huxley remarked:

Santayana has come close to the central idea of Evolutionary Humanism in sane and splendid words. "There is only one world, the natural world, and only one truth about it; but this world has a spiritual life in it, which looks not to another world but to the beauty and perfection that this world suggests, approaches, and misses."

If we aspire to realize this potential beauty and perfection more fully, we shall have to utilize all the resources available—not only those of the external world but

those internal resources of our own nature—wonder and intelligence, creative freedom and love, imagination and belief.[6]

The experience of what it is to be human in the world needs neither
revelation nor the intervention of some singular institution. Through this
experience we can understand both Humanism's appeal and its willingness
to settle happily for what is to be found in the world. It is this experience
of world and person that is prior; the Humanist's ideas are derivative. This
is both good science and good sense. So when ideas grow overly complicated
or lead us to dead ends, we must go back to our experience to make a new
start.

The return is never easy. Ideas are not simply intellectual toys. They are
embodied in institutions and powers that are interested in sustaining themselves and so resist a return to experience. Ideas also shape our consciousness,
give us the comforts of explanation, and so we hold on to them and defend
them even against our experience. Consciousness conspires with the powers
that support these explanations and is fearful of letting them go. We know
that experience breaks into our comforts and habits. Paradigmatically, and
no doubt apocryphally, Galileo's inquisitors refused to look through his
telescope for they already knew what they would see. We are each kin to
the inquisitor.

Experience is never "mere experience" unattended by past history and
by current ideas. Primitive as it is, it nevertheless comes to us and we to
it shaped by what we are and how we have been taught. In other words,
experience is both had and constructed, and all too often our constructions
stand in our way. For human beings, then, there is a pattern of perception
and responsiveness, of integration, of connectedness in the moment. At the
same time, the actual experiences are quite particular to person and place.
What is evocative for some is neutral for others and what can be experienced
in one period of time is mere background in another. Those who live with
the sea are differently experienced from those who live with the desert. The
city-dweller is not the suburban commuter and certainly not the farmer.
My experience is not yours and what I bring to experience is not what you
bring to yours. I do not, however, want to exaggerate the separations.
When we encounter each other, even across alien cultures, we remind each
other of ourselves. I see a cave painting and know connection across ages
of time; I listen to the song of a stranger and know it is music in spite of
its strangeness. The experience of experience is common to us all.

Ideas shape what will be allowed to count as experience and either support
or undermine our ability to take experience as it happens. There are traditions that derogate our moments here and now. We erect a vast paraphernalia to this end—rites and rituals that direct attention and feeling away
from the world, arts and architectures that point the senses and feelings to
another world. Of course, the best of these succeed in spite of their message

and just because they hold us within the moment they create here and now—as a Bach mass or a *Pietà* hold us to this world whatever our theologies. Non-natural ideas oppose us in this effort, ask us to use our appreciations of the mass, sculpture, architecture for other purposes and, as it were, deliberately violate the integrity of the moment.

Little wonder then that a duality afflicts experience and that discomfort with the world and in the world is its outcome. In this dualism, the primitive having and happening which is the center of naturalism are assigned to the background or, in some stories, to the work of the Devil. Sensuality—condemned as the "sins of the flesh"—is disdained not so much because it is immoral as because it denies the values of another world and affirms our connectedness to this one. Nor is it incidental that despite centuries of effort to eradicate the "Devil," he or she is an ever-present possibility. Our sensuality does not vanish. And finally, it is not incidental that the reality of the Gods is most convincingly affirmed by the mystic who overcomes duality by incorporating self and world into a single moment. Like the poet, he or she touches upon what is common to all of us, the priority of experience over argument. By contrast, proofs of God's existence and their counter-arguments only speak to those who have already agreed on the conclusions. Typically, then, the mystic is a problem to the institution that gives him or her language and meaning as much as he or she is a problem to the non-believer who confuses what is said about the experience with the experience itself.[7]

A duality of worlds is understandable. If I have spoken thus far of the moment in its affirmative and sustaining qualities, there are other moments that are fearful and terrifying, and still others that are demeaning. Recalling these, we cannot help but seek elsewhere for solace. When life is "brutish, mean, and short," it makes a certain practical sense to turn one's back on the moment in the hope of another life. There are times when the world seems to stand against us, when it seems to oppress and defeat us. There are times, too, when the world seems to have no connection to us at all and when aesthetic sensibility seems only a luxury. The urgencies of giving and getting can overwhelm the moment. Even then, the poorest of us still sing and dance. However, we encapsulate the activity in separated moments of celebration as in the holidays and festivals that interrupt the daily round.

We can be overwhelmed by the world as it is and so turn to another world. This is not only a conspiracy of kings and priests, an effort to manipulate us for the sake of power and control. There are times in our lives when we are unable to meet the world and what it is doing to us. I think of the parents whose child has been killed in an accident; of the friend betrayed; of the news of incurable illness. At such times, it seems cruel to affirm our comfort with and in the world and foolish to celebrate the moment. Indeed, we simply refuse to accept the moment at all, draw further into ourselves, and retreat from other human beings and from the world.

When someone we know and care for dies, we are isolated from others, from the world, and even from ourselves. We grow numb. We need ways to reconnect. This is precisely what rituals of mourning set out to achieve. They do so not with their promises—say, of life after death or of some ultimate justification for what is an unjustifiable event—but because they dramatize an ending and move us to a new beginning. In our numbness, we need to be reminded of experience had and to be had. So our rites and rituals are communal, standing symbolically for and serving actually as a process of reconnection. It makes little difference what is said and done but a great deal of difference that it be said and done. Typically, a Humanist funeral or memorial service meets just such a need, and more directly than most. It centers on acceptance and association, on putting back together what death has broken apart. Often, this is effective, moving, and responsive to what is needed, if the comments of participants, even those who are traditionalists, are to be believed. At such times, explanation of the event is hardly relevant and we become aware in a concrete way of the priority of the moment and of the feelings attached to it.

There are other and different moments that call for explanation, and mysteries that tantalize and elude us. Cognition is itself an experience laden with feelings and responses. It unbalances us, leaves us unsatisfied, asking, doubting, and curious. As experienced, it is resolved by insight. This cognitive moment is as rich as other aesthetic moments. The difference between cognition as discipline and as experience may be illustrated by the difference between working out a correct answer to a problem and grasping it. We may review arguments, proofs, and evidence. When we have an insight—typically an insight is "had"—we cry out with Archimedes, "Eureka!" Discipline leads us to the skills of search and research. Insight asks for metaphor in the effort to help others to "see." Indeed, as the history of discovery demonstrates, it is the latter which comes first—an "intuitive" answer or a hunch—and it is the arguments that are developed later.

For ages, it seemed that another reality, eternal and intelligent, was needed to explain our own. It just "made sense." Events seemed to call for agents that remained invisible, and we had not yet learned how to naturalize invisible forces. So we populated the world with Gods and ghosts. The reappearance of the sun each day, the phases of the moon, the coming of spring, and the harvest spoke to us of patterns too dependable to be merely incidental. Naturalism as feeling was thus undermined by the inadequacy of naturalism as idea. The latter could not meet what was demanded of it; it did not "make sense." Efforts to interpret the experience of cognition were compromised by introducing non-natural powers or by portraying natural powers unlike any that could be encountered in experience—thus, the history of theological experiment on the one hand and of classical science on the other.[8]

Under such conditions, we were surrounded by structures—political and

intellectual—that compromised our primitive naturalism. We were reminded repeatedly of immediate experience, but we were unable to deal
intelligibly with life in and of the world. The Humanist story was told as
a speculative physics, as in the work of the great classical naturalists like
Democritus and Lucretius, or through an aesthetic celebration of human
powers, as during the Renaissance. But the duality of this world and another
was more convincing, sustained by the inadequacy of science and by the
oppressiveness of society. This duality, however, was inherently unstable.
The Gods were simply too fickle. The idea that this duality embodied was
inconsistent with the experience that it sought to interpret and explain. It,
too, finally did not "make sense." The stories of theological mysteries like
the "trinity" or the "problem of evil" or the anger and viciousness of God
toward the creature whom he knew had to disappoint Him only put mystery
to work solving mysteries.

Dualism became a story of apologetics and suppression much more than
a story of cognition. Above all, it turned out to be a story that derogated
human beings. They were portrayed as rebellious, heretical, lost, sinful,
and deceitful . . . the lexicon of dualism is a record of rejecting people. Even
where the tone was not hostile, human beings were viewed as helpless
creatures who needed extra-human resources to escape what was otherwise
their character and fate. Left to themselves, they were, in one way or
another, damned. Thus, despite much that could be said in its favor, the
anti-naturalism of the Judaeo-Christian story. This rejection of natural
world and person was not, however, unique to the West; otherworldliness
was to be found in the asceticism of the Hindu and the rejections of the
Buddhist. In too many traditions, the world is mere shadow and human
life only an illusion.

The empiricism that announced the modern world was not simply a
change in the nature of inquiry but a recall to the primitive quality of human
experience itself. In effect, the modern world began when people were asked
to respect it. They were invited to look more carefully at themselves in the
world, to see afresh what was necessarily of it and what was changeable
about it. We thus come to the Enlightenment from another point of view.
We see it as a call for a different kind of attention. Among its messages
was the permission it gave us to pay attention to our experience. With the
Enlightenment, naturalism as idea took another turn and now could support, in ways hardly possible in an earlier age, naturalism as feeling.

When a Humanist talks about what the world is all about, there is a
background of appreciation, of unspoken feelings that may be summed up
in the notion that he or she is at home here and now. A Humanist's opponents, by contrast, are still looking for a home and feel alien to this one.
As they argue for some extra-natural source for meaning, the passion of
the argument is supported by a basic need to be situated and a basic feeling
that they cannot be situated here.[9]

We find ourselves again in the familiar territory of God and no God, of heaven and no heaven, of hell and no hell. We affirm that the world and all that is in it can be understood in and of itself, or insist that it must have an external cause and justification. We rehearse the clichés of theism, deism, skepticism, and atheism. We divide over materialism and spirituality. We point a finger at superstition or defend the presence of supernatural powers. We assert or deny the evolution of fascinating complexities, arguing that the human brain or life itself can happen by accident or must have a designer. We urge the necessity of an eternal lawgiver or exhibit the possibility of a worldly ethics. Finally, it comes down to the question: How can we make sense of our world? On one side are those who insist that the answer lies in some other reality; on the other are those who say that another reality is neither necessary nor intelligible.

Despite the fact that we find the arguments on all sides so familiar as to be boring, that which is hidden by the game is serious. For some it is the salvation of the soul and doing "God's will"; for others it is the defense of truth and conscientiousness. But these are not issues at a distance; they are felt before they are debated. We need ways of making sense not just of reality, but of our reality. Naturalism as idea offers to put together the primitive qualities of our experience and the ways in which we reflect on, interpret, and understand it. Anti-naturalism insists that this is not possible and that human beings must remain separated beings, in but not of this world.

In some places, tolerance and a secularized politics—in themselves achievements of the Enlightenment—hold us back from religious warfare over the ideas of naturalism and extra-naturalism. However, the virulence of religious warfare is never far from the surface—in Ireland, Iran, Lebanon, India, Israel, and too many other places. Less dramatic, but no less intense, the struggle for freedom of conscience is never entirely won. A film like *The Last Temptation of Christ* stirs the censors; the "abortion issue" leads to violence. Whether to teach creation or evolution divides communities, intimidates teachers, and puts people out of jobs. A publisher is accused of blasphemy in England for portraying Jesus as a homophile. In West Germany freethinkers are charged under the law with "insulting religious or other conscientiously held beliefs in ways liable to disturb the public peace."[10] The idea of naturalism, then, appears in a setting that is laden with emotional and political baggage.

Important as that baggage is for understanding what is involved, the meaning of naturalism as an idea is neither difficult nor mysterious. As Corliss Lamont put it:

Humanism believes that nature or the universe makes up the totality of existence and is completely self-operating according to natural law, with no need for a God or gods to keep it functioning. . . . Humanism holds that the race of man is the present culmination of a time-defying evolutionary process on this planet that has lasted billions of years; that man exists as an inseparable unity of mind and body, and that therefore after death there can be no personal immortality or survival of consciousness. . . . Humanism relies on reason and especially on the established facts, laws, and methods of modern experimental science.[11]

Naturalism, however, is not simply a description of the universe. As the heat of the debate suggests, naturalism is a felt alternative to extra- naturalism as the setting for human life and as a directive to its conduct. It is an idea that both gives and deprives us of things we care deeply about. What, then, does naturalism convey and why is it a matter of passionate controversy? John Herman Randall summed it up when he wrote:

At last, the humanism of the Renaissance, supported by the methods of scientific reasoning, was able to make a breach in the Christian tradition . . . the Renaissance emphasis on man's moral and intellectual worth . . . the new science by a spirit of subjecting all beliefs and practices to the tests of reasonableness and utility in this life. . . . Here is the religious system with its hoary antiquity. Judged by the standards of the simplicity, order, rationality, and usefulness of the system of Nature, what is it worth? . . . The whole spirit of such a[n] . . . ideal . . . is admirably illustrated by the remark of one of the characters in an early work of Diderot. . . . "Supposing him initiated in all the mysteries of transubstantiation, consubstantiation, the Trinity, hypostatical union, predestination, incarnation, and the rest, will he be any the better citizen?" Such is the test—good citizenship, social utility; and all that can pass this test is the religion of reason. All that cannot is relegated to the other field of revealed or supernatural religion.[12]

Modern naturalism began as a criticism of the ways in which the traditions had demeaned human life and the world around us. It was supported by the successes of new forms of inquiry. Like all interesting ideas, it emerged as a response to the puzzles and possibilities of experience. It was the philosophic incarnation of a world in which a democratic ethics and politics could develop and in which an experimental science could be fruitful. Most of us today are in some sense attuned to this environment and at least partially attuned to its conceptual expression. This is what it means to say we live in a secular culture. But the Humanist makes an explicit commitment to the values that underlie it. In doing so, he or she unmasks the ambivalence that permits the rest of us to keep the past while living in the present. More radically, he or she insists that naturalism is the only view that can ultimately sustain science and democracy and that other philosophies will, sooner or later, betray them.

The Humanist knows that there are democrats who hold traditional beliefs and scientists who go to church. Obviously, in their lives, the traditions meet genuine aspirations and needs. Clearly too, churches and temples have contributed significantly to the advance of democratic causes. They are partners in the liberalism of alliances and are found supporting civil liberty, fighting against racism, and defending world peace. Nor would I want to challenge the sincerity with which such views are held. But I hope that I may be forgiven a lack of charity when I suggest that, however sincere and whatever their achievements, traditionalists hold views that are philosophically incoherent.

I have little doubt that the traditionalist who is a democrat manages to hold both positions at the same time. Nor do I want to deny the validity of the science or the intensity of the faith of the believing scientist. Surely there are illustrations enough of the latter. Einstein, faced with the statistical implications of quantum theory, is said to have remarked, "God doesn't play dice with the universe." But these traditionalist and modernist views dare not meet. In fact, they depend on deliberate blindness or implicit self-censorship. I have heard physicists, when challenged, talk about something that was "science" and something else that was "religion" and maintain that these were unconnected. They do not clash but, as it were, miss each other. We illustrate thereby our capacity for sustaining contradictory ideas at the same time. We are intellectual opportunists who use one set of ideas for some purposes and another for other purposes without trying to bring these ideas together in a reprise of the medieval notion of the "two truths." Ironically, given the impulse toward "unified" theory that is so much a part of the history and temperament of modern science, the willingness to settle for two realities is striking.

We can choose to excuse certain claims from inquiry for religious, political, or psychological reasons. We do that constantly and what we exempt depends on the climate of the day. The Inquisition centuries ago and the Fundamentalist today set religious limits on what may be asked and what may be answered about man and God. Stalinist Russia decided its genetics and its physics before the research began. More felicitously, we may, on occasion, suspend criticism where it is inappropriate and when belief seems to provide psychological sustenance to someone in trouble. I am not going to get into philosophical arguments about naturalism and extra-naturalism in times of the death or terminal illness of a friend. We join in our human connection and not in our theory. It is not possible, however, consistently to set such limits and, at the same time, follow inquiry wherever it takes us.

It is possible to separate saved and damned in eternity and still treat each other as equals in secular society. In order to get away with it, however, we must erect a wall within ourselves between one view of human beings and another or else we need to keep silent about what we really think. We divide, however, when these conflicted loyalties force a choice as when a Roman Catholic civil libertarian, often with a troubled conscience, supports state interference with personal rights based on theological beliefs as in the abortion issue and, not so long ago, as in the issue of providing information about contraception. Ultimately, too, a traditionalist view of human nature undermines confidence in the possibilities of democracy itself. This, I am sure, was in John Dewey's mind when he remarked:

In a book that G. K. Chesterton wrote after a visit to this country he spoke as follows... "So far as that democracy becomes or remains Catholic and Christian, that democracy will remain democratic.... Men will more and more realize that there is no meaning in democracy if there is no meaning in anything... if the universe has not a centre of significance and an authority that is the author of our rights" (*What I Saw in America*, New York, 1922, p. 296).... The nub of the passage resides clearly in the assertion that the rights and freedoms which constitute democracy have no validity or significance save as they are referred to some center and authority entirely outside nature.... This intrinsically skeptical, cynical, and pessimistic view of human nature is at the bottom of all asseverations that naturalism is destructive of the values associated with democracy, including belief in the dignity of man and the worth of human life. This disparaging view (to put it mildly) of man is that upon which rests the whole enterprise of condemning naturalism.... The fact of the case is that naturalism finds the values in question, the worth and dignity of men and women, residing in human nature itself, in the connections, actual and potential, that human beings sustain to one another in the natural environment.[13]

Traditionalists are troubled by all of this maneuvering. Their difficulty is illustrated by the radical separation between literalists and liberals and by the efforts in modern theology to reinterpret traditional ideas. Some even go so far as to reduce theology to literary metaphor and to deny that it has any ontological concern at all. God becomes symbolic and questions of His existence are simply not germane. Yet it is difficult to understand the Hebrew notion of a "chosen people" except as a claim of some sort of transnatural superiority. It is true that Jesus' saying, "in my Father's house are many mansions," invites a pluralism of faiths. At the same time, subservience remains the root metaphor, the relationship of father as authority and child as dependent. I recall an "interfaith" discussion some years ago. Naturally the "three faiths" were represented and somehow I too was invited. In an effort at toleration, the Protestant spokesman suggested that we were all climbing the "same mountain" but from different sides. I asked, "What if there's no mountain?" and "What if I'm on a different mountain?" My questions were met by disapproving silence. Pushed to the wall—say, about the damnation of non-believers—the more generous traditionalist replies that the interpretations of scripture are but human efforts to explain the ways of God to man. Ultimately, God's ways are "unknowable." Like the literalist, he or she is thus finally forced to meet inconsistency with mystery.

Naturalists are not immune to mystery. We are often puzzled, piqued, even anxious. We are not insensitive to the size of things, the vastness of time, or the beauty and complexity of a snowflake or flower. Mystery, however, is not "the mysterious." It retains its integrity as that which we do not know or that which happens without available explanation. That is rather different from converting mystery from a question into an answer or confusing mystery with the feelings caught up in responsiveness. The naturalist does not separate inquiry and belief, politics and destiny. Naturalism provides for a coherent view of ourselves in our surroundings and sustains the more primitive naturalism of our experience of the connected moment.

As an idea, modern naturalism had its roots in the democratic impulse. It began with a concern for human beings as such and with confidence in our capacities to know and rule ourselves. It had an earlier source in the celebration of human powers, the Renaissance achievement. But neither politics nor art could have sustained naturalism without modern science. The road it took from Newton to Darwin is marked by a radical shift in human perspective, as well as by the acquisition of ideas and evidence that this shift made possible and by which it was confirmed.

Modern science—or better, the insights of modern scientists—really began with a return to classical naturalism, which held that the world we live in was worth knowing and was responsive to our need to know. To this belief, however, the sciences brought a different sense of the size and pace of things, an appreciation of the values of change, an interest in how things worked, and even a sense of adventure. As they developed, the sciences encouraged human activity in all things and welcomed human energies in practice as well as in the acquisition of knowledge itself. Despite a naive empiricism, Francis Bacon caught the spirit of the enterprise with his emphasis on the power and productivity of inquiry. The scene shifted from monastery to laboratory and observatory, and from the groves of academe to the whirl of secular society. Early modern natural philosophers were fascinating letter writers and actively engaged in a scientific social life in their cities and towns. It was no accident that a century of global exploration and of meeting the needs of exploration—astronomical, technical, geographical, economic, and cultural—accompanied the development of the sciences. Finally, the new sciences made peace with a different kind of symmetry, finding in numbers and quantities a source of orderliness and intelligibility which the Greek had found in the harmonics of geometry.[14] Above all, they insisted on a return to experience, the so-called "hypothetical-experimental" method. Ideas were not to be permitted to escape their mundane origin.

In a discussion of modern scientific ideas, Stephen Hawking writes:

You have to be clear about what a scientific theory is. . . . [a] theory is just a model of the universe . . . and a set of rules that relate quantities in the model to observations that we make. . . . It must accurately describe a large class of observations on the basis of a model that contains only a few arbitrary elements, and it must make definite predictions about the results of future observations. For example, Aristotle's theory that everything was made out of four elements, earth, air, fire, and water, was simple enough to qualify but it did not make any definite predictions. On the other hand, Newton's theory of gravity was based on an even simpler model, in which bodies attracted each other with a force that was proportional to a quantity called their mass and inversely proportional to the square of the distance between them. Yet, it predicts the motions of the sun, the moon, and the planets to a high degree of accuracy.[15]

Unlike all that had gone before, modern science has a sense of humor. This is hidden in and yet caught by the philosopher's notion of "disconfirmability." A scientific idea qualifies only if it can in principle be denied or disproven. We must be able to imagine what such a disproof would look like. If we cannot, then we do not have a scientific idea at all, and if we cannot accept the possibility of error then we must doubt that we are scientists. So, we may propose that the moon is made of green cheese and we can imagine tasting it. If, on the other hand, tasting is impossible in principle, which is not the same as being difficult to do—if we believe that our taste buds must always mislead us, or if we insist that tasting simply ought not to be done, then the proposal is not scientific at all. The moon, of course, may still be made of green cheese—although that will remain a matter of speculation—but the idea will never be able to find a place in our science.

So it is that despite the natural human propensity to hold on to our ideas almost as we hold on to our children, we must always be prepared to give them up when the evidence takes us elsewhere. Of course, we resist. The history of theory is a history of the struggle to accommodate and then, often reluctantly, to surrender cherished notions. When an observation or event does not cohere with an idea, then we look for all kinds of interpretations of the event that will save the idea. But we are not so wedded to our ideas that we are prepared to pay any cost to hold on to them. Extranaturalism, on the other hand, has developed the disciplines of interpretation to brilliant perfection in order to accommodate the event to the idea. Even the Holocaust requires that we justify the benevolence of God through an appropriate interpretation.[16] For the anti-naturalist, the mere contemplation of the non-existence of God is blasphemy; the thought cannot legitimately be entertained.[17]

Modern science succeeded in creating coherent ideas for explaining the autonomy of the universe and, with Darwin, the autonomy of life and human life itself. Neither the stars nor human beings needed an extra-natural force in order to exist. In its earlier forms, modern science did hypothesize some natural power to initiate matters, to create from nothing. Thus, for a time, we experimented with transitional "natural religions," a "god of nature and nature's god," like the Deism of Paine or Jefferson or the transcendental naturalism of Emerson's "over-soul." To abbreviate a long and complicated process, it turned out, however, that the world did not need an "unmoved mover" to get it going nor did the pattern of cause and effect need a "first cause" to establish itself. It became possible to understand the world as it is against a whirl of natural energies and processes over time that could account for what had happened and could happen.

Newton's "laws of motion" described the way in which worlds exist, come into being, and pass away—all without the necessity of outside interference. With Darwin, this cosmic panorama of space, time, and matter came home. Human beings, just like stars and planets, come into being and pass away—all without the necessity of outside interference. Neither Newton's nor Darwin's ideas could be imprisoned within a compartment called "science." Catching the destructive import of these ideas for dearly held beliefs, the struggle against naturalism was a struggle against the scientific adventure itself, even where the effort was made to save science while denying naturalism. As Julian Huxley wrote:

To all save those who deliberately shut or averted their eyes, or were not allowed by their pastors or masters to look, it was at once clear that the fact and concept of evolution was bound to act as the central germ or living template of a new dominant thought-organization. And in the century since the *Origin of Species*, there have been many attempts to understand the implications of evolution in many fields, from the affairs of the stellar universe to the affairs of men, and a number of preliminary and largely premature efforts to integrate the facts of evolution and our knowledge of its processes into the overall organization of our general thought.[18]

To be sure, Huxley addresses the promise of naturalism. But it is a promise that is being kept.

Naturalism as an idea acquired believability with the development of the sciences and so could support the primitive naturalism of our experience. Naturalists drew upon the sciences for their images and these shaped human life, not simply modern thought. With that, however, arises the problem posed by naturalism for modern Humanism. Metaphors, drawn from seventeenth-century physics are inadequate to capture all that we need captured in experience. So, as we have seen, the notion of the "individual" and of a "contractual society" succeeded by excluding from consideration the experiences of intimacy. Similarly, the ideal, moral, aesthetic, and emotional qualities of experience were isolated from the work of rationality. The former were resigned to matters of taste and opinion, and the latter were said to be objective and dependable. The philosophic unification of reality that naturalism provided had as its cost the emergence of its own dualism, a cognitive and psychological dualism.

Adventurous science thus was marked by the successful spread of two imperatives that grew into general cultural ideas: that the world was neutral and value-free, and that everything could be manipulated.[19] Where natural law ruled, it was impersonal, objective, and uncaring, and natural law ruled everywhere. The result was a denatured world, a flat world of motion, time, and space that was measurable but qualitatively empty. Beauty, goodness, and love were resigned to the vagaries of human subjectivity and the human subject, like Newton's atoms, was separated from all other human subjects. Extending this imagery into the life of the marketplace, the notion of natural law led to the notion of natural social laws as well. In the marketplace—the worlds of commerce, industry, and labor—persons became objects again. But now they were natural objects moving not in accordance with will, intention, and choice—not even the will, intention, and choice of history's villains—but rather in accord with the imperatives of law. Law, moreover, was all the more irresistible because it was embedded in the world itself and not in the powers of men and women.[20]

The same inspiration that defeated the ghosts and goblins of the past moved us into a philosophic prison of our own making. We resigned our passions to some "inside" experience while the "real" world went on "outside." Pointing to the price we paid by excluding so much that we cared about, the anti-naturalist had ready ground for denying the adequacy of naturalism as an idea and Humanism as a life-philosophy. Thus, he or she finds the naturalist guilty of "materialism" and of a lack of sensitivity to the "spiritual" needs of human beings. The anti-naturalist may even admit that in its time, the Enlightenment had to use reason to destroy the powers of the few over the many. But the war is won, with only some mopping up to do. We are overdue for a return to a chastened anti-naturalism.

There is a certain appeal in this notion of return, for most of us are touched by tradition and moved by its familiarity. Most of us, too, recognize some justice in the claim that naturalism—and so Humanism—has not overcome its limitations. But must modern Humanism remain within the Enlightenment boundaries that surrounded its birth? Within the genius of naturalism itself—in democracy, science, and art—we find the possibility of self-correction, of reconstruction. That is the final import of naturalism as an idea, the ability to engage in self-critical behavior even at the point of our basic assumptions.

NOTES

1. William James, *The Varieties of Religious Experience* (New York: MacMillan, 1961): 74. Originally published 1902.

2. In thinking about the meaning of interruption in the aesthetic experience of events, I am reminded of Goethe's description of Faust's bet with the Devil. Faust will lose his soul if he ever asks that any single moment remain, become eternal. Often this is interpreted to mean that for life to exist, experiences must be varied

and plural—an ever-changing tapestry. Changelessness is itself hell. To this I might add—particularly in consideration of the moment in Part II when Faust finds salvation in service to humanity—that the devil loses when individuals willingly accept the interruption of the appreciated event by others. Human connectedness takes priority over aesthetic response; denial of it is also hell.

> If ever well content I'll lay me on a bed of ease.
> Then ended be my course, I say . . .
> If to the Moment I shall ever say,
> "Ah, linger on, thou art so fair!"
> Then fetter me without delay;
> Gladly I'll perish then and there.

Johann Wolfgang von Goethe, *Faust*, trans. J. F. L. Raschen (Ithaca, NY: Thrift Press, 1949): 81–82, lines 1692–1702.

3. I am sure that this is what Martin Buber, Jewish philosopher and mystic, meant when he said that "community is where community happens."

4. It is this utterly abstract notion of "sense data" that generated so many of the epistemological puzzlements we have inherited from the empirical tradition of John Locke and David Hume. Alfred North Whitehead called it the philosophy of "misplaced concreteness." It was to correct it that William James developed his "radical empiricism"—an empiricism that included relationships and not just separated events.

5. On this point, it seems to me that Humanists have neglected for far too long the insights of another American thinker, George Santayana, who worked out an aesthetic basis for Humanism in modern form. See Santayana, *The Life of Reason* (New York: Scribner, 1954), and in particular "Reason in Art" pp. 301–79).

6. Julian Huxley, *Essays of a Humanist* (New York: Harper and Row, 1964: 114–15.

7. In his own way, with characteristic sharpness, George Bernard Shaw captured this in *Saint Joan*, which is well worth reading.

8. Aristotle's naturalism—see his *Metaphysics* and *Physics*—despite his empiricism, was compromised by the need to postulate an "unmoved mover" and a "first" and "final" cause. It is not surprising that St. Thomas was able to adapt Aristotle quite easily to his metaphysical and theological dualism.

9. William James is helpful in grasping this point and was talking about it when he described the "once" and the "twice" born, the "healthy minds" and the "sick souls." See *The Varieties Of Religious Experience*, Chapters 4–7.

10. These examples are drawn from cases reported by the International Humanist and Ethical Union Commissioner for Human Rights. Utrecht, The Netherlands, 1986–1988.

11. Corliss Lamont, "Naturalistic Humanism," *The Humanist Alternative* Paul Kurtz, ed. (Buffalo, NY: Prometheus, 1973): 129–30.

12. John Herman Randall, Jr., *The Making of the Modern Mind* (Boston: Houghton Mifflin, 1940): 282–83.

13. John Dewey, "Antinaturalism in Extremis," in *Naturalism and the Human Spirit*, ed. Yervant H. Krikorin (New York: Columbia University Press, 1944): 8–9.

14. On the Greeks, see Plato, *Timaeus*, and for a discussion of the development

of modern cosmology, see Timothy Ferris, *Coming of Age in the Milky Way* (New York: William Morrow, 1988).

15. Stephen W. Hawking, *A Brief History of Time* (Toronto: Bantam, 1988): 9–10.

16. The German philosopher Leibniz provides us with an eighteenth-century model of this pattern in his *Monadology* which concludes that "all is for the best in this best of all possible worlds." Voltaire, in *Candide*, satirized the notion and in his description of the Lisbon earthquake makes the same point I am making about the Holocaust.

17. Of course I know that there are classrooms in seminaries and in church-sponsored schools where the existence of God is discussed—I have even participated on occasion. But, essentially, the game is fixed, and the intention of the debate is to sharpen a conclusion already present and unchallenged. I am not blind, either, to the fact that believers experience a crisis of faith—"Lord I believe, help me in my unbelief." But again, the existence of God is not ordinarily at issue; rather, attention goes to the psychological and religious state of the believer experiencing the crisis.

18. Julian Huxley, *Essays of a Humanist* (New York: Harper and Row, 1964): 77.

19. In these passages and for my discussion of the impact of the sciences on an age of industrialism and industrial labor, I am going back to some studies I did of the workplace and the problem of "humanizing work." See Howard B. Radest, *The Work Ethic and Its Meaning* (New York: American Ethical Union, 1978): 27–29.

20. The literature of law and laws is large and familiar. Thus, David Ricardo's "iron" law of wages, and Thomas Malthus' laws of population. Marx and Engels rely on the laws of political economy and of history. Adam Smith, the granddaddy of them all, describes the laws of supply and demand and of a free market. For a compact view of these in one place, see Robert Heilbroner, *The Worldly Philosophers* (New York: Simon and Schuster, 1972).

8

A Humanist's Companions: Democracy Reconstructed

The Enlightenment was once a believable story, but it no longer is. Yet we need our narratives. They connect our ideas to our feelings and dreams. We use words, shapes, tones, or colors; we organize movements or build monuments; we express ourselves in image, song, and dance. There is in us this constructing and construing capacity—I would dare the word "creative," except that it has been so damaged, or the word "myth," except that it has been so confused with fiction.

Love, friendliness, and care populate our stories as do hate and fear. The arts gather and celebrate these feelings. The sciences need insight and imagery too; rationality is itself a passion. Intuition, inspiration, and feeling, however, lure us into worlds of imagination and their power often leads us to forget their mundane origin. When the world becomes frightening, we are tempted to confuse imagination with reality. A natural and primitive poetry is projected outward and reified as another world. We separate the world of fact from the world of meaning, the world of flesh from the world of spirit. We are tempted down a road to unintelligible dualities.

Humanism must tell its story too, as once it told the story of freedom and revolution. We need images and metaphors in order to do the work of reason, in order to argue and know and do. We cannot account for our actions without this aesthetic activity. We move out from facticity. When we fail to do so, we get lost in routines, which is another way of saying that we echo someone else's imagery without realizing it.

These considerations may make my devotion to reason suspect. Yet, it was Immanuel Kant, no stranger to rationality, who began his *Critique of*

Pure Reason with a discussion of the "transcendental aesthetic."[1] While not a storyteller, he nevertheless shaped connections and continuities. Knower and known are reciprocal; subject and object are in tune. Before we can connect specific causes and effects or measure actual distances and durations, we need a sense of time, space, and causality. Of course, we can imagine other kinds of knowers and other kinds of worlds. Philosophic science fiction[2] is invited by this partnership between knower and known. Useful and exciting, it exhibits our activity in the world by the contrasts it reveals. But the Kantian point is that any act of imagination cannot be verified nor can it show us a world in itself. Although we might prefer to see the world "as it really is," we cannot step outside ourselves. No matter where we try to go, we carry ourselves along. So I am in good rationalist company when I suggest the marriage of reason and imagery.

In a similar way, Ernest Nagel in *The Structure of Science* remarked:

The widespread use of metaphors . . . testifies to a pervasive human talent for finding resemblances between new experiences and familiar facts. . . . In any event, the history of theoretical science supplies plentiful examples of the influence of analogies upon the formation of theoretical ideas. . . . For example, Huygens developed his wave theory of light with the help of suggestions borrowed from the already familiar view of sound as a wave phenomenon; Black's experimental discoveries concerning heat were suggested by his conception of heat as a fluid . . . and nineteenth-century theories of electricity and magnetism were built in analogy to the mechanics of stresses and strains in an elastic solid. . . . Perhaps no scientist of first rank has been as clearly aware as was (James Clerk) Maxwell of the place of analogies in the conduct of physical research and in the formulation of theories. . . . Maxwell believed that the resemblance in mathematical form between some of the laws for these distinct subjects (gravitation and heat conduction) is useful "in exciting appropriate mathematical ideas."[3]

Imagery can make for chaos, and this is all the more likely since the Enlightenment's "individual" has become today's cliché. We interpret ourselves in radically individualistic ways. Often this is an indulgence; individualism betrays ignorance of our actual connections with others. One instance of a chaos of feeling was the subjectivity of the "flower children" of the 1960s. Their legacy survives in the motto, "do your own thing," and in a culture where judgments are only "matters of taste." This subjectivism run wild has little to do with our sensitivity to personal differences or with moral and cultural diversity. Instead, it tells us that the "individual" is the hero of a narrative that has lost its way. What happens between us and the world, however, corrects both us and our poetry soon enough, at times painfully.

We can create a varied aesthetic menu but it is not indefinitely large. An image "rings true" or else it does not work. Poetry in politics, in science, or in the arts is a transaction between its maker, its receiver, and the world "out there."[4] We respond just because a poem, story, dance, or sculpture—

or less explicitly, a memory or a feeling—enables us to recognize, appreciate, know, and act. We learn that it is genuinely a trans-action—we and our poetry change together. A novel or play, a painting or sculpture or an idea takes on a life of its own. Even its creator learns unexpected things from it, finds new and unexpected things in it. We are prepared for some of our inventions and not for others. We might even say that poetry is empirical, even experimental, were these terms not reserved for more prosaic activities. For all the apparent inwardness of the poet's craft, it is a social activity in a natural world.

Poetry works within history and has a history. Our feelings and their expression appear in some contexts and not in others, have foreground and background; not just any transaction but only this or that one will do. There are times when certain images are believable and other times when they are not. As William James put it, there are "live options," occasions when response is likely because some particular choice touches us and illuminates what is before us. The varieties of human intervention only feel chaotic; their occurrence is not random. Convincing images beget kindred images and generate relevant vocabularies as in "schools" of painters or literary genre. At certain times and places some possibilities strike home, while others remain entertainments, and still others are ignored. Relationships, too, are shaped by what is believed to be possible and impossible in a given time and place. The feelings between husband and wife, child and parent take the forms that context makes available. We name historic eras by picking up and picking out characteristic responses. We call it the Age of Reason or the Age of Faith, the Romantic Era or the Dark Ages. Yet, men and women lived and died, earned their bread, made love, quarrelled, dreamed, suffered, and achieved all without knowing—or caring—that later we would give them a collective name. We suppress this knowledge of the ordinary, as it were, for the sake of an image that captures another reality within the ordinary. Of course, there are many such "realities," but we pay attention to some and not to others.

There are dangers and opportunities in all this. We are not audience but actors in the world and so we work with these "other" realities. Thereby, a story brings with it a politics and an ethics. For example:

It was not till toward the end of the decade—and especially with the publication in 1958 of [John Kenneth] Galbraith's *The Affluent Society*, and its chapter xxiii on "The New Position of Poverty"—that chronic poverty began to impinge on the national consciousness as a distinct issue. . . . Then, in 1962 *The Other America*, a brilliant and indignant book by Michael Harrington, translated the statistic into bitter human terms. If Galbraith brought poverty into the national consciousness, Harrington placed it on the national conscience.[5]

Poetry can be destructive, even devastating. When we name some things we blind ourselves to other things. Feminists rightly point out that much that we call attention to—even with justifiable pride—uses a masculine vocabulary. We ignore by naming out of existence the dreams, sufferings, and achievements of women. The same can be said of racial minorities or colonized peoples, of all the other made-invisible communities of history. The act of narration quite literally identifies what we take to be real. It is this calling attention to that, for good or ill, characterizes among other things, the Enlightenment notion of the "individual."

Poetry is never simply an aesthetic exercise. The placidity of a pastoral scene is freighted with energies. The presentation of experimental data is embedded in unconfessed commitments. The feelings we entertain are never simply given. Foreground and background shift. As they do, we feel differently and give a different content to love, friendship, and care. We resurrect some images and relegate others to the dust heap. The story of the arts is marked by the "rediscovery" of lost artists; the story of the sciences is marked by aesthetic shifts; the story of relationships is marked by breaks with convention.

It may disturb the rationalist to suggest that poetry is unavoidable and the realities it describes never provable. Poetry can be overcome only by another poetry, image by an image, and ideal by an ideal. The resistance of our stories to argument and evidence does not, however, require us to desert reason. But it tells us that without connection to aesthetic and emotional strategies reason is powerless. Long ago, Spinoza, like Kant, no stranger to reason, remarked:

Proposition VII.—An affect (an emotion or feeling) cannot be restrained nor removed unless by an opposed and stronger affect.

Corollary. An affect . . . cannot be restrained nor removed unless by the idea of a bodily affection opposed to that which we suffer and stronger than it . . . it cannot be removed unless by the idea of a bodily affection stronger than that which affects us, and opposed to it.[6]

The natural history of our feelings and the ways we express them goes a long way to explain why even good argument does not "change the mind" or does so only over time and with a great difficulty.[7] Our need for stories helps to account for the philosophic incoherence of the scientist-believer or the democratic-dogmatist. A primitive poetry organizes the non-logical spaces in us, allows for what we might call emotional coherence.

The Humanist is not alone in being frustrated by the inadequacies of reason. Many a traditionalist is frustrated by its failure too. He or she learns rather quickly that the best "proofs" of the existence of God do not convince the skeptic and do not convert the heretic. I recall a dialogue between Humanists and Catholics in 1972. Arguments flew across the table. Suddenly, a Roman Catholic participant said that Humanists simply did not understand the nature of his belief and by implication of any belief. The logic of our presentation would not convince him and his argument would not convince us. His belief, he continued, was not a matter of argument or demonstration, nor was ours. He was not even prepared to use the word, "know" as in "I know that God exists" except in elliptical fashion. God's being was simply a reality for him much as breathing, seeing, and feeling were realities for him. He had not, he went on, argued himself into belief and so could not argue himself out of belief.[8] I had no quarrel with his comment; we Humanists are alike in "knowing" our realities too. Rationality is also a passion and argument is never mere argument.

There is something in the Humanist that resists the thought that we are the products of our passions and of the accidents of time and place. It smells too much of an unconfessed determinism, and seems to disable us from becoming agents of our own development. We also remember that destiny has been, all too often, the tool of tyranny. Reason and destiny were themselves hero and villain in the Enlightenment story, the story we needed to connect idea and action. As it grew dimmer in time, rationality became an icon. Meanwhile, the facts have changed. In today's pluriform world, the cosmopolitanism of the Enlightenment is untruthful to experience. In ways that were not actually or emotionally available a century or two ago, I "know" that had I been born elsewhere, I might have been Confucian, Taoist, or Muslim; or been speaking Greek, French, or Tagalog. Had I been born at another time I might have been a monk, a serf, or a Crusader. The Humanist story, however, still echoes the ultimate victory of reason as if the world had not changed, and still has as its lead character the individual freed from histories and traditions. At the same time, the Humanist has learned about the social context of individuation and that surprises are sensible and permanent reminders of *fortuna* in the "affairs of men," to use Machiavelli's phrase. Today, the Humanist story is caught in ambivalence.

We have learned that our failure is not only a consequence of tyranny and ignorance. We have learned too that we cannot be secure in our truth because we cannot ever leave ourselves. We have, in other words, departed the absolutes of early modern science—the certainties of space, time, and causality—and yet we have not surrendered the guarantees which that science offered. Like the traditionalist, the Humanist too faces the disappearance of ontological and historical securities. Therefore, Humanists celebrate reason ambivalently. It has its virtues but it is also a defense against the allure of another world and the terrors of this one. Symptomatically, the celebration all too often looks backward.

Under conditions of insecurity I am tempted to be a deserter. When I act, I intend to shape the world and those in it because I have confidence in the truth and value of my ideas. I close out all possibilities but one—and not only for myself. This burden of action and, indirectly, of all that leads to action is the ontological meaning of responsibility. At the same time, I have lost confidence in the story that allowed me to accept responsibility. So I run the risk of quietude and the feeling of guilt. At the same time, I know that passivity is also an illusion. To do nothing is also to choose.

Feelings and passions and the forms in which they are expressed pose special problems for Humanism. They seem to subvert science and rationality, values that in the present circumstance demand ever more vigorous defense. To move us toward a less backward-looking strategy, I have deliberately chosen to highlight the work of poetry in the sciences. I realize that by selecting rationalist examples—for example, Kant and Spinoza—I seem to ignore the artist as such. Yet we must not be misled by the empiricism that is the modern foreground of philosophy, science, and politics. The poet in them is never absent. More direct than most are the comments of Albert Einstein who spoke of the scientific adventure as "holy curiosity." Recalling his discovery of Euclid, he wrote:

It is quite clear to me that the religious paradise of youth, which was thus lost, was a first attempt to free myself from the chains of the "merely-personal," from an existence which is dominated by wishes, hopes, and primitive feelings. Out yonder there was this huge world, which exists independently of us human beings and which stands before us like a great eternal riddle, at least partially accessible to our inspection and thinking. The contemplation of this world beckoned like a liberation. . . . The road to this paradise was not as comfortable and alluring as the road to the religious paradise; but it has proved itself as trustworthy, and I have never regretted having chosen it.[9]

It is the transactional features of experience, our responsiveness in a responsive world, that evoke our primitive naturalism. Traditionalists have tamed this transaction with its double promise of achievement and chaos by locating it in another world. So their style is comfortable with story, myth, and parable, and with song and dance. This points out the irony of otherworldliness, for nothing so demonstrates the richness of the natural world or the inventiveness of the human being in it as those who deny both. It is not surprising to find great art and architecture at home among those for whom the worlds of Gods and demons are a commonplace. By contrast, the Humanist's political, scientific, and secular roots in the Enlightenment tend not only toward the prosaic but to suspicion of its opposite.

There is historical warrant for Humanist suspicions. Poetry counts on the richness of ambiguity. This is precisely why and how it, unlike logical symbols, experimental data, and legal rules, evokes unexpected and original responses. The Humanist, however, cannot forget that the move toward transcendance has been used to obscure the truth and to manipulate human beings. Consider the many uses—to be sure, the traditionalist might say abuses—of the word "God," or of promises of salvation. Humanist prosiness, then, is an aesthetic strategy growing from a particular history. In its anxiety to avoid manipulating people with persuasive symbols, however, Humanism exhibits a certain blindness to human capacities. Useful in its time, this is today destructive of Humanist values. Feelings and passions and the poetry through which they are expressed are unavoidably human. Precisely because of this, on Humanist grounds, we cannot dismiss them. The narrative of the Enlightenment must be overcome.

I have heard the richness of Humanism's history in the voices of its adherents. I have heard its celebration of liberation and equality, its songs and slogans, and its protests against injustice. Even a manifesto is an art form. I cannot help but note, at the same time, how repetitive this poetry seems today. We have hardly caught the grandeur of a new cosmos and an emerging global environmental consciousness. Before the magnitude and complexity of our world, we retreat to fixed categories that in their rigidity betray their Enlightenment inspiration. It was a daring idea to put the human being at the center of all values given the vulgarity, obstinacy, and vicious-ness we so amply exhibit. When we add the possibilities of world destruction by a massive technology, Humanism seems not so much daring as unbe-lievable. By contrast, the traditions make a much lesser demand on credi-bility. Yet so much of Humanism seems to have become "common sense" that there is little reason for it to make the effort of developing a distinctively modern story. Post-*Manifesto I* Humanism is thus in the ambiguous position of having achieved cultural success and of having failed to explore its own reconstruction.

The problem of a convincing narrative, however, is posed for everyone and not just for Humanists. Joseph Campbell put it:

For the democratic ideal of the self-determining individual, the invention of the power-driven machine, and the development of the scientific method of research, have so transformed human life that the long-inherited timeless universe of symbols has collapsed. . . . The spell of the past, the bondage of tradition was shattered. . . . The dream-web of myth fell away. . . .

It is not only that there is no hiding place for the gods from the searching telescope and microscope; there is no such society any more as the gods once supported. The social unit is not a carrier of religious content, but an economic-political organization. . . . Isolated societies, dream-bounded within a mythologically charged horizon, no longer exist except as areas to be exploited.

. . . today, no meaning is in the group—none in the world; all is in the individual. But there the meaning is absolutely unconscious. . . . The lines of communication between the conscious and the unconscious zones of the human psyche have all been cut, and we have been split in two.[10]

Humanists are not alone in having lost the comforting boundaries that shaped the traditions and the Enlightenment. The metaphors that put things together—a "father in heaven" or a "free individual"—no longer serve. This is as true of modern politics as of modern religions. The latter, which not so long ago were moving toward religions of reason, nature, and social reform, are now trapped in neo-Fundamentalism, sectarianism, superstition, and cultism. Politics has deteriorated into opportunism and social engineering. We know that we are neither the darlings of creation as biblical faith held nor have we become as gods as Enlightenment Humanism believed.[11] Both providence and progress with their assurance of human destiny have vanished before the incommensurable spaces and times of modern cosmology. Something happened while we were not looking:

Beyond the Milky Way lie more galaxies. Some . . . are spirals. Others are ellipticals, their stars hung in pristine, cloudless space. Others are dim dwarfs. . . . Most belong, in turn, to clusters of galaxies. The Milky Way is one of a few dozen galaxies comprising a gravitationally bound association that astronomers call the Local Group. That group in turn lies near one extremity of a lanky archipelago of galaxies called the Virgo Supercluster. If we could fly the sixty million or so light-years from here to the center of the supercluster, we would encounter many sights worth seeing along the way—the giant cannibal galaxy Centaurus A, an elliptical busily gobbling up a spiral that blundered into it; the distended spiral M51, with its one outflung arm stretching after a departing companion galaxy; the furious glowing spiral M106, with its bright yellow nucleus and its shoal of blue-white stars; and, at the supercluster core, the giant elliptical Virgo A, wreathed in thousands of globular star clusters, harboring some three trillion stars, and adorned by a blue-white plasma jet that has been spat from its core with the velocity of a bolt of lightning.

Beyond Virgo lie the Perseus, Coma, and Hercules clusters, and beyond them so many more clusters and superclusters of galaxies that it takes volumes just to catalog them. . . . Beyond that, light from faraway galaxies riding the contours of curved space, become as dappled as the moon's reflection on a pond in a gentle breeze.[12]

Stories rooted in a homely geography or a manageable duration are no longer convincing. We hold on to them, no doubt in desperation, but we live in another place and time. Even where we give some hypothetical "initiating event" of this fascinating universe the name of "God," only the name is familiar. No longer is it so that "He walks with us and talks with us and tells us we are His own," as the Protestant hymn has it. A different preparation has been made but our poetry is still untuned to what is going on.

For the Humanist, the loss of Enlightenment is doubly poignant. With the traditionalist, he or she experiences the dissipation of boundaries that once shaped the structures of life and living. There was an analogy between the ideas of progress and of salvation, between natural law and God's justice. The patterns were recognizable even as their content was changing. But the Humanist also experiences a crisis of faith in the loss of Enlightenment. Once, the politics of revolution and the dream of plenty were its felt outcomes. Freedom and reason stirred mind and blood. The Humanist has been demythologized too. Freedom has become mere negation and reason mere method. We scarcely use a democratic vocabulary any longer; we seem almost ashamed of it as if it were merely some sentimental aberration in a world that demands "realism" of us. Our poetry is shrunken and private, or else it is destructive, as in the terrifying totalitarian myths of our age. Our architecture, by and large, ignores human dimensions and is contented with mechanistic repetitions. We confess our needs by our affection for those epic excursions that look backward like novels of great wars and great loves, or we turn to Classic and Romantic literature and art. Shamefacedly, we confess that these are only acts of sentimentality and call them, derisively, "nostalgia trips."

To be demythologized means to live without stories. Popular culture, while expressive enough, deals in privacies, miniatures, and unintelligibilities. Functionalism becomes the foreground of experience so that our revealing question is: What's the bottom line? We ask it everywhere without realizing that function is itself a metaphor and without paying attention to how it chooses our very perceptions for us. The pain we feel in our impoverishment is masked by the glibness with which we speak of our disillusionment.

We are not unique. Like those who have gone before, we experience what it feels like to leave a dearly held past without finding its replacement readily to hand. Our position is lost—the place where we live and from which our living proceeds. This is only secondarily a matter of concept; it is first a matter of existence. In other words, I despair of finding myself in position. Sooner or later, this becomes intolerable and I turn from it to an illusory inwardness or an illusory past. Psychologism and Fundamentalism are thus the great anti-modern moves that tempt us all. Loyalties turn into shadow loyalties and are proclaimed with great vigor. Alienating and alienated prescriptions become attractive. I read the world as a battle of friends and enemies, or I simply retreat from it. I fight my way back to my lost illusions and defend them all the more angrily precisely because they no longer serve.

Humanist conversation looks longingly backward to revolution or Renaissance or Greece and Rome, or enviously to Humanism's traditionalist neighbors. Some retrace yesterday's path in a Humanist fundamentalism and reincarnate eighteenth-century rationalism—but they do so angrily, which betrays their doubts of its adequacy. Others move toward psychologism and turn Humanism into a celebration of personal fulfillment. Still others turn to "community" and "intuition" as if merely to announce them is to announce anything at all. There is, in short, a symptomatic turn inward and backward and this betrays the fact—as it does in others—of the absence of a usable post-Enlightenment metaphor.

If I am correct in this diagnosis, then it is urgent to find new metaphors that invite story and song. Their present-day homelessness is revealed in the inward and intimate turn of modern music and art and in the almost pathological focus on the utterly private. Yet, for the Humanist, the person was never purely inward. From the Greek to the Renaissance, "man the measure" has been the token of all Humanist poetry. The children of the Enlightenment, inspired by a new science and a new politics, announced a radical vision of the person as a free individual in a free world. He or she became a cultural ideal and then, almost without realizing it, moved from foreground to background, leaving behind a mere shell.[13]

In some places, to be sure, the free individual in a free society is still a political battle cry. When uttered in Eastern Europe, China, or South Africa, we listen with approval, even pleasure. When closer to home—say, from an excluded minority—we are more likely to be uncomfortable than supportive. Yet, under its inspiration, we once found interesting narrative connections between politics and physics, ethics and astronomy, economics and biology.

Once, traditionalists looked to the "heaven beyond the heavens" for connections between what counted here and what counted ultimately. In a remarkable shift, even religious ideas began to take their inspiration from scientific ideas just as moral and political ideas did. This sense of the way things are still lingers. So the argument is made that a particular moral, political, or religious view is "proved" by "science." The "indeterminacy principle" of quantum mechanics has been used inappropriately as an argument for free will. Similarly, using the slogan, "the survival of the fittest," we have seen alleged scientific justification for the selfishness and greed of *laissez faire* and more recently in a changed social climate for the virtues of social cooperation.[14]

Inspired by metaphor, these connections told us where to look and helped us figure out what we were seeing. But the free individual, like the impenetrable atom of Newtonian physics, was locked into a compartment that had only one occupant.[15] Admittance was not possible, although interaction—itself a revealing image—was inevitable. Among those interactions, some were invited and we could then say we were choosing our relationships, and some were rejected and we could then say we were respecting privacy. Even the invitation to interaction was written in a crabbed hand. Free individuals were destined to remain a mystery to each other; the individual was hidden away from all other individuals. While Enlightenment psychology struggled with sympathy and association, there was a certain finality to the notion that my experience was closed within my own mind and senses. I could only speculate on yours.

The free individual lacked the dimension of intimacy. Thus the Enlightenment metaphor was blind—and blinded us—to the passions that were either dismissed as aberrant and irrational or else reduced to behavioral interactions. Society replaced community and was imagined as a contract between coordinated privacies. Predictably, the mechanism—like the colliding of atoms against each other—that connected free individuals was the lawful state. We could enter society from a "state of nature" by an act of rational will, as in "enlightened self-interest," and could depart by an act of objection. Told well, the story of the free individual was exciting and promising. Its drama, undeniably heroic, was a tale of courage. Still today, when freedom and reason are under attack, it sings a promise of liberation from tyranny and superstition. Even when other children of the Enlightenment like Marxists criticized the "free individual" as a token of "false consciousness," an instrument of alienation and control by rulers over ruled, their description of a revolutionary elite and their dream of a worker's paradise still drew upon Enlightenment imagery.[16]

We need to capture the contrast between the Enlightenment story and an earlier imagery. In tribe and community, relationships were given by birth and place. Ancestry was destiny, and the person was shaped in the image of others. Self-chosen images—in career, family, or faith—were simply unavailable. The root heresy of tribe and community was the person who broke the boundaries and departed the ways of the fathers. The extreme punishment was exclusion. As a reminder of our tribal past, a child who leaves Judaism is still mourned as dead; the "return of the prodigal son" is still celebrated above all others. Traditions are filled with stories of turning one's face away and turning one's back.

Today, we have learned to notice another blindness from the feminist revolution, but the lesson is more general. Mothers, sisters, and daughters were seldom universal models. Mary was the model for all women but the "imitation of Christ" was the model for all persons. In Judaism, the child gained tribal identity through the mother, but membership in accordance with the Law was a masculine prerogative. The intimacies of the traditions, even where there were efforts at universality, were shaped by metaphors of paternal authority. By transforming intimacy into privacy, the Enlightenment sought to protect the person from invasion as much as to open the person to choices. Yet blindness lingered. The Declaration of Independence and the Rights of Man spoke of "all men. . . . " Denying hierarchical authority, they still exhibited a masculine foreground.

Nothing calls attention to the limitations of the eighteenth-century story of the free individual or the traditional story of the connected individual so much as modern feminism,[17] although there were hints enough in imperialism, colonialism, and racism. Feminism reminds us that while the Enlightenment released us from an imposed connectedness, it simultaneously impoverished us. It is a cultural instrument as much as it is a demand for social justice. We want to be free *and* we want to be connected. Consequently, we join together frequently but apparently without satisfaction. We reveal in our associations what Stephen Toulman called an "ethics of strangers":

In dealing with our children, friends, and immediate colleagues, we both expect to—and are expected to—make allowances for their individual personalities and tastes . . . our perception of their current moods and plans. In dealing with the bus driver, the sales clerk in a department store, the hotel barber, and other such casual contacts, there may be basis for making these allowances. . . . In these transient encounters, our moral obligations are limited and chiefly negative—for example to avoid acting offensively or violently. So, in the ethics of strangers, respect for rules is all, and the opportunities for discretion are few. In the ethics of intimacy, discretion is all and the relevance of strict rules is minimal.[18]

So we move on, frenetically, to other joinings whether it be in marriage, politics, or hobbies. We make and break connections often and at will. We are, as we say, "liberated," which reflects the fact that the metaphor of the free individual is still very real to us. Yet we exhibit our longings for intimacy in this pattern of broken connections. In uneasy compromise, friendships become utilitarian—"office friendships" or "contacts." Families are in trouble. We seem not to know how to be together without surrendering freedom, how to be free without losing intimacy.

I have puzzled over our need for association and intimacy, and I suggest that "companionship" may well be the metaphor for rebuilding our narrative. It ranges from the momentary connections we feel when a dramatic event unites a group of strangers to the deepest intimacies of love and friendship. It can have the single-mindedness of a sports club or the complexity of a tribe. We may find companionship over a drink or we may feel companionship across separations of time and space while reading a book or seeing a painting. The varieties of companionship we enter and leave seem to catch our double desire, to be both free and connected. Companionship also conveys a mood of comfort and welcome and so responds to our feelings of alienation from others.

A metaphor should help to construct an interesting foreground. Companionship promises to do this for us. It reminds us that we are never really alone, as the image of the free individual implies, and that we are never entirely captured by others, as the image of tribal life suggests. We are always in the company of others—at the moment of birth, when learning and growing up, in the excitements and routines of work, in the passions of loving. In dying, memory dwells on connections and we are remembered by others in and through those connections. We are in the company of others while walking the streets of a city or the paths of a forest. Even when apart, like some Robinson Crusoe, we carry our companions with us. They populate our reflections. Indeed, we might imagine the person as a company, or as a friend once put it, "I have a zoo in me."

Intimacy and friendliness are coordinate themes of companionship as is the sharing of feelings, values, ideas, and activities. Companionship allows for ranges and intensities of connectedness; it celebrates loosely coupled relationships and provides both for collective identities and for movement toward and away from identities. Companionship is thus responsive to the plurality of identities so typical of modern life and turns these into an opportunity rather than a problem. Our world is peopled by the possibilities of novel relationships and by the reconstruction of traditional relationships. Family, work, and politics are varied and changing forms. Avocation and leisure are no longer only aristocratic opportunities. For the first time in human history, we pose the "quality of life" as a universal theme here and now.

Companionships are not contracts although some may also be contractual. This frustrates us for we are caught in the prejudices of lawfulness. We tend to reduce relationship to legality, to meet human needs by passing a law, and to resolve conflicts by going to court. But legality is superficial. We learn this painfully from all that lingers after divorce. The parting is never only a rule-governed arrangement. Companionship speaks to what happens to us in ways that the metaphor of the free individual cannot. In other words, it catches an image of the person as a living, responding, and energetic organism in a world of organisms. In such a world, boundaries are seldom rigid and sharply edged. Companionship is more suited to our experience than the mechanisms of cause and effect or of give and get that shaped the story of the free individual and that were shaped by it.

We can choose our companions. Thus, the metaphor is not really an invitation back to tribalism with its authoritarian roots. Companionship does not subject us to the rule of our ancestors and their Gods, and it does not rely on exclusive loyalties. We enter and leave a company, indeed belong to many companies and enjoy many companionships. The new geography in which we live invites such movement and predicts their increase. It makes biographical experiment both available and believable. The new literacy about cultures opens to us invisible companies from past and future. No longer fixed in time, place, and destiny, companionships respond to the flow of our interests and our development. Some may be narrow and momentary; some may be lifelong. Age calls for certain relationships and childhood others. Masculinity and femininity are the source of multiple companies. Interests lead into and out of differing companies. Companionship is not merely a reflection of experience in an expanding world, but directs that experience as well. From it we learn to enjoy possibilities.

The traditionalist will find his or her own difficulties with companionship. It subverts the notion of one truth and one faith but not as liberal tolerance does. Companionship poses a different question and offers a different possibility. If we take companionship seriously, then the person may well enjoy a plurality of loyalties and even a playfulness of faiths. The habit of exclusivity, particularly in Western religions, is affronted by this possibility. It is also difficult to imagine human beings as servants of Gods and Devils and Angels. The metaphor carries with it a pervasive democracy. Companions, after all, resent being told that certain companies are, like exclusive clubs, the sole possessions of hierarchs. Finally, for the traditionalist, the freedom to enter and leave is a problem. The appreciation and enjoyment of diversity celebrates heresy.

Humanists will not have these difficulties with companionship. Indeed, it illuminates those Humanist themes that have grown tired and worn in their eighteenth-century incarnation, themes of individuality and liberation. Reflecting a development along pluralist lines of Enlightenment cosmopolitanism, it is an alternative to the free but faceless individual of the Enlightenment and the bounded individual of tradition. Yet it owes a debt to both.

Today, the children of the Enlightenment choose up sides between freedom and equality, as in debates over "affirmative action." They neglect the third term of the Enlightenment trinity—fraternity. Of course, its masculine bias needs a gender-inclusive translation. Fraternity was a cosmopolitan notion and revealed once again the Newtonian metaphor. Free individuals were alike just as atoms were like all other atoms. Diverse lives and lifestyles which developed within ethnic, religious, and historic boundaries were, like loudness, color, or hardness, only secondary qualities. In other words, much that I cared about was to be put aside and, indeed, was unimportant. The ideal to be achieved was of one human race with legally equal and morally indistinguishable members. Equality was collapsed into identity. The public arena was all that counted, and was where I really counted. If, instead, I tried to pay attention to history and personality, I would be unable to defend the view that we are indistinguishable from each other. Yet I needed that sense of equality as identity in order to achieve democracy—or at least I thought I did. The issue posed by fraternity then is not only an issue of male-biased language.

Like equality and liberty, fraternity was a revolutionary metaphor. Cosmopolitanism was an instrument of liberation from traditional communities and tribes. Two hundred years later, however, we look toward fraternity from within mass societies. These are, as it were, a satire on the cosmopolitan ideal. A tendency toward homogeneity is the rule. The universalized individual is not really free to be himself or herself. The scene shifts from social and political to psychological imagery. The Enlightenment is turned upside down, and public life becomes secondary and superficial.

I recall the struggle in the 1950s to find ways of "being oneself," by oneself. A literature of alienation developed; small communities and ethnicity became an ideal; intellectuals and social critics addressed what they called a crisis of meaning.[19] A mass society and a mass culture, however, were quite skilled in exploiting all possibilities. The post-World War II struggle with "conformity" was neither won nor lost, but transformed. Effective marketing converted individuation into yet another consumer good. Costumes, automobiles, and menus were touted as individualized and produced identically in the tens of thousands. The move from the free individual toward subjective individuality was a clue to inadequacies of the

Enlightenment metaphor, just as the frustration of that move was another clue. Its failure tells us that a psychological shift will not do. The person by himself or herself—the center of any psychological strategy—cannot meet society on equal terms. Ways must be found then for persons to come together, for them to deal with law and power, with money and morals, to live again in a public life and not with the illusion of the self by itself. At the same time, individuality remains in the foreground, calling attention to our need for personal identity.

Companionship raises an obvious question. Who is a companion? Like the notion of the free individual, the answer seems self-evident. But we know that in many places women and children are not regarded as persons, or not fully as persons. Nationalism, tribalism, and sexism still draw a line between persons and non-persons. Personhood then is not a fact of biology or psychology, but the outcome of a political, moral, and aesthetic struggle.

When the struggle is successful, then we find that "dignity" is attached to new populations, marking off new boundaries between persons and things. The idea of dignity tells us that a person—unlike an object—is a being that may not be violated. Non-violation, however, is a minimal condition. It comes to us embedded in the language of justice and rights, or alternatively, in the idea that a person is created in God's image. Instead, the diversities and energies of companionship suggest that personhood emerges through supporting relationships like nurture and friendliness and is subverted when these relationships are absent. Dignity is reconceived as a developmental idea and not as a fixed attribute. To deprive a person of dignity is always possible, just as any development can be truncated or crippled. Dignity is at risk and its deterioration is marked by the breaking of connections, the denial of companionship.

Even if companionship is denied, we think we can still meet the obligations of the social contract through social welfare programs. But in the outcome, we find "welfare dependency," the denial of dignity. Reformers, frustrated by the failure of their efforts, do more of the same or decide that reform is simply impossible. They do not look to the inadequacy of the contractual metaphor itself. Yet, contracts must miss the features of actual relationships in their variety. For the Enlightenment, this suppression of actual relationships was morally necessary. For us, it has become a problem.

Of course, a person may sever connections by isolating himself or herself, or by reducing relationships to interactions—thus depriving the self of dignity and forsaking personhood even without knowing it. The so-called "rugged individual" is from this point of view a comic and a tragic figure, comic because of the unreality of the pose, tragic because success would defeat his or her very intention. John Dewey called attention to this when he wrote:

It is not too much to say that the whole significance of the older individualism has now shrunk to a pecuniary scale and measure. The virtues that are supposed to attend rugged individualism may be vocally proclaimed, but it takes no great insight to see that what is cherished is measured by its connection with those activities that make for success in business conducted for personal gain. Hence, the irony of the gospel of "individualism" in business conjoined with the suppression of individuality in thought and speech.[20]

Being forced to sever connections is an ultimate form of punishment, as in segregation, solitary confinement, exile, and death. Certainly, there is evidence enough in the experience of loneliness on the one hand, and of racial discrimination on the other, to suggest that this is not a far-fetched idea. Unlike both traditional and Enlightenment images, which are quite close together, dignity does not attach once and forever to a free individual, or to a being created in the image of God. The metaphor of companionship suggests that dignity is a relational idea that generates moral obligations for the person—to act connectedly—and for persons—to make connections available.

Companionships like families, schools, clubs, congregations, and work-places acquire moral status precisely because of their potentialities for de-veloping personhood in their members. For example, this sense of mem-bership was once conveyed by the notion of the "dignity of labor." When labor was a cause and not an establishment, companionship was its ideal. Today, the "dignity of labor" is reduced to contractual obligations and benefits, and to the legal autonomy of those who enter agreements. Com-panionship suggests ways by which parents or teachers may nurture the dignity of children through mutual activities. The focus shifts from rules and rights; we instead look to develop the capacity of the child to be a companion. The teacher or parent who seeks inheritors and successors only tries to duplicate himself or herself. Rather than nurturing a member of the company, a replacement is sought. In a similar way, we can test the moral qualities of marriage by the capacity of its members to sustain connections, by the renewal and reconstruction of their relationships. Such marriages are both comfortable in their memories and varied in their activities. In its romantic form, marriage can only be temporary—for romance builds on the illusions we have before we are companions. The unbreakable marriage, as in the days before divorce was respectable, relied on the powers and pressures of law and tribe. The metaphor of companionship, in other words, moves moral attention from attribute toward development with all its risks and possibilities.

Worth is a correlate of dignity. I dignify myself and understand that I am doing so. Unlike an object, I need not be presented by another, need not have someone else exhibit me. My presence is active; I present myself. When I meet a person, he or she conveys a sense of his or her own worth. I know people who deny worth to themselves. Meeting them I experience a sense of emptiness in them and pity in me. Their denial, literally self-denial, may show itself in retreat or in aggression—as if by pushing the world away or by pushing it around they could compensate for worthlessness. I think of the angers of the oppressed or of the nastiness of the petty bureaucrat. Self-deniers may even seem amiable, but it is a troubling amiability afflicted by an uncritical agreeableness. Aggressive or acquiescent, they become things to be maneuvered from outside of themselves.

The encounter with a person signals a special claim on my attention. Things may legitimately be treated as instances of categories, as pencils, chairs, clouds, or stars. I understand the unsolved problem posed by the unique and precious object—a painting, sculpture, or something peculiarly personal. Such an object does not merely exemplify a category and this suggests that the distinction between persons and things itself needs revision. Of course, we need the benefits of momentary blindness in order to subsume persons under functional headings—as when we deal with clerks, toll-takers, or bus drivers. But, these are "convenient fictions," necessary and dangerous fictions. A person is a subject and not an object, a being for whom there are no replacements.

If history shows anything of progress, it is in an increasingly more generous definition of persons. At the same time, our complaints about the failures of democratic society arise precisely because the Enlightenment raised our moral and political standards. Whatever the limits of its metaphor, an ethical transformation was at the heart of its project. Personhood has been recognized in serfs, blacks, Latinos, Native Americans, women, and children. What has yet to occur is the transformation of collectives into companies.

The moral imagination released by the Enlightenment has extended personhood. There are hints today that its boundaries cannot be drawn only around the human race. True, we already seem to have non-human companions as when we assign "personality" to our pets. But this is a pose. We can withdraw the assignment at our pleasure. We are not permitted to act this way toward persons. We cannot arbitrarily give and take membership away. The relation of owner and pet is then only a shadow companionship, although it may be felt as quite real.

We move beyond such subjective occasions when we establish the moral category of "cruelty to animals." With that, a transformation is underway. Recently, we have also begun serious and controversial discussion of "animal rights"[21] stimulated by the moral problems of medical experimentation. Thus far, however, the power seems all on one side and concerns only the human conscience. The "victims" are not invited to the table and are only exhibited, even by their defenders. But power was never a sufficient moral argument. An alternative criterion for membership in a company, that is, for personhood, is the ability to use symbols in order to grasp relationships of ends and means as well as to reflect on possibilities and impossibilities. Another criterion of companionship might be the ability to exhibit affectionate relationships, even to the point of placing the good of another above ones own good. And we do have evidence that rationality and altruism are not found only in human beings. As anthropologist Harvey Sarles wrote,

As naturalistic observation has informed us in the past decades, other species are quite different from how we had thought and imagined them. The field of ethology/ behavioral biology, has taught us that most species live complex social lives; that they raise and teach their young with some care; that they live in different sensory worlds, orientate and navigate differently from humans. But they are not so simple and savage as we had thought. They seem to communicate with one another, suggesting that they possess some senses of "meaning"—at least within their own species. Seeing other species as they actually live: as "feral" (not "wild"); in social intercourse (not as marauding solitaries); and knowing much more about their sensory abilities and their "surrounds"—ethology provides a comparative framework for looking "back" at humans from the perspectives of other species, as well as a "critique" for the re-examination of our comparative habits and thinking.[22]

Other beings use symbols and show affections that cannot be explained away as simply instinctive. We can imagine a moral company that includes higher apes, whales, and dolphins who have been shown to use symbols and perform symbolic acts. We realize that our judgments about what ought or ought not be done with non-human animals are corrupted by our power. In other words, we get away with treating other species as we do because we are able to. Morally, however, our knowledge and our experience suggest the likelihood that it is not possible to restrict companionship to any particular population.

Criteria like rationality and altruism call for caution. Using the exercise of symbolic capacities as a sign of moral capacity may well be a case of special pleading. Perhaps then an ethics derived from the metaphor of companionship had better be based on sensitivities and appreciations rather than in languages and rationalities. This suggests merging ethical and aesthetic ideas, ideas of right and good with ideas of responsiveness and fittingness. The merger suggests a basis for a more comprehensive environmental ethics.

By putting appreciation into the moral center, we can correct the reduction of ethics to matters of rights and justice. Companionate relationships occur—say, between an infant and its mother—on moral grounds quite distinct from those of fairness and equity. Friends may do with and for each other without regard for the give and take of distribution or merit. A number of moral ideas orphaned by the Enlightenment find an intelligible ethical home, ideas like love, friendliness, concern, empathy, loyalty, and pride.

Companionship brings to light an unavoidable problem. As we breathe, move, and eat we destroy other living things. Thus, we carry with us into the world a deeply felt sense of tragedy. It becomes an ontological feature of moral experience, an ever-present corrective to the optimism of a Humanism that asks human beings to play God. Companionship, even in this preliminary exploration, "thickens" moral experience.

The metaphor of companionship offers new imagery for naturalism as well. Humanist naturalism is reducible to the notion that everything that was, is, and shall be is included within a single universe. But the relationships involved in that inclusiveness were scarcely described. A common-sense distinction between persons and things led to contract relationships between persons and utilitarian relationships between persons and things. We are accustomed to thinking of human beings on one side and everything else on the other. That this leads, sooner or later, to an "arrogance of power" and a pride of place is not surprising. Nor should it be surprising that the world, in some senses, is inhospitable to the easy assumptions of this person-and-object view of things.

Companionship suggests participation, an inclusive and even democratic naturalism. No doubt there will be inarticulate members of the company for whom surrogate voices must be found. We understand this clearly enough when attending to the moral status of infants, the terminally ill, the unconscious patient, and the brain-damaged human being. A companionate naturalism suggests that there could be many other inarticulate members, although we need be wary of presuming that they are necessarily or permanently inarticulate. Participatory naturalism raises the problem of human responsibility in a novel way. There are hints of it in the Christian notion of "stewardship" but it is disabled by the fact that it is tied to an image of sheep and shepherd, possessor and possessed. Companionship is a move toward naturalistic partnerships and away from the hierarchies of stewardship. Thus, we might open up moral and political terms, terms of participation, which have been strictly anthropocentric even for the most radical of Humanisms.

Nature may also be appreciated as a presentation, indeed as a number of presentations. It is, however, not only a theater for our enjoyment and use. Orderliness and disorder, coherence and incoherence are categories that we bring to the world, but also that it brings to us. Certainly unifications and integrations are evident in our experience of ourselves with the world. We are hardly justified in concluding that it is only our experience that consists of such unifications and integrations. We cannot conclude that all animals but one have nothing like that experience. Historically, however, we have controlled orderliness through tools and knowledge and have thereby claimed a unique privilege in the world and over the world. Companionship suggests a Humanism that is less arrogantly centered on itself and less given to the virtues of manipulation.

Classical naturalism reminds us of a companionate metaphor.[23] Aristotle's "nature" was dynamic and Spinoza long ago proposed that all existents have a "tendency," a characteristic direction that shapes the world-for-them.[24] An appreciation of all contexts and points of view, even those of non-humans, is not beyond our imagination and is fruitful in addressing where and how we live today.[25] Of course, this takes away our special status as lords of creation. At the same time, it offers a world that is rich with beings that we need to take into account and that may, in ways we do not yet grasp, take account of us.

Finally, I want to take a look at tools and artifacts through the lens of a companionate metaphor. Ordinarily, these are treated as things, and ordinarily, this is quite justifiable. On the other hand, unique and aesthetic objects are evocative and personal. A different sense of activity is possible. As the craftsman or craftswoman knows, there is vitality in tools and materials. The grain and texture of wood resists or invites carving. We speak of respect for, and not just of appreciation for, paintings, sculptures, buildings, and bridges. To dismiss these as mere things or to interpret our experience of them as only instrumental is to ignore both what we do and they are.

One consequence of our surrender to a mechanistic metaphor is a disposable world with its economy of discards. Our experience is narrowed to the merely useful or aesthetically superficial. This encourages a discard morality. Consequently, our lives are not only impoverished but actually put at risk by the garbage heap we create.[26] A precious object, however, is never only an object, whether it is a favorite chair, a tool, or a musical instrument. As children, we learned the lessons of participation taught by a favorite toy, pillow, or blanket. As we grew up we were expected to forget the lesson but we never quite do. We were transformed by our unique objects just as we transformed them; we entered into a transaction with them. This was marked by the fact that such an object ceased to be simply "out there." The painter cannot tell where brain, eye, hand, brush, paint, and canvas separate. As an athlete or workman achieves competence, he or she achieves continuities. Artifact and human being cease to be alien to each other. By way of reminding us that objects can be genuinely active in our experience, we need only recall our stumbling efforts as novices and the reciprocities of mastery.[27]

The metaphor of companionship takes us down some familiar and some not so familiar pathways. It illuminates in an interesting way Enlightenment values that have grown tired in use and that have been inadequate in dimension. This it does by bringing into the foreground the third term of the Enlightenment—fraternity. Certainly, companionship fits with a shift in the sciences from mechanism to organism, from atomism to system. At the same time, it gathers together realities of experience as human beings move among a fascinating variety of other human beings and cultures, and among a fascinating variety of other beings. A willing exploration of possibility is no stranger to Humanism. As Julian Huxley wrote:

I feel that any such religion of the future must have as its basis the consciousness of sanctity in existence—in common things, in events of human life, in the gradually comprehended interlocking whole revealed to the human desire for knowledge, in the benedictions of beauty and love, in the catharsis, the sacred purging of the moral drama in which character is pitted against fate, and even deepest tragedy may uplift the mind.[28]

Companionship, then, is an alternative to the free individual of the eighteenth century, a metaphor that could very well do.

NOTES

1. Immanuel Kant, in "First Part. Transcendental Aesthetic," *Critique of Pure Reason*, trans. F. Max Muller (New York: MacMillan, 1949): 15–39.

2. There are many examples of the imaginative construction of worlds and persons. Some are permanent contributions to our literature like Lewis Carrol's *Alice in Wonderland* and *Through the Looking Glass* and others are fascinating curiosities like Edwin Abbott's *Flatland* published about 1880 in England. "An anonymous letter published in *Nature* on February 12, 1920 entitled "Euclid, Newton, and Einstein" calls attention to the prophetic nature of *Flatland*:

[Dr. Abbott] asks the reader, who has consciousness of the third dimension to imagine a sphere descending upon the plane of Flatland and passing through it. How will the inhabitants regard this phenomenon?... Their experience will be that of a circular obstacle gradually expanding or growing and then contracting, and they will attribute to *growth in time* what the external observer in three dimensions assigns to motion in the third dimensional space. Transfer this analogy to a movement of the fourth dimension through three dimension space. (James R. Newman, ed., *The World of Mathematics*, New York: Simon and Schuster, 1956: 2384).

3. Ernest Nagel, *The Structure of Science* (New York: Harcourt Brace and World, 1961): 108–09.

4. I am deeply indebted to John Dewey's aesthetic views for this notion of "transaction." See John Dewey, *Art as Experience* (New York: Capricorn, 1958).

5. Arthur M. Schlesinger, Jr., *A Thousand Days* (Boston: Houghton Mifflin, 1965): 1010.

6. Baruch Spinoza, "Of Human Bondage, or of the Strength of the Affects," *Selections*, ed. by John Wild (New York: Scribner, 1930) pp. 292–93.

7. For a discussion of the pedagogical implications of this point and for an analysis of how we learn, see Howard B. Radest, "The Map Is Not the Territory," *Can We Teach Ethics*, Chapter 5 (New York: Praeger, 1989): 77–97.

8. The complexities involved in the readiness to respond to one image or another, to enter the transaction, is brilliantly argued by James Turner in *Without God, Without Creed* (Baltimore: Johns Hopkins, 1985). The book is aptly subtitled, "The Origins of Unbelief in America," and the thesis may be summed up in the notion of social and cultural readiness to entertain an idea—in this instance, the idea that there is no God.

9. Albert Einstein, "Autobiographical Notes," *Albert Einstein: Philosopher-Scientist*, ed. Paul Arthur Schilpp (La Salle, IL: Open Court, 1969): 11.

10. Joseph Campbell, *The Hero with a Thousand Faces* (New York: Meridian, 1956): 387–88.

11. Eustace Haydon's *Biography of The Gods* (New York: Ungar, 1967, 1941) is an example of the view that the gods evolved from "primitive" tribal deities to personal cosmic powers to ultimate dissolution in the idealistic capacities of human beings. In *A Common Faith* (New Haven: Yale, 1934), John Dewey uses the word "God" to represent the summing up of human ideals. His context is emergent evolution. Later, he came to regret using the word because of its historic connotations and inevitable misunderstandings.

12. Timothy Ferris, *Coming of Age in the Milky Way* (New York: William Morrow, 1988): 175.

13. Prophetically, John Dewey spoke of the "new" individualism and the "old" and ironically of what he called "ragged" individualism. See *Individualism Old and New* (New York: Capricorn, 1962), and particularly Chapter 4, "The Lost Individual" and Chapter 5 "Toward a New Individualism," pp. 51–100.

14. If I understand the debate about psychobiology and a modern genetic interpretation of evolution, we have identified both the agent and the beneficiary of survival as the species itself, particularly the persistence of its genetic structure. For such a collective entity to survive, cooperation among its members would be necessary, and even self-sacrifice for the sake of the species would make good sense. See Richard Dawkins, *The Selfish Gene* (New York: Oxford, 1976) and Edward O. Wilson, *Sociobiology: The New Synthesis* (Cambridge, MA: Harvard, 1975).

15. Consider, for example, the solipsism implicit in Bishop Berkeley's empiricism or the impenetrability of Leibniz's "monads."

16. See, for example, Erich Fromm, *Marx's Concept of Man* (New York: Ungar, 1977).

17. The literature of feminism is rich with descriptions and suggestions of connections and relationships. It radically distinguishes privacy from intimacy. It also calls attention to the different intention and outcome of a society legitimated by a theory of "rights,"—that is, a society of laws and a community legitimated by a theory of concern. See Nell Nodding, *Caring, A Feminine Approach to Ethics and Moral Education* (Berkeley: University of California Press, 1984) and Debra Shogan, *Care and Moral Motivation* (Toronto: Ontario Institute for the Study of Education, 1988).

18. Stephen Toulmin, "The Tyranny of Principles," *The Hastings Center Report* 11, no. 6 (December 1981): 35.

19. The classic text of this phenomenon was David Riesman's *The Lonely Crowd* (New Haven, CT: Yale, 1950).

20. John Dewey, "Individualism Old and New" in *The Philosophy of John Dewey*, vol. 2, ed. John J. McDermott (New York: Capricorn, 1973): 616.

21. For a discussion of animal rights, see *Animal Rights and Human Obligations*, 2d ed. (Englewood Cliffs, NJ: Prentice-Hall, 1989) Tom Regan and Peter Singer, eds.

22. Harvey B. Sarles, "Humanism and Human Nature: Recovering the Individual," *Humanism Today*, no. 4, (1988): 57.

23. I can well understand the shakiness of this proposal. Further, I do want to distinguish my suggestion from traditional views of "panpsychism." I am testing a metaphor and not at all claiming that the world and everything in it is inhabited

by spirits or by spirit. For a useful discussion of the theme, see Paul Edwards, "Panpsychism," in *The Encyclopedia of Philosophy*, vol 6, Paul Edwards, ed. (New York: MacMillan, 1967): 22–31.

24. See Spinoza's *Ethics* and Aristotle's *De Anima*.

25. A recent article is suggestive of the creative power of point of view or, following my earlier analysis, of the poetic:

Two decades ago, a British scientist named James Lovelock put forth an imaginative and poetic view of how the Earth functions. . . . Dr. Lovelock said, the Earth itself appears to behave like a living organism. He named the organism Gaia after the Earth goddess of the Greeks. The Gaia hypothesis beguiled environmentalists and others. . . . The concept acquired mystical overtones, and not least for that reason, it was shunned by other scientists, some of whom ridiculed it as a fairy tale. But times change. . . . And today . . . the Gaia hypothesis, whether true or false, appears to have significant influence on the way some scientists study the Earth and the questions they ask about it. [it] has provided an organizing focus for research as they step up their efforts to learn more about how the enormously complex global environment functions. . . . And it has stimulated a spirited debate over the role of life in governing the Earth's climate. (William K. Stevens, "Evolving Theory Views Earth as a Living Organism," *The New York Times*, August 29, 1989), p. C1).

26. For a discussion of this theme, see Howard B. Radest, "The Virtues of Wastefulness," in *Humanizing the Workplace*, ed. Roy P. Fairfield, (Buffalo, NY: Prometheus, 1974): 239–56.

27. For a related analysis of experience, see John Dewey, *Experience and Nature* (New York: Open Court, 1958).

28. Julian Huxley, *Religion without Revelation* (New York: Mentor, 1957): 168.

9

A Humanist's Journey: Without Endings

In nineteenth-century America, Unitarians were called "God's frozen people." Today, we Humanists have joined them. Accusations of intellectualism are frequently heard among us. Mixing nostalgia for lost communities and guilt at departing the ways of the elders, we accuse ourselves of neglecting friendliness and care. We seem to doubt that what is true and best to us is enacted by us. In this alleged failure to live out Humanist principles is an unspoken doubt about their validity. The credibility of Humanism itself is at stake in the actualities of biography and relationships.

To be sure, friendliness is not necessarily a feature of traditional communal life. God and His agents are as likely to condemn as to praise, to ignore as to welcome. Churches are not immune to snobbery and elitism. Intellectualism is no stranger to the traditions either. Church fathers dedicated themselves to arguing theology just as Talmudists did to debating the finer points of *Torah*. The day-to-day life of people was all too often resigned to the merely routine. No doubt in holidays and worship, the congregant was saved from the indifference of scholars and priests. The beauties of story and ritual or of native poetry and dance nurtured those who had little regard for what was going on in the monastery or university. It would not do, however, to romanticize the parish, congregation, or synagogue. Often scenes of pettiness, manipulation, and bigotry, they were not always the places of warmth, love, and acceptance demanded by Christian communion or Hebrew tribalism. Humanists then are by no means unique in exhibiting blindness to their fellow human beings. They do, however, tend to have a rather sentimental view of other people's successes and their own failures.

Abstractions are alluring and safe. It is easier to love mankind than to love a man or a woman, to love an invisible God than to love His all too visible creatures. The more abstract the ideas, the easier it is to excuse my inability to confirm my faith by the way I live my life. I can find protection from the demands to "love my neighbor as myself," or to take all human beings as companions. So it is that argument replaces action and rote replaces relationship. That will not do for the Christian or the Jew; it will not do for the Marxist or Muslim. Each must fault the dehumanization of idea and belief. For the Humanist, however, failure in human relationships leaves emptiness everywhere. He or she has neither God nor History to fill the void.

We are all caught up in the unpredictability, fascination, joy, and sadness of personal living. Humanist and traditionalist alike are shocked out of their defenses by "crisis." We turn to other human beings in times of achievement, celebration, or trouble. We betray abstraction by our passionate quarrels about even the most abstruse ideas.[1] Obviously, something is hidden in them that stimulates our passions. In fact, when passion is absent, we do not succeed in discovering, clarifying, or understanding our ideas. They become merely routine. In that sense, the only truth worth having is personal truth, although this is by no means the same as mere opinion.[2] In other words, the passion of our quarrels tells us that we have made the truth of Humanism genuinely our own. No matter how distantly our ideas may seem to wander from experience, or how far the symbols we use in talking about them depart from ordinary language, the ideas of Humanism, like the ideas of Marxism, Christianity, Judaism, or Islam, are not simply entertained and are not simply entertaining.

Ideas work in many ways and we do not always realize how much of ourselves is in them. There are some kinds of ideas—say, in mathematics or physics—where personal attachment is less visible than others, but it is there. Routines have their uses too. They are habits of thought rather than occasions for thinking. Any idea, however, can become a matter of passion when it becomes a matter of inquiry. The idea that the earth moves became a cause of battle between the new scientists and the Aristotelians as much as between investigators and inquisitors. The nature of number can still stir controversy among mathematicians and philosophers. Toys and playthings can stir loyalties in the child, in the followers of team sports, or in the patriot. Common sense itself becomes a passion, as when adolescents test their parents and teachers with a deliberately irritating refusal to accept the "self-evident."

Some ideas evoke our feelings more frequently than others. Even when hidden by the paraphernalia of denial—abstractness, routine, and authority—they are just below the surface waiting to break through. More obviously than the patterns of mathematics or the discoveries of the sciences, these ideas inhabit a permanent battlefield where our lives are at risk. We find them gathered under the names of morality, politics, and faith. There, argument will not easily succeed, frustration will arise, and angers will remain uncalmed. We will divide into friends and enemies—even if only temporarily—and we will, for reasons of fatigue if nothing else, seek the benefits of suppressive silence in others and in ourselves.

So it is with Humanism. Whatever the outcome of the quarrel about whether it is a "religion,"it lives in the arena of faith, morals, and politics. In that arena, our passions and our truths are engaged. Humanists, however, have a special problem because of their roots in the values and methods of the Enlightenment. Arguments from reason and evidence are supposed to make quarrels about belief pointless. The personal and the passionate are for Humanists under the cloud of unreason, and thus an embarrassment. More than most, they are taught to move away from the personal encounter and toward the abstract idea. That is implicit in making the claim of science everywhere and, most particularly, the claim of objectivity. Even where they are engaged in social reform,their style is still distanced. It is the cause and not myself-in-the-cause that is in the foreground.

A bias for objectivity has its merits. Many a cause has been lost in an egoist's agenda. That is the other side of Humanist "coldness." But at the same time, it invites the hazard of self-induced blindness, as if the cause had a life of its own, and as if passion and interest had not chosen and shaped this cause for me. This blindness also makes it difficult to identify the personal agendas of Humanists which, in principle, are not supposed to be present at all. It leads to the strange notion that Humanism does not entail a personal life. It is not surprising then that the literature of modern Humanism neglects the lives of Humanists. What the Humanist does is alienated from what he or she is by this inheritance. That, and not the superficial judgment about intellectualism, is the real issue to be faced.

The other faiths of history center on a person and a personality. Whatever the wanderings of theology and ideology, they become models of personal life for others. Examples are the lives of Jesus, Moses, Mohammed, Buddha, or Lenin. Suspicious of a cult of personality, Humanism goes to the other extreme, ignores its Humanist personalities, and so does not offer actual models. It fails to work out the place of Humanism in the biographies of its participants.

There is thus a missing part of the Humanist story and without it, Humanism can neither be finally understood nor validated. As with others in the arena of faith, politics, and morals, a Humanist is as a Humanist does, feels, and believes. The Christian has been taught that it does not "profit a man to gain the world, if he loses his soul." The Jew must perform *mitzvah*, the "good deed." These show the way from abstract belief to personal conduct. At the same time, neither these, nor the quiescent pessimism of the Buddhist or the revolutionary zealotry of the Leninist will do for the Humanist. The Christian's double view of world and soul will not serve nor can an idealism embedded in the commandments of God or

History suit the Humanist temperament. Yet, although hardly expressed, Humanists do live differently from others. What then is the personal outcome of Humanism for the Humanist?

Without formal Humanist biographies,[3] I must rely on my own encounters with Humanists. I have already said something of my personal path toward Humanism. Let me add by way of background to some future undertaking something, informally, about the "sociology" of Humanists. The first thing that strikes me is that there are very few "birthright" Humanists. Free-thought, Deism, secularism, or atheism, for these few, were likely family ancestors. When I meet them or visit in their homes I hear about Robert Ingersoll, Bertrand Russell, or Tom Paine. Others, for whom Humanism is a family matter, often found their way from politics or to faith. A few remember *Manifesto I* and its signers.

Since Ethical Culture is still young, older members still speak from personal knowledge of Felix Adler. I have heard affectionate stories about John Lovejoy Elliott, successor to Felix Adler, as Leader of the New York Ethical Culture Society. His biography, one of the few available, reports that for the Elliotts and Lovejoys, Lincoln and abolition played the role of religion.[4] When I visit Unitarian and Ethical Culture Societies I meet second- and third-generation members, many of whom are quick to tell me of their ancestry. Among Unitarian-Universalists I hear about John Dietrich, Curtis Reese, or Ray Bragg. These modern contributors toward Humanism in Unitarian-Universalism are vivid and very personal. But overall, those who inherited their Humanism are very few indeed.

America's immigrant history contributes another part of the Humanist population. For today's European Humanists, ideology typically played a major role and when they arrive here they do not leave ideology behind. Indeed, American "pragmatism" is a puzzle to them and they express their dissatisfaction with the "superficiality" of American Humanism, its lack of ideology. Anti-clericalism, secularism, and socialism served them as Humanism's seedbed. Their Humanism started out and remained a cause and thus an occasion for philosophic criticism and political attack. When I worked in northern New Jersey, I came to know a small community of European socialists, now transplanted to the United States. For them, socialism was a way of living and not simply an economic and political program. Growing older, they needed to deal with death and dying. This led many of them to embed their socialism in Humanism, although they did not really see it as much more than a matter of naming differently. For a period, I served the group, informally, as a kind of secular "chaplain." At the same time and to their frustration, their children had left socialism, and so Humanism, behind.

But the "birthright" Humanist and the first-generation immigrant are only a minor part of the Humanist story in the United States. Most Humanists are likely to have started out as adherents of Christianity or Judaism.

There does not seem to be any correlation, however, between the intensity with which a family held its faith and the chance of its producing a Humanist heretic. Like so much faith in the United States, the Humanist's transition is usually a private matter. The break with the past is personal and seldom public and ideological. It can occur early or late, angrily or peaceably. Felix Adler, for example, wrote:

The separation was not violent. There was no sudden wrenching off. There were none of those painful struggles which many others have had to undergo when breaking away from the faith of their fathers. It was all a gradual, smooth transition, the unfolding of a seed that had long been planted. I have never felt the bitterness often characteristic of the radical, nor his vengeful impulse to retaliate upon those who had imposed the yoke of dogma upon his soul. I had never worm the yoke. I had never been in bondage. I had been gently guided. And consequently, the wine did not turn into vinegar, the love into hate. The truth is, I was hardly aware of the change that had taken place until it was fairly consummated. One day I awoke, and found that I had traveled into a new country.[5]

Others are not as peaceable. This is particularly the case with those who grew up in Fundamentalist and orthodox environments. If they do break out, they must wage a battle in order to gain their freedom. Meeting them, I realize that it has left its scars. The break is, however, still a personal matter. Despite the angry and unforgiving rhetoric of what we sometimes call the "come-outer," it is only secondarily a matter of loyalty to some public agenda and hardly ever the result of reasoning to a conclusion. It is felt and interpreted privately.[6] To be sure, things were somewhat different in the nineteenth century when the substance and not just the politics and pageantry of faith were likely to be newsworthy matters.[7]

Because the break is personal, it leaves its mark in remembered angers and resented authorities. Indeed, as I recall meeting newcomers to Humanism, I have the impression that the later a person came to it, the greater the intensity of resentment toward the past and the more passionate the negativities. It is as if they had lingered over their angers, rehearsed them repeatedly, and allowed them to grow beyond reference to any particular event or stimulus. Humanism for them, and at least initially, was not so much an affirmation as a cry of anger and outrage.

Except for the few born into it, childhood in all likelihood finds the future Humanist in a Christian or Jewish Sunday School, receiving communion, singing hymns, reciting bible lessons, being confirmed. On the surface, there is little that forecasts the turn away from tradition that would later be taken. Somewhere in adolescence, however, a teen-ager's typical challenge to authority takes an atypical direction. The move of the young proto-Humanist is only apparently intellectual, a criticism of the unbelievability of the traditions. Obviously the struggle for autonomy against parental authority is at work too. Naively, the teen-ager "tests" God or the "power of prayer"—usually late at night, looking for a sign that, of course, does not come. A bit later, he or she might turn toward an attractive or interesting alternative. Unlike his or her friends, the future Humanist does not settle for outward conformity and inner indifference. Of course, the alternative he or she finds may wear the guise of political cause or scientific truth. Occasionally, the adolescent, to the dismay of his or her parents, will even indulge in religious experimentalism. I can remember more than one young- ster who would visit church after church looking for something he or she could not find at home. Nor, as far as I am able to determine, is Humanism suddenly available as in a conversion experience. Instead, I witnessed in myself and in others a pattern of development, moving from rejection of tradition and toward a different possibility. Typically, this movement is intimate and has little or no institutional context. Perhaps a few close friends might share in the news.

Most young Humanists don't know they are Humanists, although they may well boast of their atheism. As one of them wrote:

I first saw the light one night when I was sixteen years old. . . . That night I was reading a Little Blue Book that had been given to me by my boyfriend . . . Shelley's *The Necessity of Atheism*. . . . I usually say that until the moment I opened the book I was a very religious young women, but I suppose I had actually been outgrowing my religion for a while. . . . I was prepared for Shelley and his atheism even though I didn't know it. . . . Shelley's logic shattered in one memorable night all the Sunday School lessons, Bible studies, and sermons I had been exposed to for years.

My first reaction was fury, a fury so strong that I risked confronting my father the next morning at breakfast "You can't possibly believe all that god stuff! Do you?" I demanded. . . . His response made me ever angrier. This pillar of the religious community, this trustee of the local Presbyterian church, this man who . . . attended services every Sunday told me calmly that no, he didn't believe what the church taught. But he did believe that without the church there would be no morality in the world.[8]

Whether shared or not, expressed or not, at root there is a sense of isolation and even of originality. The discovery not only doesn't have a name but the idea that others have been there before or are there now is unavailable. For example, the biologist E. O. Wilson wrote:

Partly because I was an only child, introverted by nature, growing up in small towns close to the woods and shoreline, I developed an intense early interest in biology. . . . By the time I entered the University of Alabama at the age of seventeen, I was a devoted entomologist with a large personal collection of insects, dreaming of a life in science. Very soon, I encountered the formal disciplines of genetics and evolutionary theory. I came upon a hard truth: I saw that all I had learned and hoped to accomplish in natural history studies made sense only from the vantage of scientific materialism. Very little of it could be fitted into the fundamentalist view of the world in which I had been indoctrinated. . . . I chose to learn as a scientist, but I never forgot the power of religion. I never lost respect for the sincere feelings of my fellow southerners, however different from my own. . . . Today, I would call myself a scientific humanist.[9]

The outcome of this adolescent process is felt to be unique . . . so much so that when later in life—in college or in the early stages of family and career—there is the accidental discovery of Humanism, it is greeted with a mix of disbelief and relief. At the same time, the echoes of earlier alienations remain so that the emerging Humanist finds other Humanists somewhat suspect despite the pleasure of recognition. In part, no doubt, this is both a cause and a consequence of the temperamental individuality that all Humanists bring to associations. There is some lingering resentment at the loss of a precious originality following the discovery that Humanism and fellow Humanists exist. It is no surprise, then, given this patterns of arrival, that Humanists guard their own positions, are wary of common agreement, and are quick to argue their own "points of the law." When this individualist temperament is reinforced by the rationalism, cosmopolitanism, and atomism of the Enlightenment, the difficulties encountered in building and sustaining Humanist associations are understandable.

The pathways to Humanism are expressed in ideological and intellectual languages but are not initiated that way at all. Matters of personality and feeling, and accidents of biography set the Humanist on his or her way. Practical concerns intervene to make Humanism a likely center of biography. As what is called "intermarriage" increases in an urban and pluralist culture, questions of where to marry and how to raise and educate children arise. Humanism—and this is quite evident in Ethical Culture Societies, Unitarian Fellowships, Humanistic Jewish Congregations, or the American Humanist Association's Humanist Counselor program—provides an appropriate meeting ground because it does not demand exclusive loyalty and is open to diversity.

Society's effort to control conscience may force others out of the church or synagogue and toward Humanism. Church/state cases, despite the elaborate paraphernalia of the law, usually have this personal quality, as when parents challenge a school board over Bible reading, prayer, or religious instruction. Isolated and often ostracized as a result, the nonconformist finds a refuge in Humanism. A similar pattern appeared with the emergence of "non-traditional" conscientious objectors during the Vietnam war. Many young men found that their objection did not fit the law which recognized only "religious" objection. Yet the grounds of their refusal to serve were not "political" either. I think too of pressures toward religious conformity in public schools. In some communities this becomes so offensive that nonconforming parents in self-defense seek protection for their children by finding a Humanist affiliation. I can recall, particularly during the growth of suburbia after World War II, the many parents who would remark: I really don't need it for myself, but my children need to know how to answer the question, "What is your religion?" and they need to be able to answer it honestly.

Humanists come to Humanism with differing needs and motivations, differing loyalties and differing purposes. The notion that Humanists are all of a kind, all rationalist and intellectual, is as false as the idea that all Christians share the same beliefs and values. But Humanism by its nature and claim is secular, democratic, and naturalist and has no reference outside of person and world. So its diversity is more of a problem. It is a participant's ideology, which means that it cannot be simply delivered to its adherents in one true and final interpretation. Its meaning cannot be authoritatively established in some dramatic event or some sacred text nor is its definition the prerogative of some council of elders. There is no Bible, Vatican, or Ark of the Covenant to mask its differences. It is, therefore, to the Humanist as he or she is, and to Humanists in uneasy association, that we must look for Humanism's evolution. Given the variety of pathways and motivations that lead into Humanism, however, its evolution is inevitably hesitant, confused, and confusing both to its adherents and to its observers. The journey to Humanism reflects not only the ideas that have accrued to Humanism but what happens to those ideas in the peculiar and varied histories of Humanists and the time in which they live.

Ironically, intellectualism serves as a mask for the personalism that marks the ways that Humanists discover who they are. The reliance on ideas and language is itself a defense against the confusions of personalism with its unpredictable mixture of commonalities and departures. By using ideas and arguments, Humanists can avoid facing the ragged-edged quality of Humanism. But the dynamics of denial contribute to making its ideas and arguments seem, all too often, rather thin and routine. In near confession of this characteristic of its development, many Humanists when challenged back away from statements of ideology. Instead, they claim that Humanism is a matter of mood and of broad general notions. Efforts to specify ideology will be resisted, not so much because there are disagreements on the ideas but because there is an implicit suspicion of the effort itself. In typical fashion, however, those who try to specify and those who think the project illegitimate will themselves become polarized on the issue of process. Indulging this argument will, in turn, become another defense against faith. The sociology of Humanism leads into a circle of frustrations.

Humanists are few and hard to find. Given the difficulties of living with us when we are found, why should we want to associate with other Humanists, and if we do associate, what are we likely to find? We can, after all, live in a secular world without the interference of priests and prophets. We can assert our individuality and our freedom without categorizing it as Humanism and without entering into Humanist associations. It is possible to do good things and to join any number of groups where social idealism can find tangible expression. Indeed, if we look at Humanism as a collection of truthful ideas or as the need to do good works, there are many possibilities that require neither Humanist association nor Humanist identity. We can be democrats, civil libertarians, reformers, and secularists without taking on the puzzles of a philosophy that seeks to integrate these. Finally, if we must have a philosophy for the sake of our ideological mental health, it seems possible to be a Humanist alone and thus to avoid the frustrations of Humanist association.

The prescription of independence is also tempting to many who have no hesitation in identifying themselves as Humanists. I confess that it is, occasionally at least, tempting to me as well. It would leave me free of entanglements and permit me to interpret my Humanism without the need to defend it to others. As some have put it to me, "I can hold my position with integrity and without compromise." This interpretation of the possibilities of Humanism is still an echo of the individualist metaphor of the Enlightenment which is very much alive in us. It builds upon the public and outward-turning sense of what Humanism is all about that we have also inherited from the Enlightenment.

A lonely Humanism serves, too, by setting us apart as radically different from church and synagogue. It helps Humanists complete their escape from their own past. With the individualist metaphor reinforcing the remembered struggle for autonomy, many Humanists reject Humanist communities and congregations much as they rejected their childhood church or synagogue. They are skeptical of the need to have anything like it in their lives at all. On similar grounds, they are suspicious of nearly all leadership and authority. I have heard the Humanist credentials of Ethical Culture and Unitarianism challenged on just such organizational grounds: since these Humanisms are "congregationally" organized and have a professional "ministry" they cannot really be Humanistic at all. Sometimes this is put more bluntly: Ethical Culture, Unitarianism, and Humanistic Judaism look too much like the traditions that have been left behind. It is not unusual to hear, too, that "congregational" organizations are really ways of avoiding the "true" implications of Humanism. Having learned the painful lesson in childhood that tribe and tradition intrude on personal choice and value, many Humanists accept a duality between public and personal life and jealously guard the latter from view, including the view of other Humanists.

It is not surprising, then, that when we find Humanists together, they are really not quite together. There is always something of a drawing away and a drawing apart. Humanists do seek each other's company and find support in it. Yet they never quite accept it. As with so much of what we have discovered about Humanism, here too we meet ambivalence. When a Humanist is challenged by the import of this kind of behavior for the survival of Humanism, he or she turns to a restatement of the truthfulness of the ideas of Humanism. Doing so, he or she will reveal yet another echo of the Enlightenment, a residual confidence in progress and a faith that "truth" will inevitably defeat falsehood. The reply is quite likely to include as well an ode to the sacred quality of personal privacy. When practical considerations are urged, it is further argued that association is only a way of achieving collectively what cannot be achieved alone. Ideally, then, Humanist associations should come into being and pass away and are to be understood as limited conveniences.

This grudging argument for association usually reveals, in yet a final echo of the Enlightenment and without anyone realizing it, the notion of a social contract. I am struck by how typical it is to find among Humanists that almost the first step in associating is to create a "constitution and bylaws," to set down the contract. Friendliness and association wait upon this formal activity in a reversal of what we know about how human beings come together. Yet we rarely reflect on what this inversion tells us about ourselves. It is as if associating were always a matter of decision, of weighing reasons for and against.

The more I reflect on my own experience, however, and on the experience of other Humanists, the more convinced I am that Humanism is finally to be found most deeply embedded in its personal practice. From this perspective, the intellectualism, the quarrelsomeness, and the individualism of the Humanist may be understood as a struggle for articulation that is frustrated because Enlightenment Humanism does not provide sanction, language, or form for exposing or celebrating personal practice. In other words, association is an existential need and not simply an instrument, and the frustration of that need forecasts the failure of Humanism. It is worthwhile, then, to take a look at the texture of a Humanist's life and experience and to ask whether or not the Humanist can encounter intimacy and friendliness as readily as justice and truthfulness.

Like all human beings, the Humanist has a rich and complicated personal life. He or she has friends and enemies, hopes and dreams, fears and angers. As these develop, they shape the path that the Humanist takes toward Humanism, and they are in turn shaped by the Humanism he or she finds along the way. We get glimpses of this transaction between personal biography and Humanism when we meet the Humanist at moments of love and death. The masks come down. Truthfulness and secularity are no longer abstract ideas or primarily philosophic or scientific propositions. It is striking that I have yet to see a Humanist retreat to the comforts and promises of his or her religious childhood when facing death or disaster. Of course, some express regret that they cannot rely on promises of immortality and assurances of eternity. Nevertheless, there are atheists in foxholes. Nor is it the case that Humanists are libertines and opportunists. They commit to marriage and family and friendship as seriously as others do. They make and keep promises, and accept obligations. Indeed, although this may sound more pretentious than I intend, they seem to take the moral side of experience more seriously than most. The lives of Humanists deny a dark and hopeless Dostoevskyan logic. It is simply not true that "if God is dead, all things are permitted."[10]

The message that Humanists listen for and deliver becomes quite clear at times of crisis. Of course there is the pain of departure and separation in the face of death, the worry and frustration in the face of failure, and the anxiety of connection and hope in the face of love. Strangely, for all the boast of individualism, however, a common thread connects the Humanist to these experiences and thereby to other Humanists. For the Humanist there is no eternity. This world is all there is. He or she knows that life is momentary and so celebrates the passing moment and is sensitive to its irrecoverable quality. Naturalism now becomes tangible in biographical form. In an example more eloquent than most, but by no means unusual, a Humanist wrote:

I believe it takes courage to live. In action, this means I surrender myself to life. To try to control your life is the coward's way out. It means there are no adventures, surprises, or magical turning points. A controller doesn't trust his or her ability to live through the pain and chaos of life. There is no life without pain, just as there is no art without first submitting to chaos. Stated another way: a neurotic solution is one that seeks to avoid legitimate suffering. You have to suffer—not every day but as a consequence of time. Perhaps a five-year old does not suffer (if the child is lucky enough to be in a good, loving home) but the rest of us must suffer at various times. You'll live through it. You can't control suffering because if you try to avoid it then you kill rapture and joy. The two are inextricably linked. Joy never comes without suffering and therefore demands courage. For myself that means that if something terrible happens to me, I say to myself what my mother used to say to me, "Worse things have happened to nicer people." You'd be amazed at how that works.[11]

I have seen enough to tell me that the inner life of the Humanist is shaped by a deeply felt temporality. For all his or her rationalism, the Humanist is far less given than others to seeking out explanations for unexpected events. Things happen and only later are they argued, debated, and studied. This felt naturalism leads to a mixed mood of regret and gratefulness. At the same time that the Humanist adopts this existential stance, his or her inner life is shaped by a commitment to truthfulness. It too becomes an existential fact and is intertwined with the psyche itself. After a funeral or memorial service, I hear repeatedly that the service had "integrity" and that it was important not to lie for the sake of false comfort. In other words, naturalism is a fact of a Humanist's psychology and not simply an abstract idea. For all the individualist metaphor, a sense of connectedness to fellow human beings is evident that is more deeply held and felt than would follow from the needs of mere practical association.

Crisis, fortunately, is not a permanent diet. On the other hand, it yields evidence of the existential reality of Humanist ideas. They become visible in the lives of Humanists just when it counts most. Humanist habits tend, however, to hide the fact that they are at work in daily life. Humanists here suffer an ideologically induced schizophrenia. The Enlightenment view of the public and the private is bridged only at moments of greatest threat, as at death, or greatest hope, as in marriage and the welcoming of children.

The inner life of Humanists is also shaped by moral categories, so much so that claims—as in *Manifesto I* and *Manifesto II* or the International Humanist and Ethical Union Statement of Principles—that "Humanism is ethical" seem to derive from a Humanist's being rather than the reverse. I am not the only one to notice that Humanists take ideas like honesty and integrity quite seriously—often much more seriously than their neighbors. Indeed, Humanists are critical of their neighbors at least as often because they sense "bad faith" as because they disagree with their theological or ideological views. Humanists are even more critical of themselves. The Humanist's denial of eternity leads to impatience, a feeling that moral conflicts cannot await eternal resolution. This sense of immediacy shapes the inner life of the Humanist. Of course Humanists are not necessarily better than their neighbors, but they are more attuned to issues of better or worse. Their intellectualism masks an almost visceral sense of good and evil. The pulpits and platforms of Humanist associations attend to current moral issues and ring with prophetic denunciation. Typically, however, these are connected to personal life—turning issue into personal issue— which may well be the way that the Humanist expresses his or her concerns of salvation. In fact, the Humanist, ironically, often exhibits a kind of moral Puritanism.

If the sociology of Humanism provides us with a pluralist portrait of association, the psychology of Humanism tends to show evident commonalities. Despite the emphasis both Humanists and their critics place upon rationalism, it is more than likely that Humanism is based in a specific experience and temperament rather than in an ideology. The joys and pains of temporality shape the inner life of the Humanist and are the existential ground of Humanist naturalism and secularity. Of course, this fact of biography does not verify the truthfulness of Humanist ideas, but it does tell us that these ideas are serious and seriously rooted in personal life. This becomes all the more interesting when set against Enlightenment categories, which may seem as masks as well as truths. It is possible to say that Humanists themselves have not been fully conscious of their own Humanism, that they have been taken in by their own defenses and by the metaphor of the free and rational individual. Humanism relies on precisely those features of experience—the personal, the temperamental, and the felt—to which its language and imagery denies primary importance. Dimly aware of this, some modern Humanists forsake the Enlightenment in the name of the personal and convert Humanism into mere self-help. That road is taken often enough in our time, but its outcome is only a mirror image of the Fundamentalism that Humanism rejects. Neither will do, for both suffer the error of dualism, the radical isolation of "in here" and "out there."

For modern Humanism, the road ahead is by no means well defined. It seems to me that our predecessors had it easier. Stimulated by the energies and loyalties demanded by revolution and reform, they achieved a clarity of purpose and direction that is missing today. The story of modern Humanism appears as a move toward ambiguity. As I noted some years ago:

I think it a chimera to believe that we can "return" to unadorned Humanism or "pure" Ethical Culture. We need to find out instead if Ethical Humanism can have a distinctive message. Adler's thought had emerged from a deeply reworked effort to understand not only Kant but the problems of industrial life. Dewey's arose from a deeply reworked Hegelianism joined with efforts to elicit the social import of the sciences. The question before us is how to build from these insights and those of others like Julian Huxley and Erich Fromm toward a new and as yet unshaped position. . . . Sadly, Ethical Humanism has not yet found a suitable conjunction of idea and practice.[12]

We lack a convincing way of putting modern Humanism together coherently and sensibly, a way of seeing, feeling, and thinking amid all the confusions and cross-purposes of our lives and our world. Once, the Humanism of the Enlightenment was just such an offering of unity. Beneath the prosiness of its style, it had its dreams of progress and freedom. As we have seen, this Enlightenment poetry no longer sings as clearly and sweetly for us.

I cannot, however, dismiss it, nor do I want to. So I look one last time, but now with an eye to the future, at the threads of an Enlightenment Humanism. The clue to its reconstruction will be found in what we do with its metaphors and in the temperament of its children. As we live day by day, we reveal that liberty and secularity are felt—not just thought. We have in fact moved into a different world than the one inhabited by our ancestors. The ideas—I almost wrote "mere" ideas, but that would not do—that describe that move are well in hand. We are, however, only in the most preliminary way attuned to the poetry of time and evanescence that gives meaning to that move.

We are only at the beginnings of a new consciousness, a Humanist consciousness, and I feel a certain sadness because I know I will not see that consciousness fulfilled. So much has happened so fast to us. Our history as a species tells us, however, that we need long preparations. We have not caught up with ourselves. As the late Julian Huxley put it:

As a result of a thousand million years of evolution, the universe is becoming conscious of itself, able to understand something of its past history and its possible future. This cosmic self-awareness is being realized in one tiny fragment of the universe—in a few of us human beings. Perhaps it has been realized elsewhere too, through the evolution of conscious living creatures on the planets of other stars . . .

Evolution on this planet is a history of the realization of ever new possibilities by the stuff of which earth (and the rest of the universe) is made—life, strength, speed and awareness; the flight of birds and the social polities of bees and ants; the emergence of mind long before man was ever dreamt of, with the production of colour, beauty, communication, maternal care, and the beginnings of intelligence and insight. And finally, during the last few ticks of the cosmic clock, something wholly new and revolutionary, human beings with their capacities for conceptual thought and language, for self-conscious awareness and purpose, for accumulating and pooling conscious experience . . .

The new understanding of the universe has come about through the new knowledge amassed in the last hundred years.[13]

As with evolution, the ideas of the sciences are not yet personal ideas, not yet genuinely our own. Perhaps that and not just the incompleteness of its ideas is why the Enlightenment seems so thin. There is work to be done. When I hear about the size and structure and organization of things, I am hardly able to take it in. I can talk as glibly as the next of light years and geologic ages, large numbers and vast spaces. At the same time, ancient images and traditional securities have their hold upon me and letting go might see me drowned in a chaos of modern realities, political and cosmological. So, I am not blind to the reasons why my neighbors remain on familiar territory, and I cannot simply dismiss them as benighted. They are, after all, just like me.

In an echo of Kant, Stephen Hawking suggests an "anthropic principle," which he paraphrases as "We see the universe the way it is because we exist." He distinguishes a "weak" from a "strong" anthropic principle and adds:

A second objection to the strong anthropic principle is that it runs against the tide of the whole history of science. We have developed from the geocentric cosmologies of Ptolemy . . . through the heliocentric cosmology of Copernicus and Galileo, to the modern picture in which the earth is a medium-sized planet orbiting around an average star in the outer suburbs of an ordinary spiral galaxy, which is itself only one of about a million million galaxies in the observable universe. Yet, the strong anthropic principle would claim that this whole vast construction exists simply for our sake. This is very hard to believe.[14]

This point of disbelief is the Humanist advantage. I know—although it is hard to confess it—that I cannot cling to what is no longer really available. An honest confession that the world is not here for me is supported by my Humanism. Like others, I am uncomfortable with changes I have not yet been able to embrace, but at least I need not experience the discomforts of bad faith. We have moved into new territories while still trying to use old maps. We must then set ourselves the cartographer's task. For this drawing of new maps, new ways of living and new realities, Humanism is an apt compass and a reprise of its themes is helpful.

The memory of Enlightenment achievement undergirds my confidence. For all its limitations, it demonstrated that we could participate in building our world. We were not doomed to repeat the stories of Greeks and "barbarians," God and victim. We were not fated to the paths of destiny and recurrence. Humanism is thus a legitimate source of confidence. The fearful and the pessimistic, convinced that we are sinners all or certain that only grace can save us, are unsuited for this cartographer's task.

At the same time, the story of these last several hundred years has corrected an optimism that too easily turns into pride. That is the moral and the intellectual message of our more complicated experience of intelligence and reason. To our Humanism, we bring the lessons learned from frustrated reforms and facile rationalism. Today we benefit from new and enlarging companionships that were only a vague promise when the call for "liberty, equality, and fraternity" was first heard. We can draw upon the strengths of many others. To be sure, we are also caught in their difficulties—but then we always were even if we did not know it. From the genius of democratic revolutions with its ideal of one human race, we can now move toward an actual and generous inclusion and connection. So if the Gods are vanished, we are nevertheless not alone. Indeed, our world is all the richer and its membership more accessible than the ghosts and goblins or the Gods and Saints of another age.

The cartographer's task looks to the future. We also need ways of living in the moment. We live on the ground, but we are also trying to draw its diagram from above and ahead. Again, Humanism is particularly apt. We can speak truthfully to each other even in the most difficult moments; we can accept what we are and what we are not. In fact, we have learned that temporality is itself a ground of celebration, reminding us to accept the moment as precious just because it must vanish. An earlier wisdom taught us that we would not pass this way again and yet it hedged with a promise of eternity. A Humanist secularity reminds us that we need to take that wisdom much more seriously.

Humanist rationality, paradoxically, is an invitation to enriching the lived personal experience. Reason is not only a reliable method that moves us from speculation to verification but is itself a passion that introduces a special quality to human life. As Santayana[15] remarked:

The inner authority of reason, however, is no more destroyed because it has limits in physical expression or because irrational things exist, than the grammar of a given language is invalidated because other languages do not share it, or because some people break its rules and others are dumb altogether. Innumerable madmen make no difference to the laws of thought, which borrow their authority from the inward intent and cogency of each rational mind. Reason, like beauty, is its own excuse for being.[16]

Although its enemies see some Satanic monolith, the Humanism we have explored is a kaleidoscope. Humanists inherited a dream of progress and envisioned a line drawn from past to future, ever onward, ever upward. But in fact, Humanism is much more playful, even if Humanists are given to seriousness. We are tourists without a guide, and we sometimes poke our noses where we are not invited. We are always in a hurry to get somewhere—only to discover that we really did not have to hurry at all. In fact, we are exploring ourselves even as we explore the world—and the two, on Humanist grounds, are not alien to one another. We are in and of the world much as it is in and of us. At the point of being and not simply at the point of cognition, this is the naturalistic theme that stirs the sciences and that animates us. Thus, ideas which seem to have so pragmatic and intellectual a cast in the Humanist lexicon reappear as motifs of living itself.

It may be urged as a refutation of Humanism that the temporality it celebrates and the nature it praises must lead finally to a dead end. The sciences that Humanism idealizes tell us that the universe itself will end and with it all memory and all hope. The anti-Humanist might well remind us that ultimately there can, on Humanist premises, only be nothingness. After we die we are recalled by our children and friends for but a short while. Perhaps we leave some slightly more lasting mark of our presence in the causes we embrace, the books we write, or the monuments we build. Yet these will vanish too, just as the Humanist will vanish. Can we make peace with the disappearance of all and everyone?

We might take the pathway of *angst*, confront nothingness in "fear and trembling," and await a grace we do not expect. We might refuse nothingness and insist that the world simply cannot be this way. The first move leads to nihilism; the second to another world. It was William James from the platform of an Ethical Culture Society who offered an argument for the denial of temporality in "Is Life Worth Living":

Once more it is a case of *maybe*. And once more *maybes* are the essence of the situation. I confess that I do not see why the very existence of an invisible world *may* not in part depend on the personal response which any one of us may make to the religious appeal. God himself, in short, *may* draw vital strength and increase of very being from our fidelity. For my own part, I do not know what the sweat and blood and tragedy of this life mean, if they mean anything short of this. If this life be not a real fight, in which something is eternally gained for the Universe by success, it is no better than a game of private theatricals from which one may withdraw at will. But it *feels* like a real fight which we, with all our idealities and faithfulness, are needed to redeem. And first of all to redeem our own hearts from atheisms and fears.[17]

These options are not really available to the Humanist. *Angst* comes close to celebrating chaos and resolves its fearfulness by an act of absolute belief. Taking advantage of the "case of maybe" suggests wishful thinking. At root, there is something in me that cannot accept either anguish or denial as tenable alternatives. I find the notion that the universe takes me so seriously or that I take myself so seriously abidingly funny. Somehow, it reflects a lack of proportion.

To be sure, my laughter is touched by regret, even sadness. I sometimes wish I were important enough to match the importance of the universe, but I am not. Events pass me by and the future extends well beyond anything I can imagine, let alone experience. There is never enough time for all that I would wish and want, never enough ability to grasp and enjoy what I would encounter, and never enough energy to do what I would do. The Humanist then faces the notion of his or her finitude, learning to enjoy what is and to accept graciously what cannot be. Humanist laughter is thus joined to a stoic's courage to face the end of things without illusion.

In fact, we really do not make the choice between eternity and nothingness. Our scope is more limited and our needs less grandiose. I face my own death and accept the fact that what I leave behind is equally momentary. I face the death of family and friends and those I care about. I face the limitations of achievement and know that even in the best of them there is a mixture of failure. I live without extending myself or my memory backward and forward to the ends of time and space—something I cannot do in any case. The argument from eternity is, I think, only a theological or philosophical game. In fact, Humanism, like any other faith, speaks to the lived present. Its warrant appears as it happens and not in the ultimate beginnings or endings of things.

I have yet to hear of a genuine choice between cosmic being and nothingness. Matters that truly matter are much closer to hand, such as why did something so evidently wrong happen, or what was served by this event, or how was that good luck justified. I may struggle for explanations because such concerns are genuine and genuinely human. At the same time, I know that answers really are not available, and that my science asks different kinds of questions and gets different kinds of answers. In all likelihood, I will confess that I do not know, that there is no explanation. These genuinely felt puzzles are drawn to biographical scale. In other words, the validation or refutation of Humanism is referred finally to personal knowledge and not to an abstract idea.

It is the radical claim of Humanism that we can live rich and full lives while denying eternity. It is the even more radical claim that such lives are more satisfying precisely because they come closer to truthfulness and do not rely on illusion. To be sure, there will be those for whom eternity remains a reality. If in reaction the Humanist yields to the Fundamentalist temptation, he or she will attempt an argument and miss the point. In fact, the Humanist is better placed than most, even when encountering those who deny Humanism itself. Appreciating the varied possibilities of the world is a capacity that grows from taking democracy as a moral and aesthetic idea and not just as a political arrangement. There is in these considerations a certain Humanist perversity. The Humanist passionately seeks to get others to agree and yet would find his or her enjoyment of diversity betrayed if that passion were satisfied. We have, in other words, come a very long way from the clear and distinct ideas of the Enlightenment and from its narrower dimensionality. Humanism, finally, takes possibility seriously as a category of experience.

Humanism's attentiveness to the world as it is qualifies it for the cartographer's task, for limning the world as it might be. When I am tempted to surrender this world for some other, I resist—and not only because it is unbelievable. Such a surrender would disqualify me for the future. When, nevertheless, I am tempted, I remind myself that the fact of our temporariness commands our present energies and our actual appreciations.[18]

NOTES

1. For example, we have been fooled by the ways in which scientific processes are described—for example, the "scientific method" and by the ways in which scientific outcomes are reported. Not the least of our difficulty in grasping the role of accident and passion in the sciences is the way in which textbooks mislead students about the nature of scientific activity. An interesting and revealing picture can be found in James D. Watson, *The Double Helix* (New York: New American Library, 1969).

2. The notion of "personal" truth should not surprise us. For example, when the therapist seeks to develop insight in a patient, he or she is calling attention to the force of the notion. In a related way, the progressive teacher who brings to students the idea of "learning by doing" is identifying the personal features of truth. In organizations seeking a democratic model the notion of "taking ownership" is yet another aspect of the same point of view. The personal truth is not at all the subjective truth.

3. There are some autobiographies and biographies around. Among the best of these, for example, is Bertrand Russell's *Autobiography* (London: Allen and Unwin, 1967–69); and Alan Wood *Bertrand Russell: The Passionate Skeptic* (New York: Simon and Schuster, 1958). Clearly John Stuart Mill, *Autobiography* (New York: Columbia University Press, 1924) is deservedly a classic. Nevertheless, biographical literature is not a matter of course in Humanist circles and often much of it is intellectual biography. Among the studies available of Humanists in groups is Robert Tapp, *Religion among the Unitarian-Universalists: Converts in the Stepfather's House* (New York: Academic Press, 1973). See also "Humanists and Their Values," *Humanism Today*, vol. 4 (New York: North American Committee for Humanism, 1988): 127–39. Before his death, Sidney Hook published his autobiography *Out of Step: An Unquiet Life in the 20th Century* (New York: Harper and Row, 1987).

4. See Tay Hohoff, *A Ministry to Man*, chap. 1 (New York: Harper, 1959).

5. Felix Adler, *An Ethical Philosophy of Life* (New York: D. Appleton–Century, 1918), p. 14.

6. I do recall in the 1950s a Presbyterian minister in Rockland County who was tried for heresy and who became an Ethical Culture leader. The public character of this transition was, however, an exception. Several former ministers and priests have become Humanist leaders and many leave church and synagogue for Humanism. Except for a few, however, the move is quiet and scarcely noted.

7. For example, the content of sermons was often reported in the press on Mondays and editorial comment was not unknown:

Professor Adler . . . delivered a communistic discourse yesterday. . . . He formally rejected "that form of social organization" [and] described his plan as "cooperation. . . . " Now there may be a technical and refined distinction between "cooperation" of this sort and communism but there is certainly no difference in spirit. . . . Who is to judge how much money a man can "use for humane purposes?" How is "humane" use to be defined? Ethical Culture such as this might well provoke a smile, if it was not in sober harmony with some of the most vicious of contemporaneous notions. ("A Communistic Sermon," *The Evening Post*, New York, NY, February 9, 1880).

When I served an Ethical Society in New Jersey, the local press would occasionally report a Sunday address and some local papers still do. But this is rare and growing even rarer. At best, a self-serving "release" is printed. Since the media tend both to reflect and lead their public, this would seem one more instance of secularization.

8. Gina Allen, "The Night I Saw The Light," *Free Inquiry* 7, no. 2 (Spring 1987): 19.

9. Wilson, E. O., "Biology's Spiritual Products," *Free Inquiry* 7, no. 2 (Spring 1987): 14.

10. It is possible, of course, to mount an argument on behalf of atheists in foxholes or about our need to have a God to ensure morality. For example, God must have known He was putting us in a foxhole. It follows that if I am not an atheist, I must at the very least wonder how and why this happened and what kind of God does these kinds of things. It is striking that after a disaster, people thank God for saving them without noting that they would not have gotten into the fix in the first place without God's acquiescence. In other words, the theist in the foxhole has at least as much of a problem as the atheist. Similarly, before we can accept God's security for our moral decisions, we must first judge whether the security is offered by God or Devil, which forces us back on our own moral resources as much as we are alleged to be forced there by a Humanist's autonomy. Again, the problems are quite similar and the believer is not necessarily at an advantage in the argument. At the very least, the Humanist need not look over his or her shoulder in fear that a moral or metaphysical error will produce eternal damnation.

11. Rita Mae Brown, "Surrender to Life," *Free Inquiry* 7, no. 3 (Summer 1987): 39.

12. Howard B. Radest, "Ethical Culture and Humanism: A Cautionary Tale," *Religious Humanism* 16, no. 2 (1982): 70.

13. Julian Huxley, "Transhumanism." In *New Bottles for New Wine*, p. 13 (New York: Harper and Brothers, 1957).

14. Stephen Hawking, *A Brief History of Time*, p. 126 (New York: Bantam Books, 1988).

15. Once again, I find Santayana a much neglected Humanist resource. A useful discussion of Santayana's notion of the "spirit" may be found in Victor Tejera, "Spirituality in Santayana," *Transactions of the Charles S. Peirce Society* 25, no. 4 (Fall 1989): 503–29.

16. George Santayana, *The Life of Reason*, p. 79 (New York: Scribners, 1954).

17. William James, "Is Life Worth Living," an address given at Harvard University and at the Philadelphia Ethical Society in 1895. The essay has been reprinted many times.

18. I am indebted to John Dewey's analysis of experience and in particular to the notion of "consummatory experience," which is the significant category explored in *Art as Experience* (New York: Capricorn, 1958).

Selected Bibliography

BOOKS

Adler, Felix. *An Ethical Philosophy of Life*. New York: D. Appleton-Century, 1918.
———. *The Reconstruction of the Spiritual Ideal*. New York: D. Appleton and Company, 1924.
———. *The Essentials of Spirituality*. New York: James Pott, 1905.
Arisian, Khoren. *The New Wedding*. New York: Vintage, 1973.
Black, Algernon D. *Without Burnt Offerings*. New York: Viking, 1974.
Blackham, Harold J. *Humanism*. Middlesex, England: Penguin, 1968.
Blau, Joseph L. *Cornerstones of Religious Freedom in America*. Boston: Beacon, 1949.
Bode, Carl. ed. *Ralph Waldo Emerson: A Profile*. New York: Hill and Wang, 1969.
Bullock, Alan. *The Humanist Tradition in the West*. New York:W. W. Norton, 1985.
Bury, J. B. *The Idea of Progress*. New York: MacMillan, 1924.
Cremin, Lawrence A. *The Transformation of the School*. New York: Vintage, 1961.
Das, Sushanto. *Dedication to Freedom: M. N. Roy—The Man and His Ideas*. Delhi, India: Ajanta, 1987.
Davies, Paul. *God and the New Physics*. London: J. M. Dent, 1983.
Dewey, John. *Art as Experience*. New York: Capricorn, 1958. Originally published in 1934.
———. *A Common Faith*. New Haven: Yale University Press, 1934.
———. *Democracy and Education*. New York: The Free Press, 1966.
———. *Individualism Old and New*. New York: Capricorn, 1962. Originally published in 1929.
———. *The Public and its Problems*. New York: Henry Holt, 1927.
Dobrin, Arthur, and Kenneth Briggs. *Getting Married the Way You Want*. Englewood Cliffs, NJ: Prentice-Hall, 1974.

Emerson, Ralph Waldo. *Selected Essays*. Ed. by Larzer Ziff. New York: Penguin, 1982.

Ericson, Edward L. *American Freedom and the Radical Right*. New York: Ungar, 1982.

————. *The Free Mind through the Ages*. New York: Ungar, 1985.

————. *The Humanist Way*. New York: Continuum, 1988.

Ferris, Timothy. *Coming of Age in the Milky Way*. New York: William Morrow, 1988.

Frankel, Charles. *The Case for Modern Man*. Boston: Beacon, 1956.

Friess, Horace L. *Felix Adler and Ethical Culture*. New York: Columbia University Press, 1981.

Fromm, Erich. *Marx's Concept of Man*. New York: Ungar, 1961.

Goldman, Eric F. *Rendezvous with Destiny*. New York: Vintage, 1956.

Guttchen, Robert S. *Felix Adler*. New York: Twayne, 1974.

Haydon, A. Eustace. *Biography of the Gods*. New York: Ungar, 1967. Originally published in 1941.

Hofstadter, Richard. *The Paranoid Style in American Politics*. New York: Knopf, 1965.

————. *Social Darwinism in American Thought*. Boston: Beacon, 1955.

Hohoff, Tay. *A Ministry to Man*. New York: Harper, 1959.

Hook, Sidney. *Out of Step: An Unquiet Life in the 20th Century*. New York: Harper and Row, 1987.

Humanist Manifesto I and Humanist Manifesto II. Buffalo, NY: Prometheus, 1973.

Hume, David. *An Inquiry Concerning Human Understanding*. Ed. by Charles W. Hendel. Indianapolis: Bobbs-Merrill, 1975.

Huxley, Julian. *Essay of a Humanist*. New York: Harper and Row, 1964.

————. *New Bottles for New Wine*. New York: Harper, 1957.

————. *Religion without Revelation*. New York: Mentor, 1957.

Huxley, Thomas H. *Science and the Christian Tradition*. New York: D. Appleton, 1899.

James, William. *Essays on Faith and Morals*. Sel. Ralph Barton Perry. New York: Meridian, 1962.

————. *The Varieties of Religious Experience*. New York: Macmillan, 1961. Originally published in 1902.

Kant, Immanuel. *Critique of Pure Reason*. Trans. F. Max Muller. New York: MacMillan, 1949.

————. *The Fundamental Principles of the Metaphysics of Ethics*. Trans. Otto Manthey-Zorn. New York: D. Appleton Century, 1938.

Krikorian, Yervant H. ed. *Naturalism and the Human Spirit*. New York: Columbia University Press, 1944.

Kuhn, Thomas. *The Structure of Scientific Revolutions*. Chicago: University of Chicago Press, 1962.

Kurtz, Paul. *Eupraxophy: Living Without Religion*. Buffalo, NY: Prometheus, 1989.

————. *The Transcendental Temptation*. Buffalo, NY: Prometheus, 1986.

Kurtz, Paul, ed. *The Humanist Alternative*. Buffalo, NY: Prometheus, 1973.

Kurtz, Paul, and Albert Dondeyne. *A Catholic Humanist Dialogue: Humanists and Roman Catholics in a Common World*. Buffalo, NY: Prometheus, 1972.

Kurtz, Paul, and Svetozar Stojanovic. *Tolerance and Revolution, a Marxist–Non-Marxist Dialogue*. Buffalo, NY: Prometheus, 1970.

Lamont, Corlis. *Man Answers Death*. New York: Philosophical Library, 1952.

———. *The Philosophy of Humanism*. New York: Ungar, 1982.

Larue, Gerald A. *Ancient Myth and Modern Life*. Long Beach, CA: Centerline, 1988.

Lippmann, Walter. *The Public Philosophy*. New York: New American Library, 1955.

Lyttle, Charles H. *Freedom Moves West: A History of the Western Unitarian Conference, 1852–1952*. Boston: Beacon, 1952.

MacIntyre, Alasdair, and Paul Ricoeur. *The Religious Significance of Atheism*. New York: Columbia University Press, 1969.

Mann, Arthur. *Yankee Reformers in the Urban Age*. Cambridge, MA: Harvard University Press, 1954.

Maslow, Abraham H. *Motivation and Personality*. New York: Harper, 1954.

Mill, John Stuart. *On Liberty*. Middlesex, England: Penguin, 1974. Originally published in 1859.

———. *Autobiography*. Ed. by John H. Robson. New York: Penguin, 1990. Originally published in 1873.

Mondale, Lester. *The New Man of Religious Humanism*. Peterhead, Scotland: Volturna, 1973.

Muzzey, David S. *Ethics as a Religion*. New York: Simon and Schuster, 1951.

Nagel, Ernest. *The Structure of Science*. New York: Harcourt Brace and World, 1961.

Nodding, Nell. *Caring, A Feminine Approach to Ethics and Moral Education*. Berkeley: University of California Press, 1984.

Olds, Mason. *Religious Humanism in America*. Washington, DC: University Press of America, 1978.

Paine, Thomas. *The Age of Reason: Being an Investigation of True and Fabulous Theology*. Buffalo, NY: Prometheus, 1985. Originally published in 1794–1796.

Persons, Stow. *Free Religion*. New Haven, CT: Yale University Press, 1947.

Radest, Howard B. *Toward Common Ground*. New York: Ungar, 1969.

Radest, Howard B., ed. *To Seek a Humane World*. London: Pemberton, 1971.

Randall, John Herman, Jr. *The Making of the Modern Mind*. Boston: Houghton Mifflin, 1940.

Rawls, John. *A Theory of Justice*. Cambridge, MA: Harvard University Press, 1971.

Regan, Tom, and Peter Singer, eds. *Animal Rights and Human Obligation*. Englewood Cliffs, NJ: Prentice-Hall, 1989.

Rogers, Carl. *On Becoming a Person*. Boston: Houghton Mifflin, 1961.

Russell, Bertrand. *Unpopular Essays*. New York: Simon and Schuster, 1950.

———. *Why I Am Not a Christian*. New York: Simon and Schuster, 1957.

Santayana, George. *The Life of Reason*. New York: Scribner, 1954. Originally published 1905–1906.

Sartre, Jean-Paul. *Existentialism and Human Emotions*. Trans. Bernard Frechtman. New York: Philosophical Library, 1957.

Schlipp, Paul Arthur, ed. *Albert Einstein: Philosopher-Scientist*. La Salle, IL: Open Court, 1969.

Schneider, Herbert W. *A History of American Philosophy*. New York: Columbia University Press, 1946.

Sher, Gerson S. ed. and trans. *Marxist Humanism and Praxis*. Buffalo, NY: Prometheus, 1978.

Simon, Walter M. *European Positivism in the Nineteenth Century*. Ithaca, NY: Cornell University Press, 1963.

Spinoza, Baruch. *Ethics*. Secaucus, NJ: Citadel, 1976. Originally published in 1677.

Stein, Gordon, ed. *The Encyclopedia of Unbelief*. 2 vols. Buffalo, NY: Prometheus, 1985.

Storer, Morris B., ed. *Humanist Ethics*. Buffalo, NY: Prometheus, 1980.

Tapp, Robert. *Religion among the Unitarian Universalists: Converts in the Stepfather's House*. New York: Academic Press, 1973.

Tarkunde, V. M. *Radical Humanism*. Delhi, India: Ajanta, 1983.

Turner, James. *Without God, Without Creed (The Origins of Unbelief in America*. Baltimore: Johns Hopkins University Press, 1985.

Wilson, Edward O. *Sociobiology: The New Synthesis*. Cambridge, MA: Harvard University Press, 1975.

Wine, Sherwin T. *Humanistic Judaism*. Buffalo, NY: Prometheus, 1978.

————. *Judaism Beyond God*. Farmington Hills, MI: Society For Humanistic Judaism, 1985.

Wood, Alan. *Bertrand Russell: The Passionate Skeptic*. New York: Simon and Schuster, 1958.

Wright, Conrad, ed. *A Stream of Light*. Boston: Unitarian Universalist Association, 1975.

JOURNALS

Free Inquiry. Quarterly. Council for Democratic and Secular Humanism. Buffalo, NY.

Humanism Today. Annual. The North American Committee for Humanism. New York.

The Humanist. Six Times per year. The American Humanist Association. Amherst, NY.

Humanistic Judaism. Quarterly. The Society for Humanistic Judaism. Farmington Hills, MI.

International Humanist. Quarterly. The International Humanist and Ethical Union. Utrecht, The Netherlands.

Journal of Humanism and Ethical Religion. Annual. National Leaders Council of the American Ethical Union. New York.

Religious Humanism. Quarterly. The Fellowship of Religious Humanists. Yellow Springs, OH.

Index

ABOUT THE AUTHOR

HOWARD B. RADEST, director of the Ethical Culture Fieldston Schools in New York City, was instrumental in developing its K–12 curriculum focusing on ethics and moral reasoning. He also serves as the dean of The Humanist Institute and the founder and chairman of Columbia University's Seminar on Moral Education. Mr. Radest is author of *Can We Teach Ethics?* (Praeger, 1989).